MW01226131

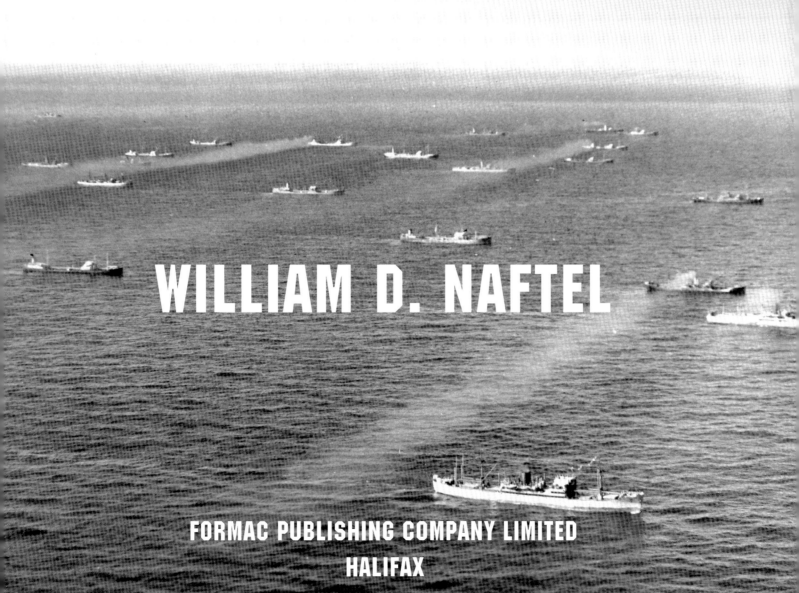

WARTIME HALIFAX

THE PHOTO HISTORY OF A CANADIAN CITY AT WAR
1939-1945

WILLIAM D. NAFTEL

FORMAC PUBLISHING COMPANY LIMITED

HALIFAX

ACKNOWLEDGEMENTS

In a work such as this, the named author is only one of the many contributors. I thank them all, but would like to acknowledge in particular the ready and willing assistance of the staff of the Nova Scotia Archives and Records Management, and especially Anjali Vohra and the helpful suggestions made by Barry Cahill. Private individuals were especially helpful, in particular Joyce Purchase, Joan Payzant and the Estate of Ralph Kane.

My thanks to you all for helping to bring life to a neglected chapter of the history of this harbour community.

© 2009 William D. Naftel

All rights reserved. No part of this book may be reproduced or transmitted in any form or by any means, electronic or mechanical, including photocopying, or by any information storage or retrieval system, without permission in writing from the publisher.

Formac Publishing Company Limited recognizes the support of the Province of Nova Scotia through the Department of Tourism, Culture and Heritage. We acknowledge the financial support of the Government of Canada through the Book Publishing Industry Development Program (BPIDP) for our publishing activities. Formac Publishing Company Limited acknowledges the support of the Canada Council for the Arts for our publishing program.

Canada Council   Conseil des Arts
for the Arts   du Canada

NOVA SCOTIA
NOUVELLE-ÉCOSSE
Tourism, Culture and Heritage
Tourisme, Culture et Patrimoine

Library and Archives Canada Cataloguing in Publication

Naftel, William D.
        Wartime Halifax : the photo history of a Canadian city at war 1939-1945 / William D. Naftal.

Includes index.
ISBN 978-0-88780-835-7

        1. World War, 1939-1945—Nova Scotia—Halifax—Pictorial works.
2. Halifax (N.S.)—History—20th century—Pictorial works. 3. Halifax
(N.S.)—Pictorial works. I. Title.

FC2346.4.N36 2009   971.6′225030222   C2009-904833-7

Formac Publishing Company Limited
5502 Atlantic Street
Halifax, Nova Scotia
B3H 1G4
www.formac.ca

Printed and bound in China

CONTENTS

PRELUDE

In 1867, the year of Canadian Confederation, the citizens of the communities around Halifax Harbour, still economically oriented towards international trade and socially oriented towards the British naval and military garrison, had been cool to the whole concept of the union with Upper Canada; but a generation later the experiment seemed to be working. Local capital funded new industries, local politicians played leading roles in national politics, and municipal infrastructure began to reflect advances in delivery of services and public transportation. This progress and integration was, however, something of an illusion, because with increasing speed the new Dominion's focus shifted to development of the fertile western prairies and the natural resources of British Columbia on the Pacific Coast. By the turn of the twentieth century, the Halifax Harbour communities were no longer a national economic focus. They were barely in the consciousness of the rest of the country.

When British forces left in 1905–1906, with them went the dignity of an Imperial role and in 1939, yet another generation later, the harbour communities were still struggling to find the level of self-esteem which they had had in the heady days of the mid-nineteenth century.

World War I had brought some prosperity to the local economy, but it was not sustained. The dull economic times that settled in about 1921 were not relieved by the economic boom that was a feature of the 1920s across North America. It can be said that when the world-wide depression hit in 1929, Halifax did not have very far to fall.

This reality is not to say that people were easily able to weather the storm, because it was a time when the "social safety net" depended heavily on private charity and if you had no job, no connections, and no money life could be a dire struggle. On the other hand, good management at the Halifax Shipyards, one of the city's big employers, ensured regular work. The Ocean Terminals of the National Harbours Board were the Atlantic terminus of the Canadian National Railways and the city was the financial and administrative centre of the province. Its small size, about 62,000 in Halifax and 8,000 in Dartmouth, meant that for better or worse people knew each other. Many of its residential areas were as good as anywhere in Canada. Its poor areas though were probably worse than elsewhere, and there were certainly more of them. At the beginning of World War II, much of the municipal infrastructure dated from the prosperous years of the nineteenth century, and while it was adequate to meet the populations' needs, it would soon require new capital investment.

In the spring of 1939, the good news came from a slowly improving economy, but the news from overseas was bad, as the German government of Adolf Hitler made increasingly aggressive moves against its neighbours. In spite of gathering storm clouds, for just a couple of days that June, life in Halifax Harbour stood still under blue skies and warm breezes as King George VI and Queen Elizabeth visited the city, ending a remarkable Canadian tour. When they sailed out of the harbour on the Canadian Pacific liner Empress of Britain on 15 June, they left behind fond memories of a good time. It was soon apparent that these memories would have to do for awhile, as the next six years brought darkness and danger.

Halifax, capital city of Nova Scotia was founded in 1749 by Hon. Edward Cornwallis.
Buildings and Places of Historic Interest
Citadel – commenced in 1828 (C4)
Dockyard – 1759 (D6)
Dutch Church – erected in 1755 (D6)
Government House – Residence of the
Martello Tower – erected in 1796 (C1)
Nova Scotia Archives – contains Collection of Historic Objects (B3)
Ordnance – erected circa 1810 (D5)
Province House – Legislative Building erected in 1811–1818 (D4)
Provincial Museum – located in the Technical Coll. – contains Collection of Historic Objects (D3)
St George's Round Ch. – erected in 1800 (D5)
St Pauls Church – erected in 1750 (D4) and St Pauls Cemetery (D3)
Town Clock – erected 1801–03 (D4)
Williams Lake
Boulderwood
Saraguay Club
HERRING COVE ROAD
NORTH
Pinehill
Old Penitentiary
SOUTH
Franklyn Park
Martello Tower
Naval Memorial
Fort Cambridge
Point Pleasant Park
Fort Ogilvie
Greenbank
R.N.S. Yacht Squadron
YOUNG AVENUE
Grain Elevator
Cold Storage Plant
Ocean Terminals
Union Station
Prominent Old Buildings in the City
Admiralty Ho. – commenced in 1814 (C6)
Acadian School – erected in 1816 (D4)
Bloomfield – erected c. 1830 (C6)
Custom Ho. (Old) – c. 1815 (E4)
Gorsebrook – c. 1820 (C2)
Halifax Banking Co. (D5)
House – No 66 Hollis St – erected c. 1815 (D3)
No 77 Hollis St – c. 1815 (E3)
Built by John Trider c. 1815 (D2)
Melville Island Prison – erected c. 1808 (A4)
Reynolds Bldg – erected in 1816 (E3)
George's Island

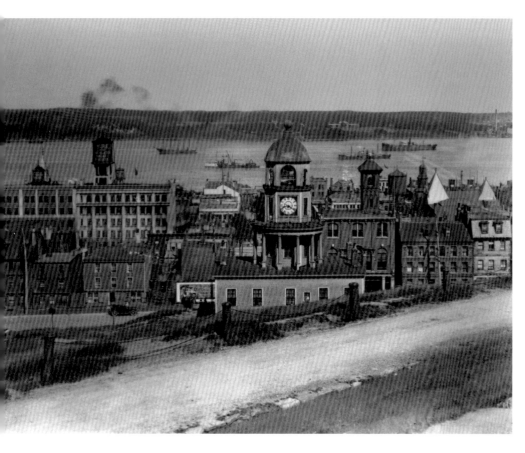

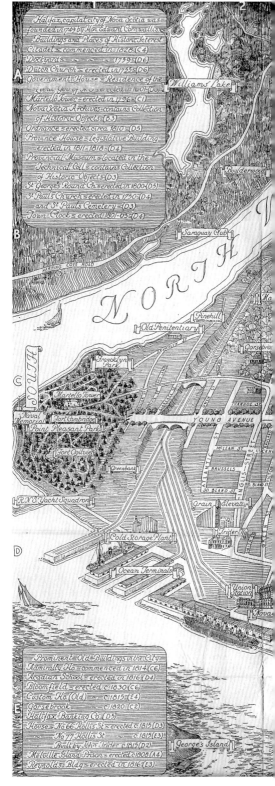

ABOVE: *Halifax changed very little between World War I and World War II and in many respects was a somewhat shabby reflection of its prosperous Victorian years. Although its role as the provincial capital, home of universities, and base for the Canadian military and other agencies of the Dominion government had insulated it from some of the worst ravages of economic depression, these agencies had not yet become the major players that they would be in the post-World War II era. This 1920s view of downtown Halifax, showing the iconic Old Town Clock, was more or less valid up until the 1960s.*

RIGHT: *This 1939 map of Halifax and Dartmouth was intended for tourists and visitors, recognized contributors to the local economy even then. It shows the communities on the eve of war. Although Dartmouth is somewhat circumscribed, it was not much bigger than it appears in this view. The northwest of Halifax peninsula is notable for its empty acreage, punctuated by the grassy fields of the civic airport and the Simpson's department store. The north of the city essentially ends with the grounds of the Provincial Exhibition at Almon and Windsor. The downtown looks eastward, as it always had, to the multitude of nineteenth-century finger piers and the more modern Ocean Terminals to the south, integrated with the transcontinental line of the Canadian National Railways.*

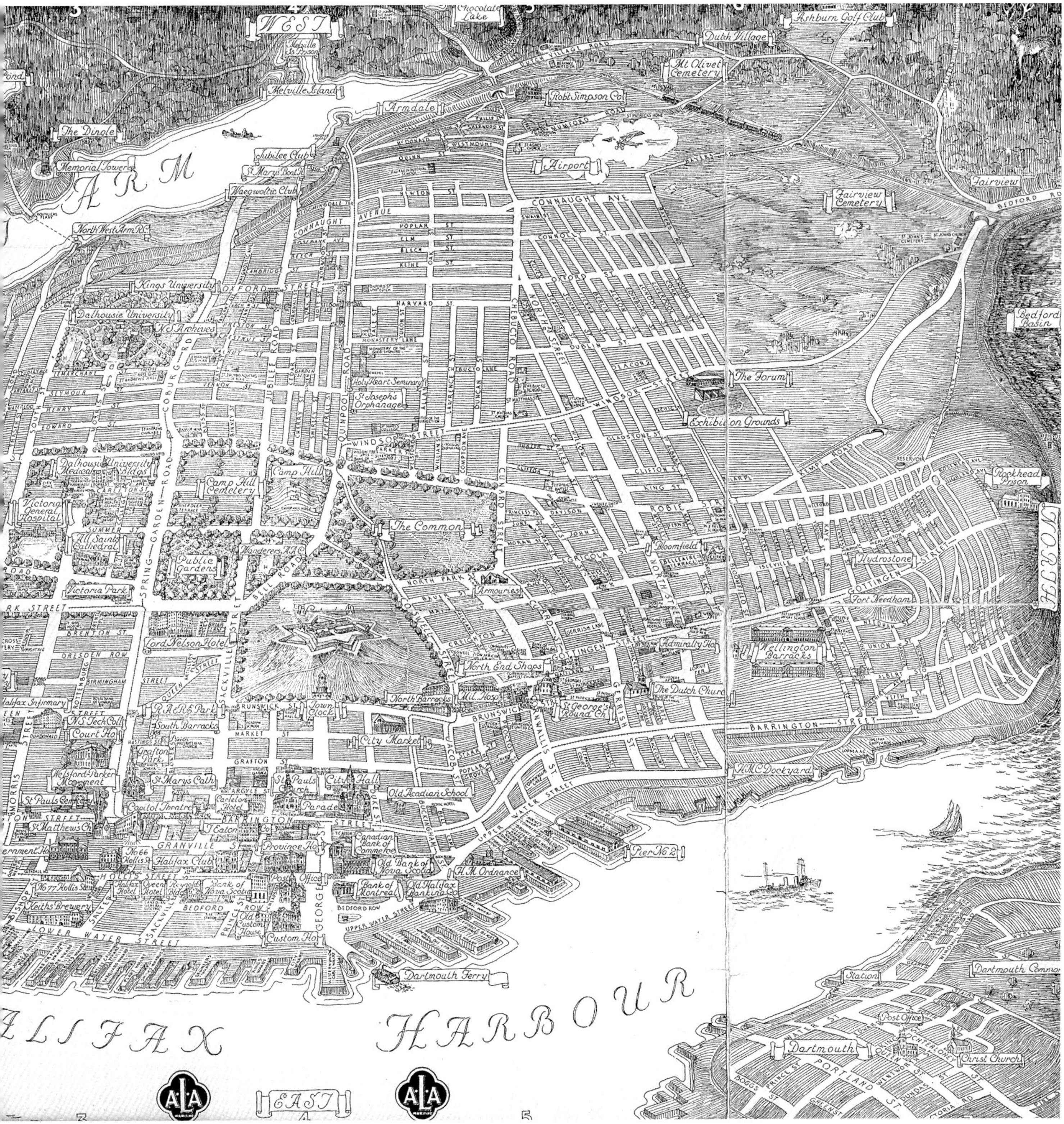
WEST
Chocolate Lake
Melville Island
Armdale
The Dingle
Memorial Tower
ARM
Jubilee Club
St Mary's Boat Club
Waegwoltic Club
North West Arm R.C.
Dutch Village
Ashburn Golf Club
Mt Olivet Cemetery
Robt Simpson Co.
Airport
Fairview
Fairview Cemetery
Bedford Basin
CONNAUGHT AVE
Kings University
Dalhousie University
N.S. Archives
Holy Heart Seminary
St Joseph's Orphanage
The Forum
Exhibition Grounds
Camp Hill
Camp Hill Cemetery
Dalhousie University Medical Bldgs
Victoria General Hospital
All Saints Cathedral
The Common
Public Gardens
Victoria Park
Bloomfield
Hydrostone
Rockhead Prison
Fort Needham
Armouries
Lord Nelson Hotel
Admiralty Ho
Wellington Barracks
North End Shops
The Dutch Church
Halifax Infirmary
North Barracks
St George's Round Ch
Town Clock
N.S. Tech Coll
South Barracks
Court Ho
City Market
St Mary's Cath
St Pauls Church
City Hall
Old Acadian School
H.M.C. Dockyard
Capitol Theatre
Carleton Hotel
Parade
St Matthew's Ch
Province Ho
Canadian Bank of Commerce
Pier No 2
Halifax Club
Old Bank of Nova Scotia
H.M. Ordnance
Halifax Hotel
Queen Hotel
Bank of Nova Scotia
Post Office
Bank of Montreal
Old Halifax Banking Co
Keiths Brewery
Old Custom House
Custom Ho
Dartmouth Ferry
BARRINGTON STREET
SPRING GARDEN ROAD
HALIFAX HARBOUR
Station
Post Office
Dartmouth
Christ Church
Dartmouth Common
EAST

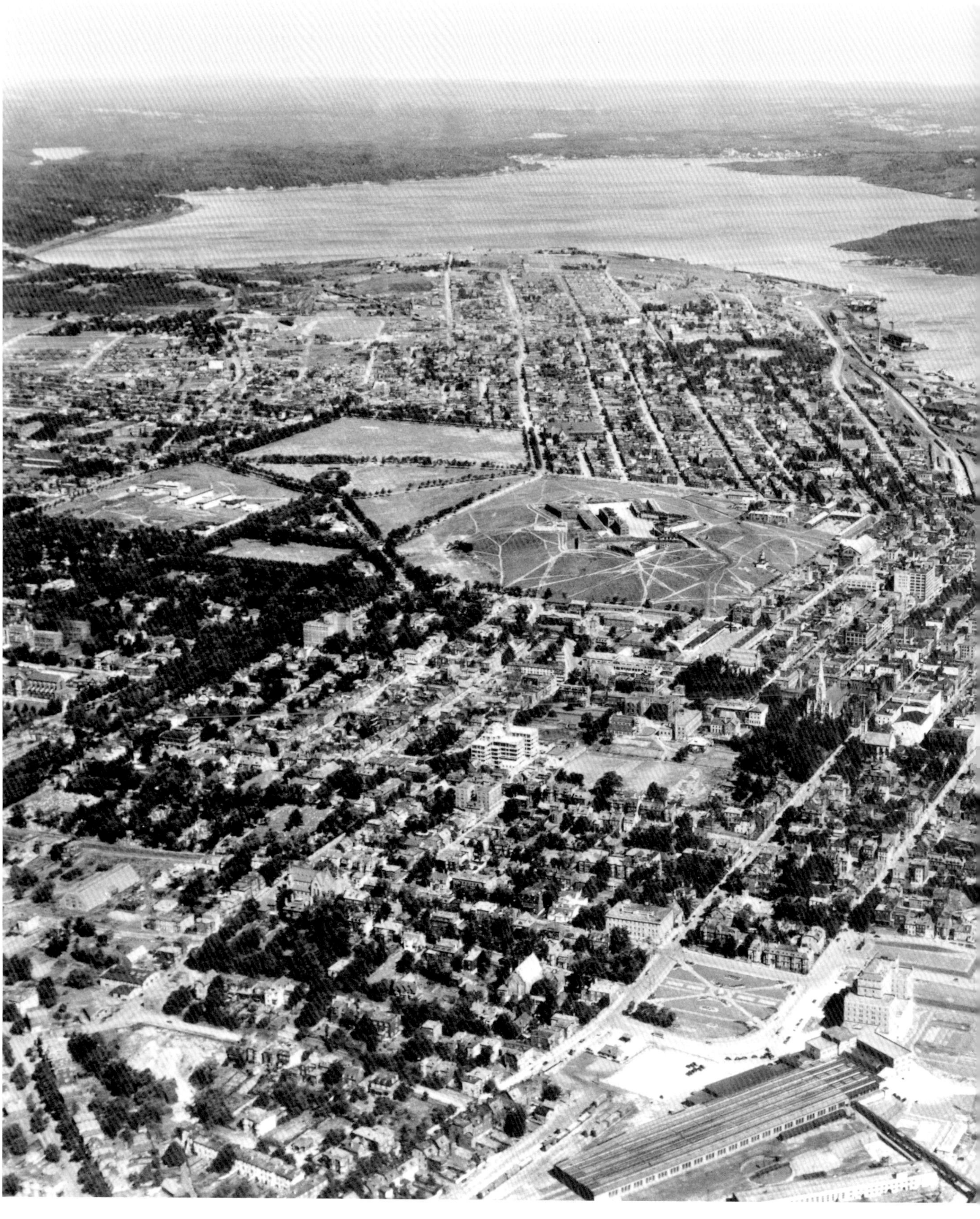

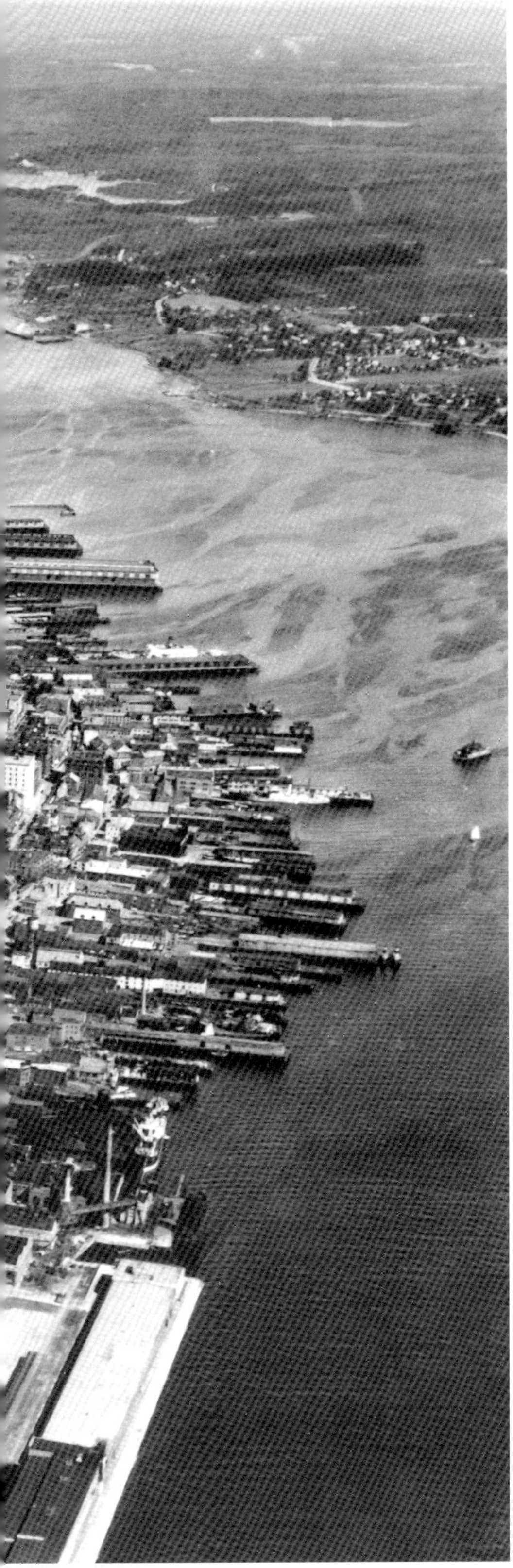

LEFT: *A bird's-eye view taken around 1930, showing the harbour communities looking north, with Bedford at the top and a sliver of Dartmouth to the right. The vast, sheltered expanse of Bedford Basin, dozing in the sun, would by decade's end be filled with the ships of many nations, gathering their resources to face the hostile gauntlet of the Battle of the Atlantic lying between them and Britain. For reasons of security, Halifax and its neighbouring communities were known to the rest of the world simply as "An East Coast Port."*

BELOW: *This 1941 aerial view shows what appears to be troop maneuvers on the Wanderers Grounds at the base of Citadel Hill and on that account alone highlights the immediate impact of the war. Temporary wartime buildings also began to appear quickly on the Citadel glacis along Jubilee Road and the Commons, almost pristine in the previous aerial, and then began to disappear with the construction of Queen Elizabeth High School and Camp Hill Hospital.*

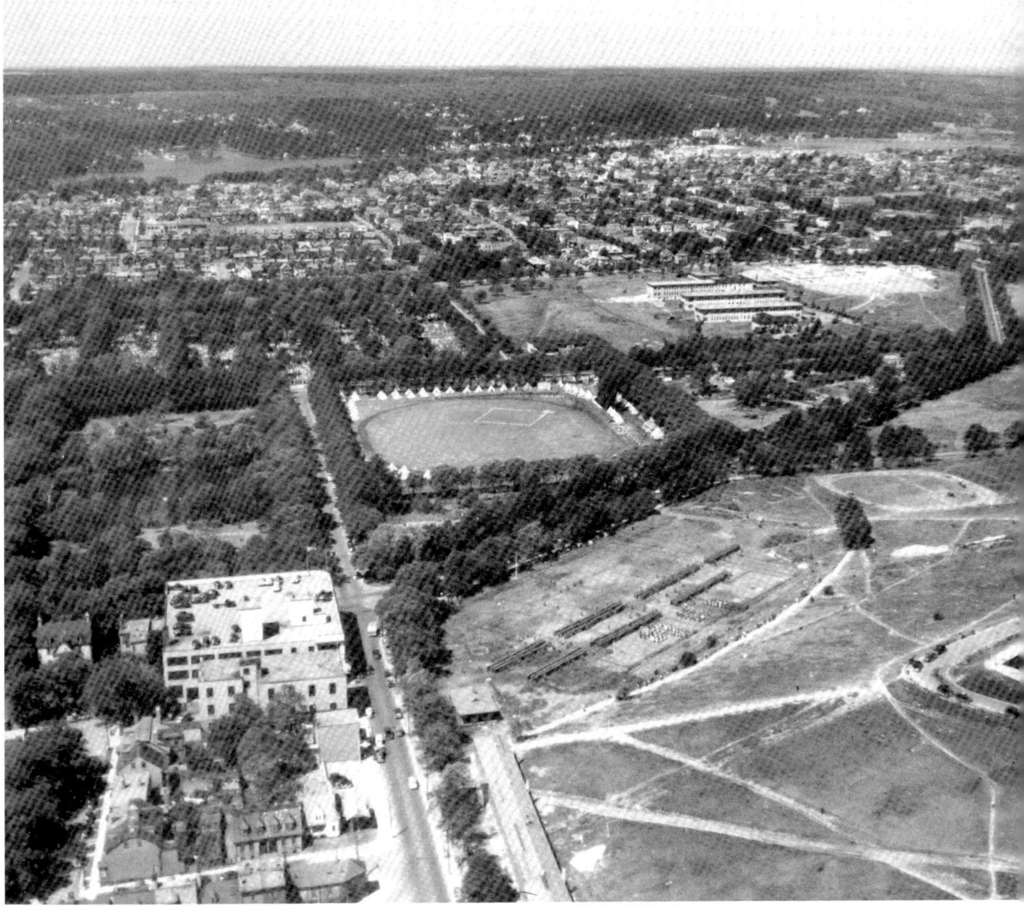

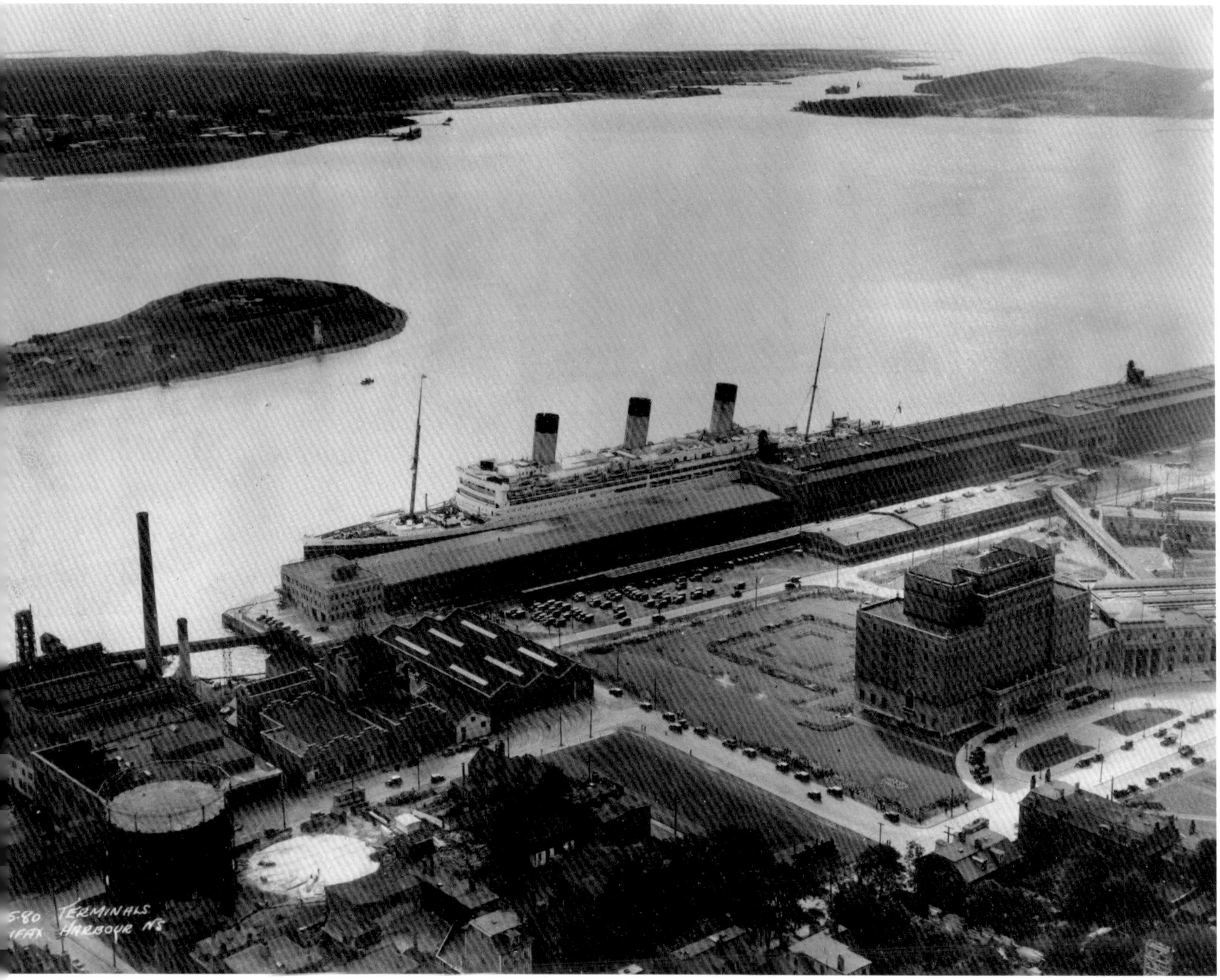
TERMINALS
HARBOUR NS

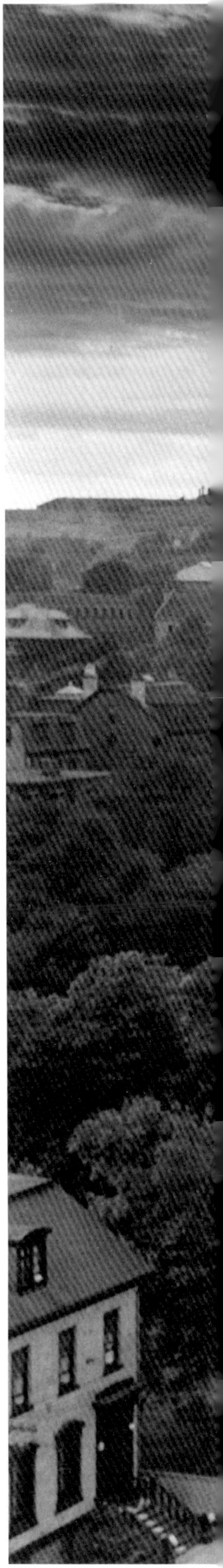

ABOVE: *This 1930s aerial view shows the Canadian National Railway's Nova Scotian Hotel and its proximity to the "Seawall," where a passenger liner is tied up at Pier 20. To the left can be seen the waterfront facilities of the Nova Scotia Light & Power Company, which included the steam generating plant, a coal gas generating plant, and car barn for the company's fleet of tram cars, known as the "Birney Safety Car." The hotel was a major component of the development of the Ocean Terminals. It and Union Station next door were linked to the Seawall with enclosed overhead walkways. The hotel was also surrounded by handsome gardens and fronted on Cornwallis Park, named in honour of Edward Cornwallis, the city's founder.*

RIGHT: *The Nova Scotian Hotel, from whose roof this photograph was taken, was a twentieth-century development in a neighbourhood which still maintained a distinctly residential and nineteenth-century air with its many wooden houses. The steeples belong to Saint Matthew's (United) Church and Saint Mary's (Roman Catholic) Cathedral. The Birney car seen in this view was "safe" because it was designed to stop automatically if the motorman was incapacitated and the doors would not open if the tram was moving. Their short wheel base made them ideal for navigating the tight curves of the trackage in the eighteenth-century layout of the downtown core.*

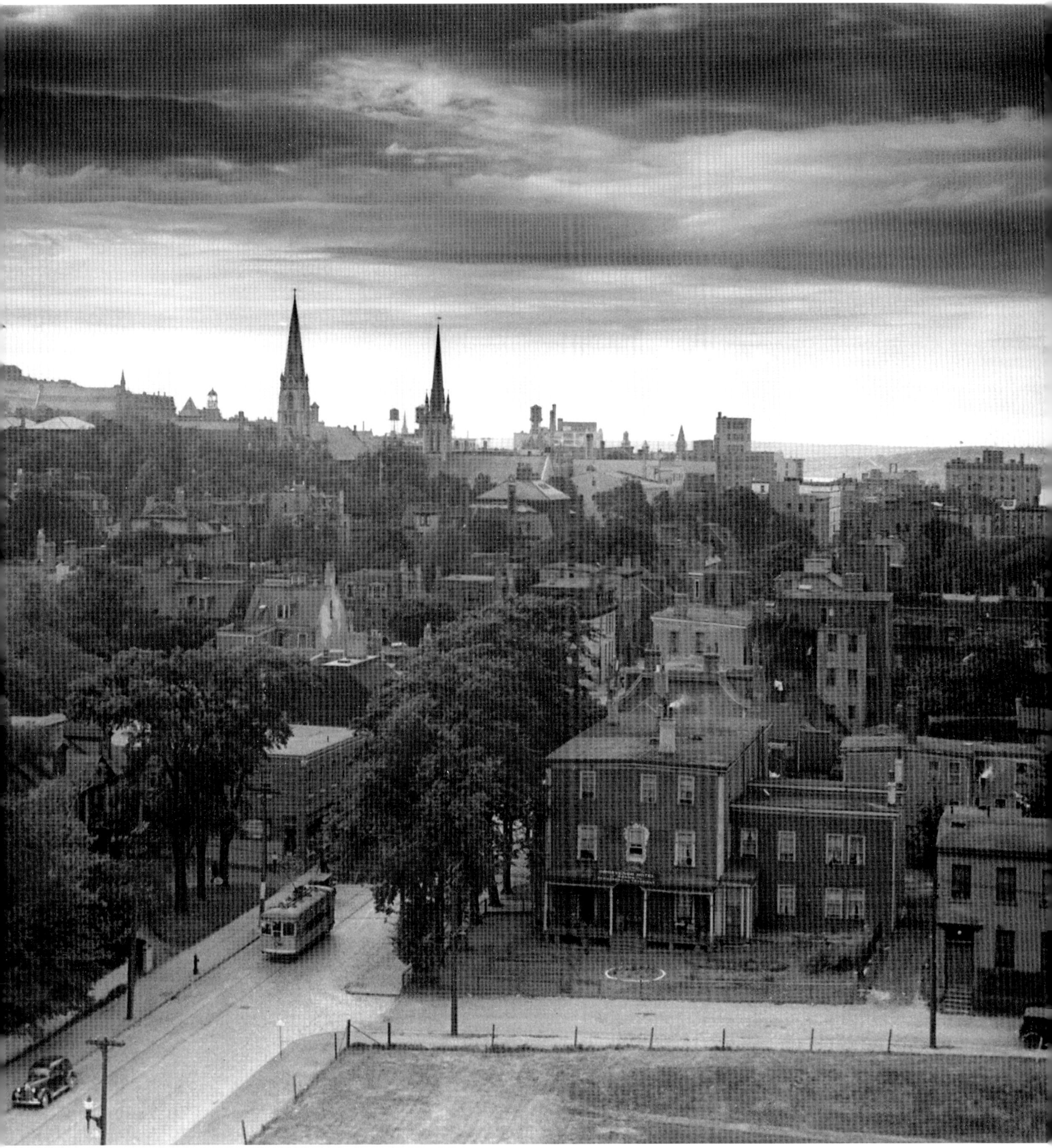

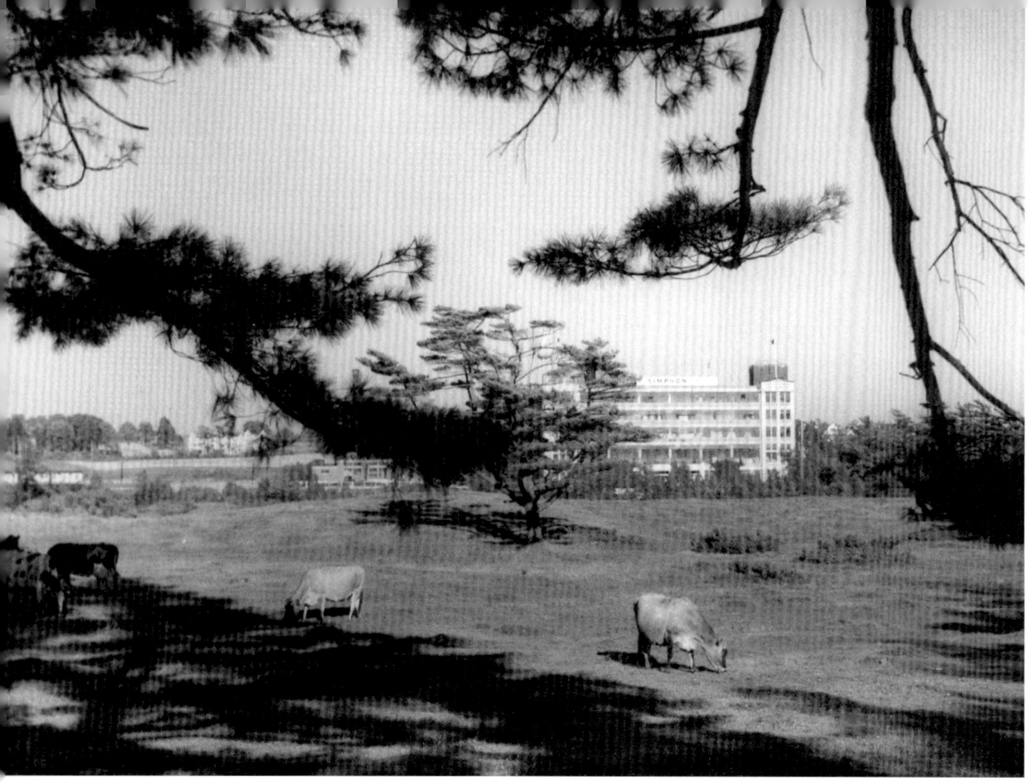

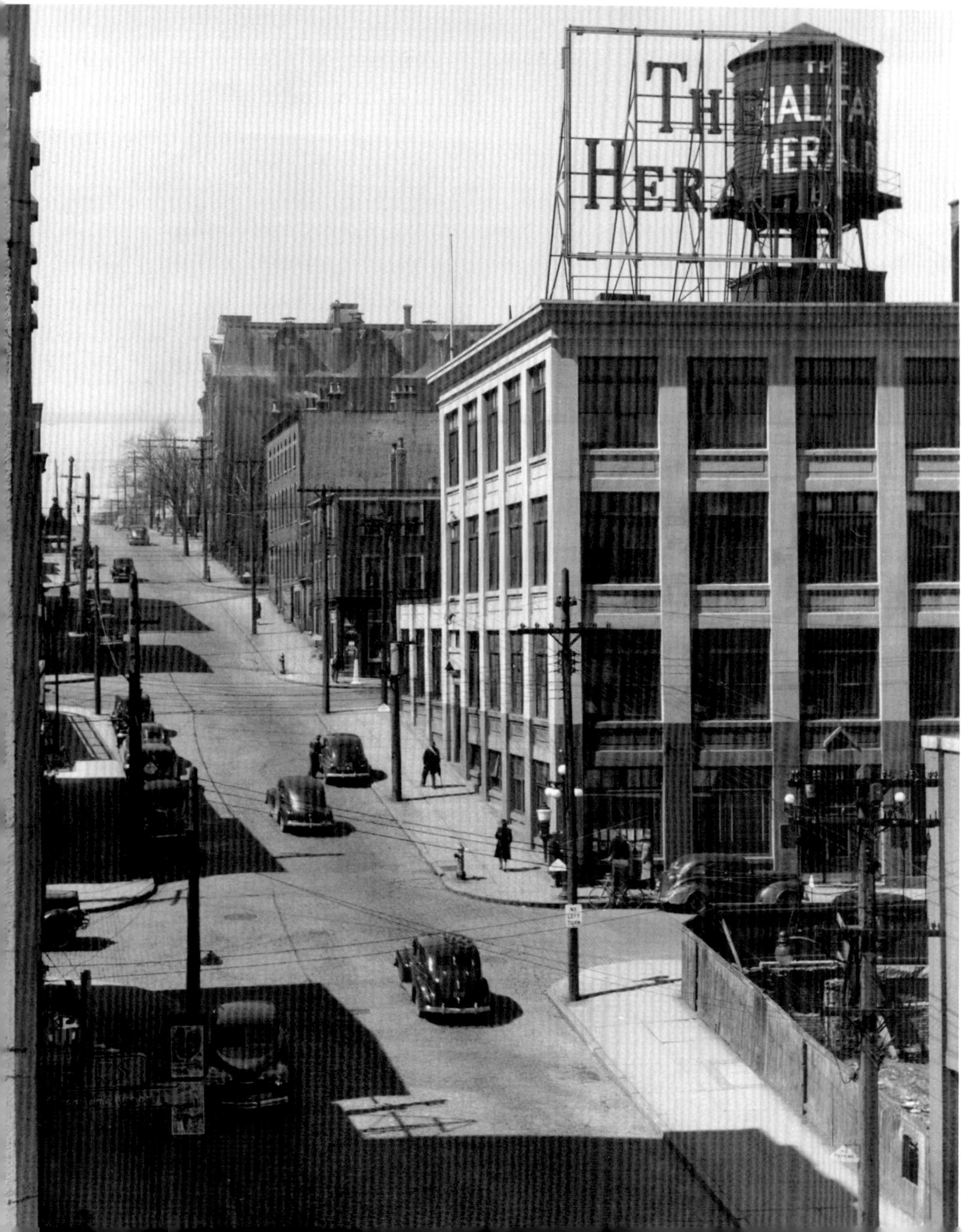
THE HERA
THE HALIFAX HERALD

TOP: *The isolation of Simpson's department store, built adjacent to empty fields which still lingered in the northwestern part of the peninsula, is clear. The cows probably belonged to the Saint Joseph's Industrial School, a boys' reformatory run by the Roman Catholic Church on a pastoral site now occupied by the Halifax Shopping Centre. After the war this bucolic scene quickly gave way to commercial and residential development, but the population in pre-war Halifax was not enough to fill up the peninsula.*

BOTTOM: *The steep climb from the harbour made Halifax a difficult city for pedestrians and horse-drawn conveyances. The Army put its Citadel at the top of the hill to overlook and protect HMC Dockyard and the anchorage. Sackville Street led up to the southern entrance of the Citadel, just out of sight on the top right in this view, and passed by the building of the* Herald and the Mail, *one of the city's two main newspapers, the other being the* Chronicle and Star *located at Granville and George.*

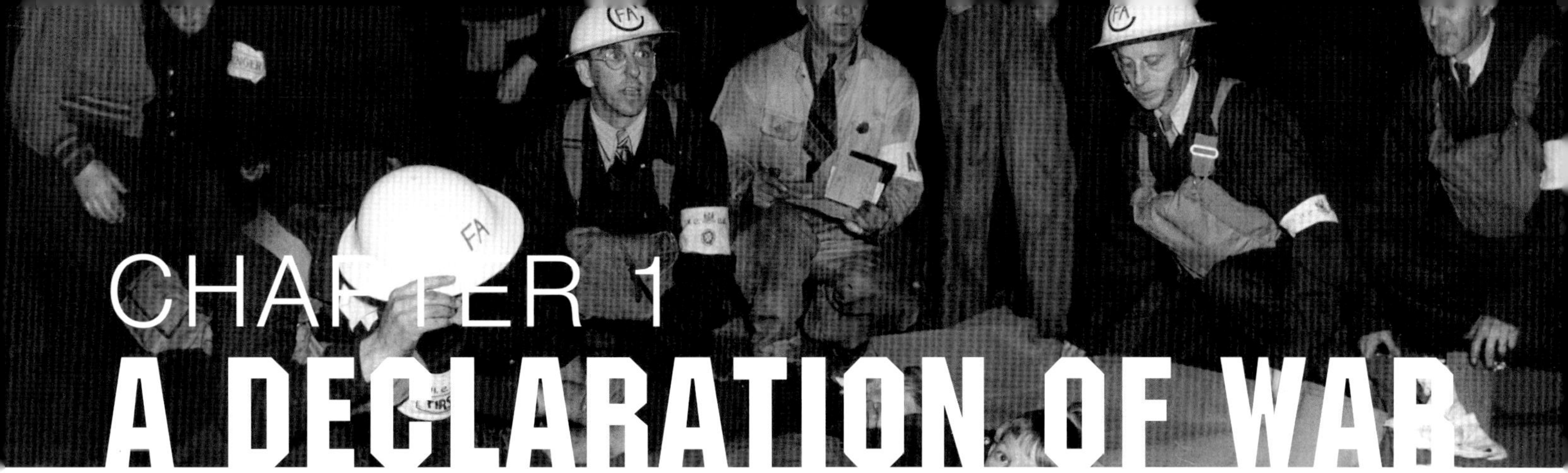

CHAPTER 1
A DECLARATION OF WAR

The visit of the King and Queen in the spring of 1939 was not just a nice idea. The hope that Hitler's territorial ambitions had been sated with the sacrifice of the German-speaking areas of Czechoslovakia in October 1938 quickly proved vain. The royal visit served to remind Canadians and, through their majesties' visit to Washington, D.C., Americans as well, of the connections to Britain. Behind the scenes military planners were furiously working to make up for lost time due to political complacency. Government and military authorities began to cast thoughtful glances in the direction of Halifax, the old Imperial naval base. Britain would need a link with North America in the event of war, and in spite of President Franklin D. Roosevelt's evident sympathies, neutrality was the long-term policy of the United States. Halifax's superb ice-free harbour and transcontinental rail links made it a logical jumping-off place for shipping to Britain. The logic that had made it such an obvious location for a western Atlantic naval base in the eighteenth century still applied.

If war came, it would be a shock for which Canada was ill-prepared, but not entirely unprepared. In Halifax, quiet organizational actions began during the early months of 1939. The Royal Canadian Mounted Police and Nova Scotia Light & Power (N.S.L.&P.) began to discuss the means of protecting the company's harbourfront generating and streetcar facilities. At this point attack from lightning-fast seaborne raids was seen as a genuine threat to the harbour facilities.

The old harbour batteries, last upgraded by the British in the 1890s, might have been dilapidated; however, even when defence spending was at its nadir in the 1930s, they had never been abandoned. A report by Major B.D. Treatt in 1936 had not only reaffirmed their role, but also outlined a five-year upgrading programme. That work was behind schedule, but no matter, a plan existed. Meanwhile, near Eastern Passage, just inland from a World War I–era American Navy seaplane base, work on new runways for the Royal Canadian Air Force, undertaken over two years earlier, was being rushed to completion.

In mid-August, with danger signs in Europe clear, the military was put on alert. On 26 August, mobilization orders were issued for Canada's armed forces. Hustle and bustle began to appear in the streets, even if it was dressed in uniforms from the last war and armed with 4.7" "Long Toms" and 8" Howitzers.

On 1 September 1939, German forces flooded across the border with Poland. KMS *Schleisen*, which had visited Halifax just two years before on a cadet training cruise amid many protestations of good will, poured shells into Polish coastal communities, and dive bombers screamed down from the skies above Polish cities. On 3 September, Britain and France declared war on the German Reich; the Canadian government followed a week later.

Most of Canada would not notice much difference for over a year, and then only when rationing began to make daily life difficult. In Halifax, which for security reasons was soon known as an "East Coast Port," the impact was immediate. Garrisons filtered out to the old forts at the harbour mouth. The first group of soldiers to head overseas, the 1st Division, gathered for a December departure. A squadron of Wapiti bombers of the tiny R.C.A.F. dropped out of the sky onto the grassy runways of the old Halifax Civic Airport from their former prairie home. Railway flatcars bearing anti-aircraft guns rolled into the railyards from Picton, Ontario. On 16 September, HX 1, the first trans-Atlantic convoy, set off from the harbour. The Atlantic, where just days before the always fickle weather had been the only problem, was suddenly more sinister. On 3 September, the very day that war was declared, a German submarine sank the passenger ship *Athenia*, loaded with tourists returning from European vacations, many of whom found their way to Halifax on the neutral American ship *City of Flint*. Thus began the Battle of the Atlantic, a struggle of savage intensity, on Germany's part to strangle Britain, and on Britain's part to survive. Initially seen as a struggle between surface navies, the German submarines, the U-boats, rapidly dominated; from a fleet of 30 in 1939, it rose to 300 by 1942, and in that year came close to winning the battle by sinking ships faster than they could be replaced. The rapid evolution of military technology was as much a part of the war story as were the men, ships, submarines, and battles: magnetic and acoustic mines, degaussing, radar, the snorkel, extended range of aircraft. In all its manifestations the struggle raged until the war ended in May 1945. More than any other city on the North American mainland, Halifax and its sister communities of Dartmouth, Bedford, and Rockingham were witnesses to this struggle.

Gently at first, but with increasing effectiveness, the civilian economy shifted to a war footing and administrative controls began to envelop the lives of those on the Home Front. For the first year or so, jobs and money, actual disposable income, increased. Even tourists from an America still at peace kept coming, eager to see this new attraction, a city wearing the trappings of war. Wit h the bombing of Pearl Harbor on December 1941, Americans, too, would don these war trappings to a degree they could not in 1939–1940 imagine.

RIGHT: *In December 1939, three and a half months after the beginning of World War II, the 1st Division of Canadian soldiers, hastily recruited from across the entire country, rolled into Halifax on the first of hundreds of troop trains. Some of these men did not see Canada again for nearly six years. Far more than most Canadian communities, the "East Coast Port" was keenly aware of the war from its first days. The soldiers in this photograph were the vanguard of 494,874 troops who embarked for overseas from here. Their lives and the lives of the citizens in the harbour communities were never the same again. From this vantage point, the enclosed overhead walkways that connected the steamship terminal to the railway station and the Nova Scotian Hotel are clearly seen.*

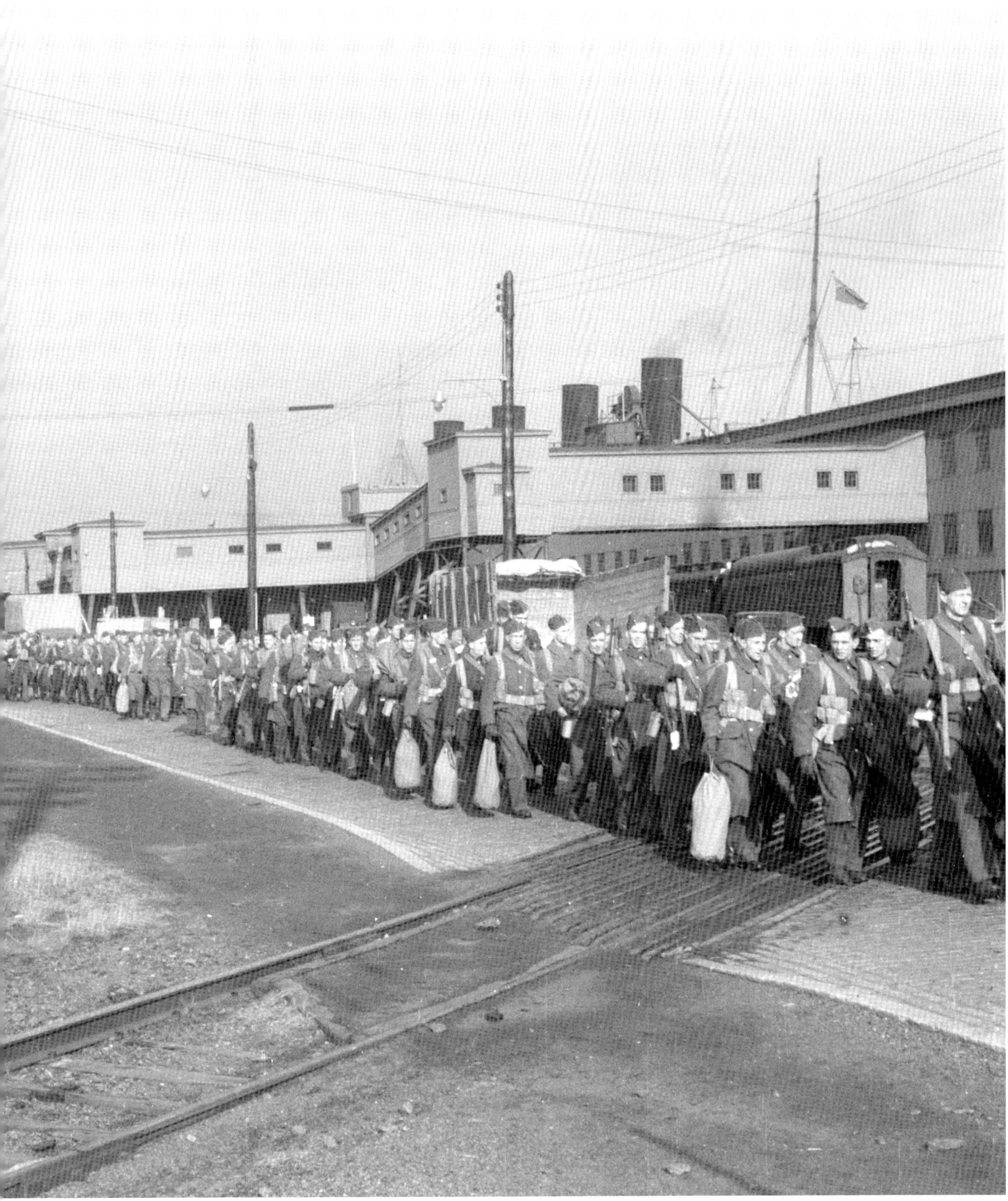

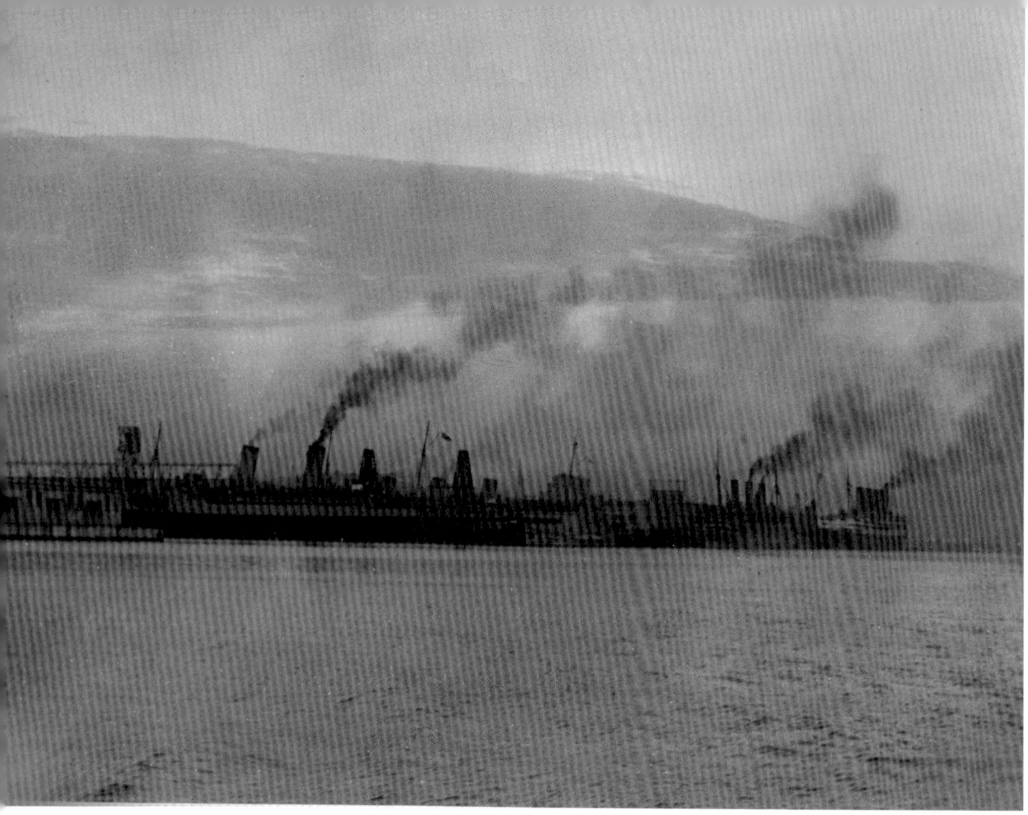

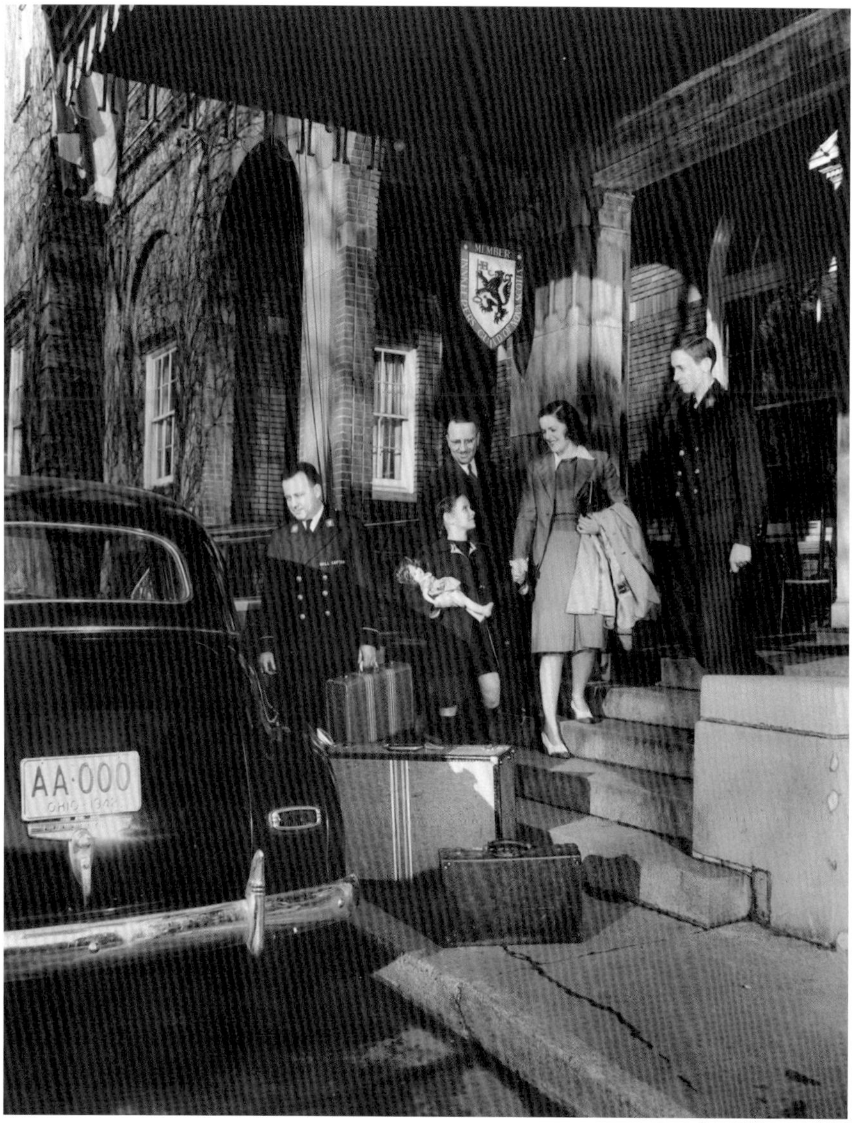

TOP: *As hastily as the 1st Division had been recruited, ocean liners, made redundant by the overnight transformation of the world's oceans into potential killing grounds, found a new life as troop transports. The 1st Division was lucky. Their transports, seen here on the eve of departure, retained most of their pre-war splendour and many a soldier who had been a hobo a year before found himself relaxing in the posh surroundings of a first class lounge. Soon, however, this luxury was swept away and endless ranks of utilitarian bunks filled the lounges, smoking rooms, and cabins. Only the names were left to the ocean greyhounds —* Queen Mary, Queen Elizabeth, Pasteur, Aquitania, Mauritania, *and many more.*

BOTTOM: *One type of visitor to Halifax in the early days before war restrictions hit hard was the tourist from a still-neutral United States. In an expression of* schadenfreude, *Americans were fascinated by the sight of a nation at war, of convoys heading out to sea, of battleships that meant business, of blackouts and recruiting posters. After December 1941, these sights would be their reality too, but not just yet, and for a time Nova Scotia made hay out of the war, theatre in the round as the city forged ahead with wartime preparations. Here tourists from Ohio arrive at the Lord Nelson Hotel on the corner of Spring Garden Road and South Park Street.*

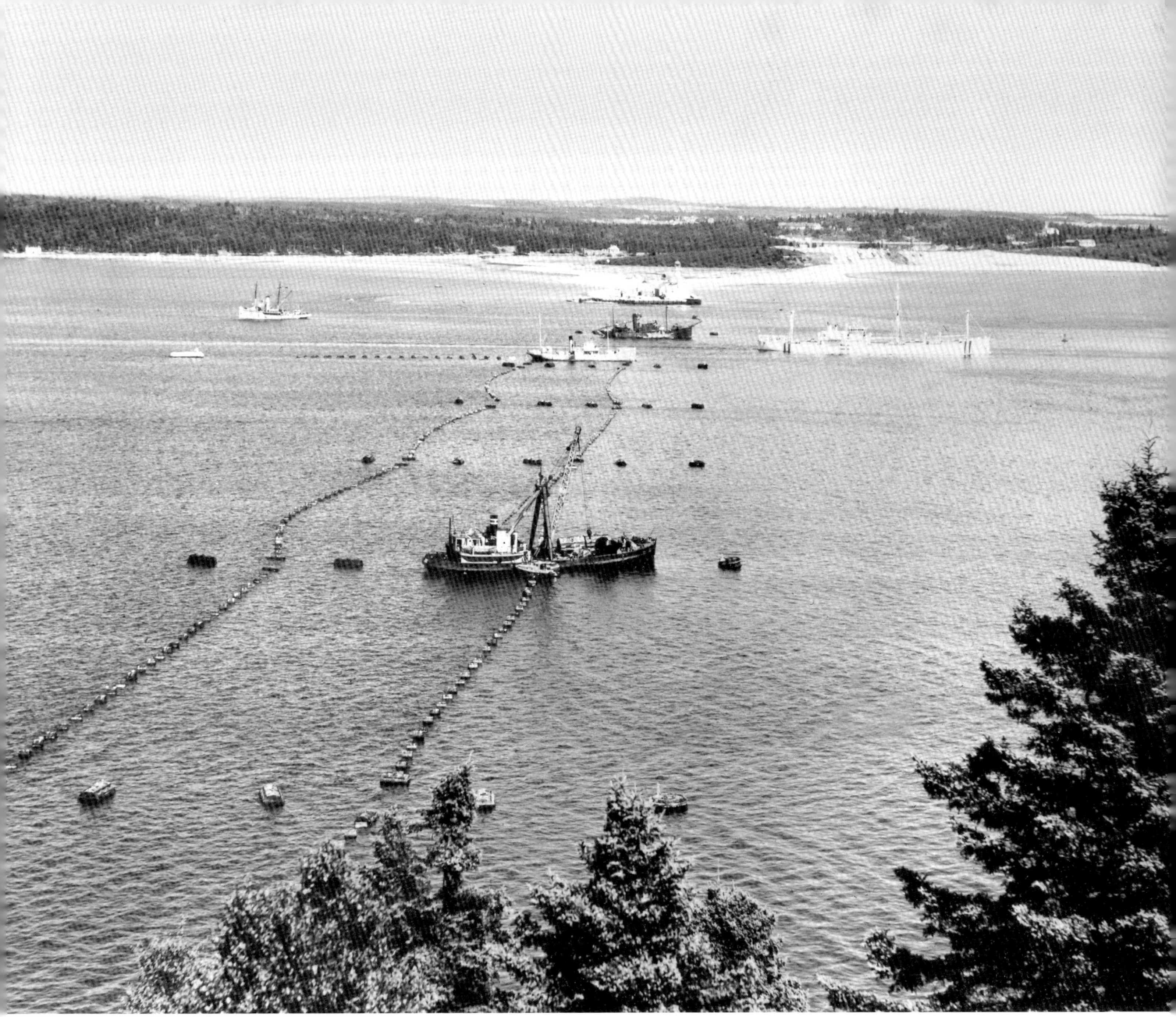

ABOVE: *Other than pilotage fees, there was nothing to prevent the coming and going of ships in and out of peacetime Halifax Harbour. It did not take the 14 October torpedoing of MS* Royal Oak *at its anchorage in Scapa Flow to convince naval officials that Halifax Harbour needed protection. That work was already in hand by the Foundation Company. By mid-November 1939, with remarkable speed, an "Anti-Submarine Boom Defence" was installed between McNab's Island and York Shore below York Redoubt. It consisted of a massive net of steel rings suspended from buoys, which touched the harbour bottom at any state of the tide. An entrance or gate was controlled by two "gate vessels," which pulled aside a section of the net to allow authorized ships to come and go.*

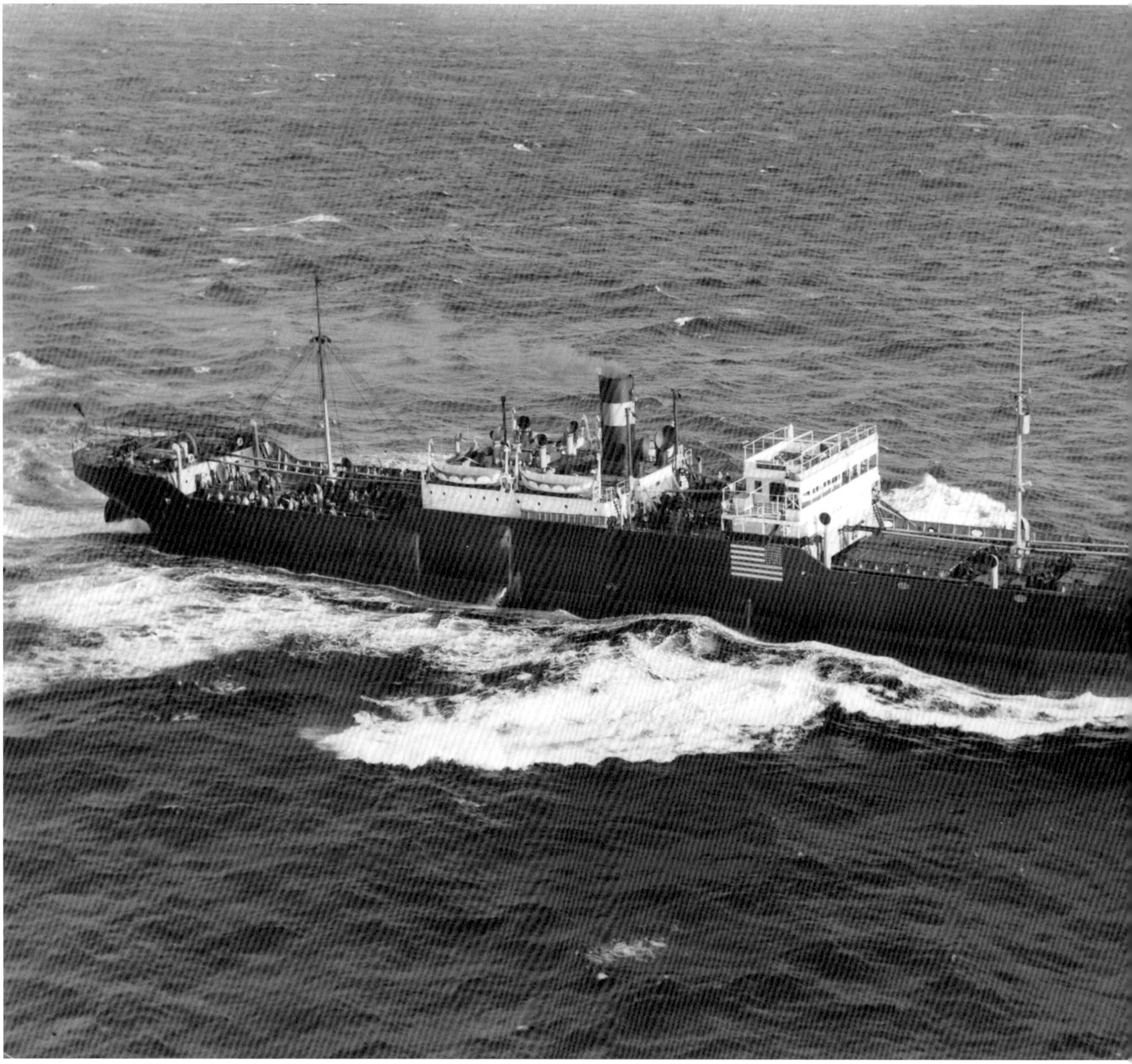

ABOVE: *That the war was going to be a serious business became apparent very quickly. On 3 September, the very day war was declared, the German submarine U-30 sank the Donaldson liner* Athenia *off Ireland, with the loss of 118 lives. The ship was crowded with passengers, including many American tourists heading home from a European vacation cut short by circumstances beyond their control. Two hundred of the passengers were picked up by the neutral American ship* City of Flint, *seen here, which brought them to Halifax where they arrived on 13 September. The German government, which still had hopes that the uproar over the invasion of Poland would blow over, was as upset by the sinking as anyone. It was well aware that the British had been handed a huge propaganda opportunity, which they indeed exploited to the full, painting the Nazis once more as barbarians attacking innocent civilians.*

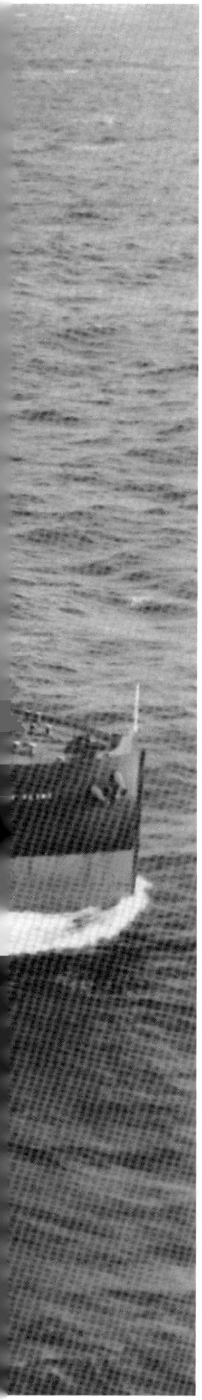

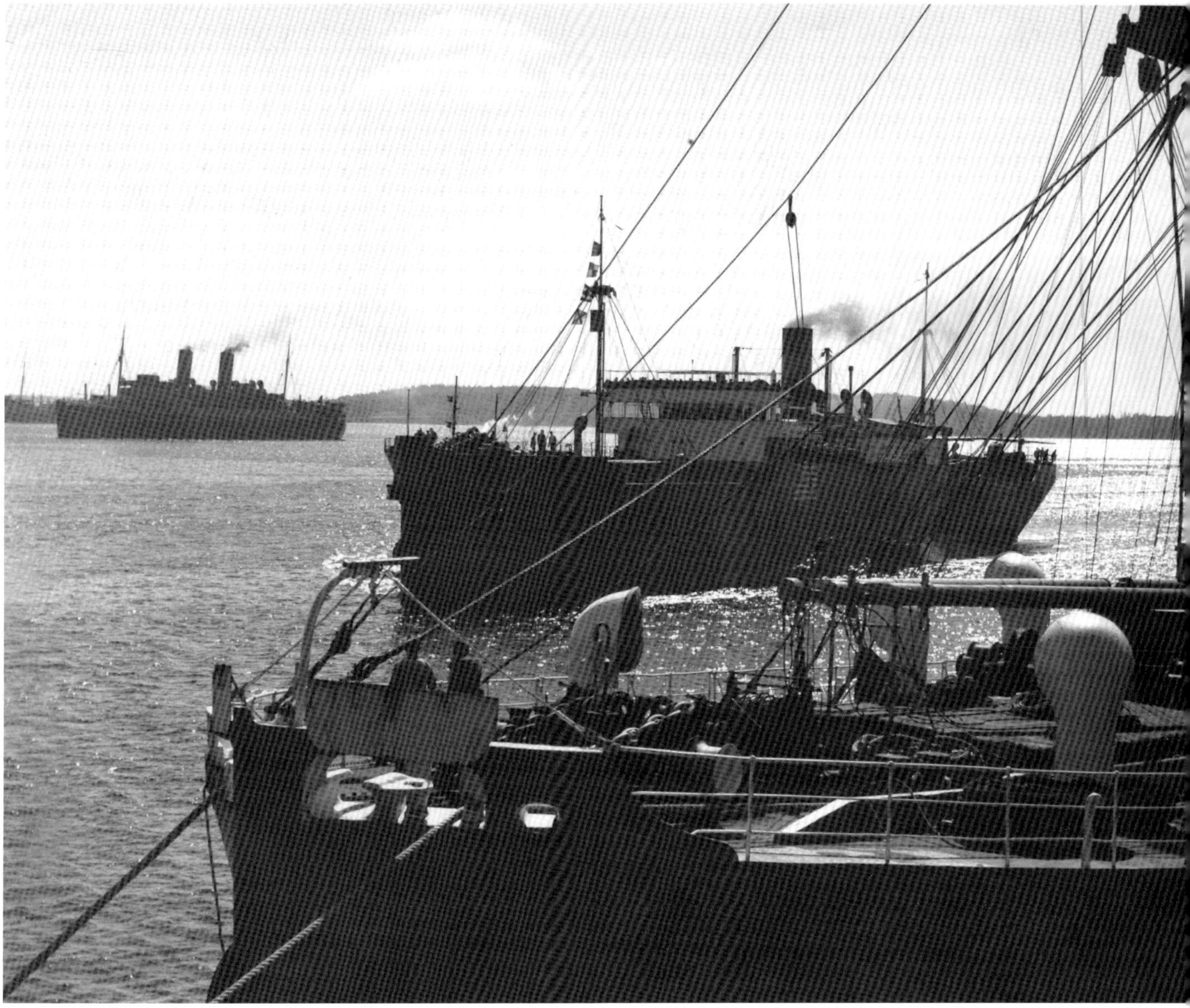

ABOVE: *Ironically, the* City of Flint, *shown here docking in Halifax with* Athenia *survivors, was within a month captured by the German pocket battleship* Deutschland; *its cargo of lubricating oil was declared contraband and seized as a German prize. After a series of adventurous manoeuvers, it was returned to the Americans by the Norwegian government, but the Germans had their revenge with a torpedo in 1943. Every convoy that left the port of Halifax contained ships and crews that could tell dramatic stories like this one of disaster or near-disaster. Sadly, many never survived the crossing to tell the tales.*

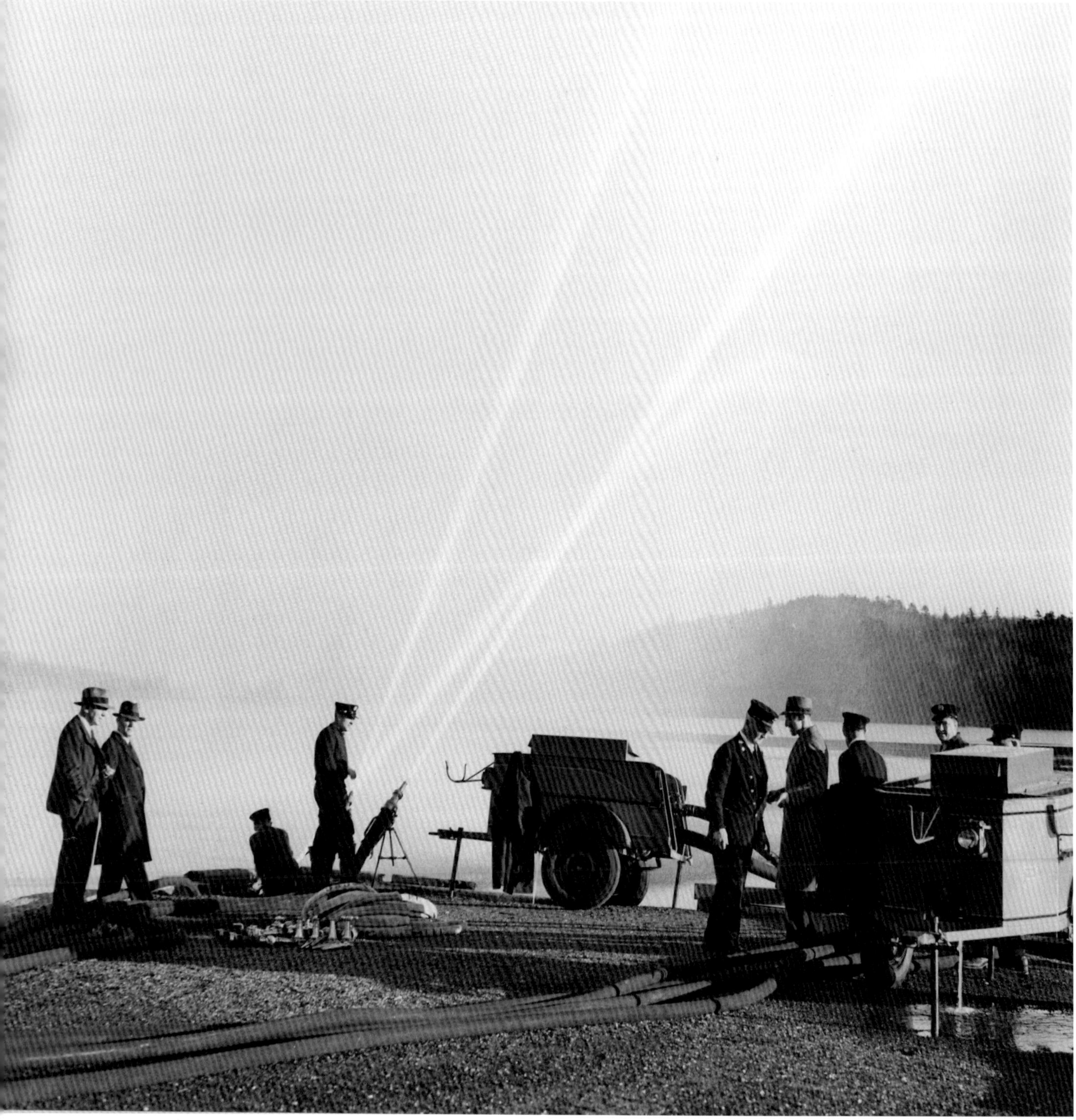

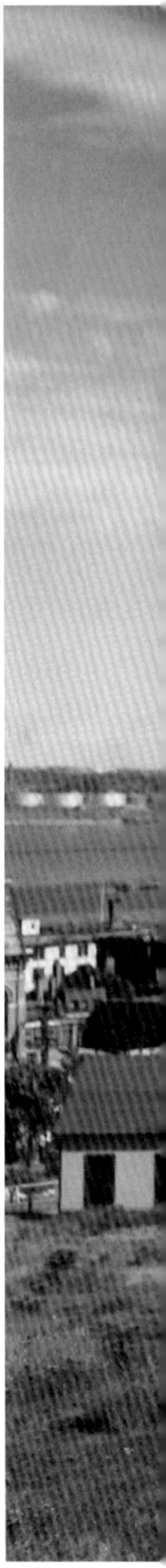

ABOVE: *From the civilian point of view, the Air Raid Precaution organization was the most high-profile component of Civil Defence. Based on 1920s British precedents, civilian society was organized to cope with the destabilizing effects of aerial bombing and even invasion. The civilian chaos which accompanied the fall of France in May and June 1940 convinced authorities that civilian society must be trained and organized like the military, under the umbrella of Civil Defence. Every sector was given a role. Here, able-bodied men are testing a new A.R.P. pumper, one of thousands supplied across the country to douse fires started by German incendiary bombs. This programme provided some communities with their first-ever real firefighting equipment.*

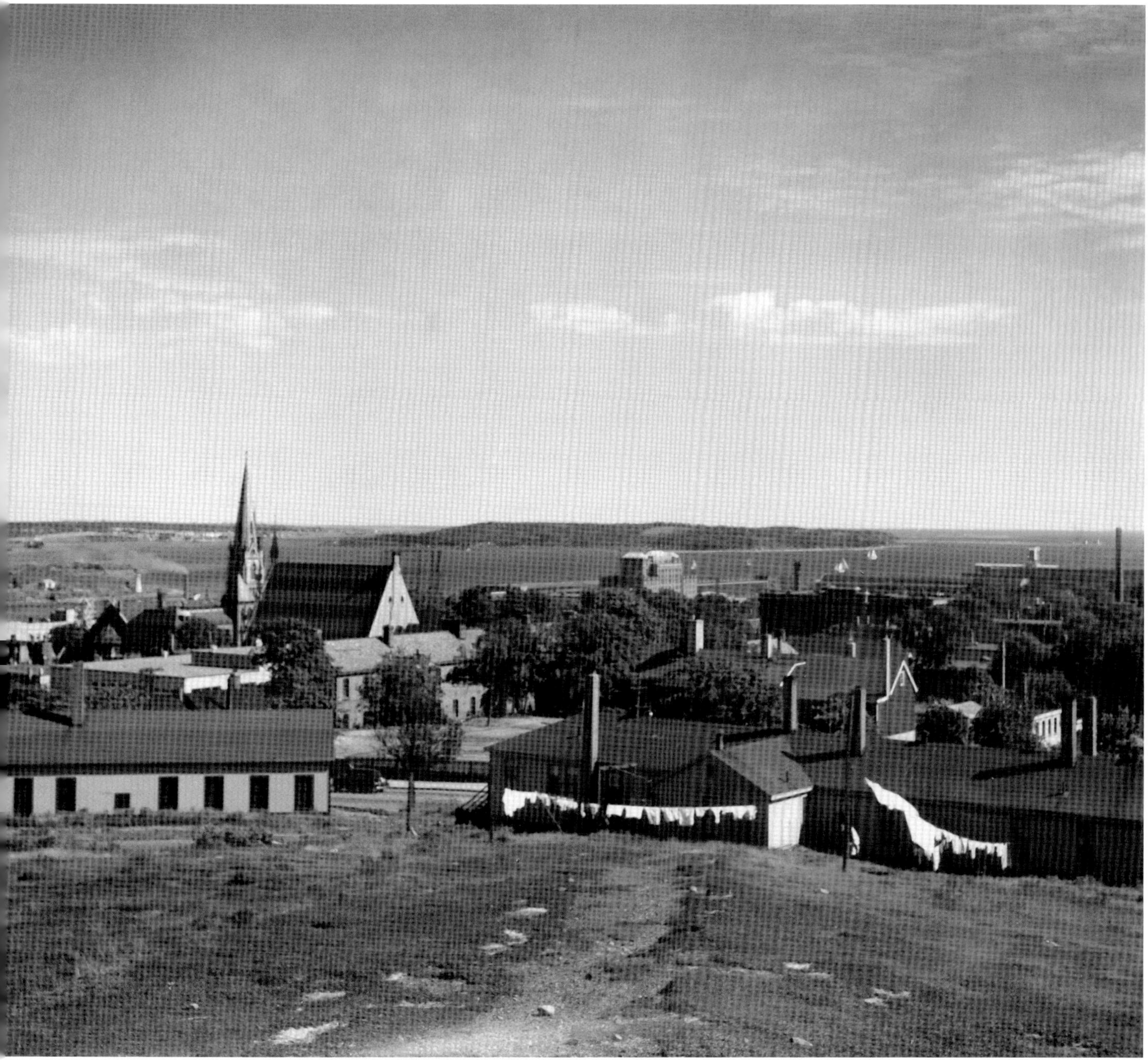

ABOVE: *In the city, old British military installations sprang into action. Below the Citadel, Royal Artillery Park became an administrative facility, a nucleus from which many offspring facilities grew. Its earliest contribution was World War I ordnance spruced up to serve for coastal defence until better stuff came along. In this photo, taken about 1940, R.A. Park remains intact, before post-war development pushed Brunswick Street through to Spring Garden Road. The old South Barracks with laundry can be seen, as well as the back of Saint David's Church, the tower of Saint Mary's Cathedral, and the top of the Nova Scotian Hotel looking towards McNab's Island. The Anti-Submarine Boom Defence is just offstage to the right.*

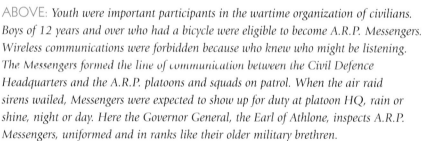

ABOVE: *Youth were important participants in the wartime organization of civilians. Boys of 12 years and over who had a bicycle were eligible to become A.R.P. Messengers. Wireless communications were forbidden because who knew who might be listening. The Messengers formed the line of communication between the Civil Defence Headquarters and the A.R.P. platoons and squads on patrol. When the air raid sirens wailed, Messengers were expected to show up for duty at platoon HQ, rain or shine, night or day. Here the Governor General, the Earl of Athlone, inspects A.R.P. Messengers, uniformed and in ranks like their older military brethren.*

RIGHT: *For many on the Home Front, joining the A.R.P. was not only a patriotic contribution to the war, but a much enjoyed social and community focus. Its meaningful activities replaced many increasingly unpatriotic pre-war pleasures such as picnics in the country or Sunday drives. Civil Defence activity also resulted in significant improvements for communities. Resources such as those shown here, impossible for many communities to contemplate before September 1939, were suddenly showered upon them as part of war's largess. After 1945, reluctant to return to the old ad hoc ways, communities were allowed to retain the wartime equipment and continued the wartime spirit by forming volunteer fire departments.*

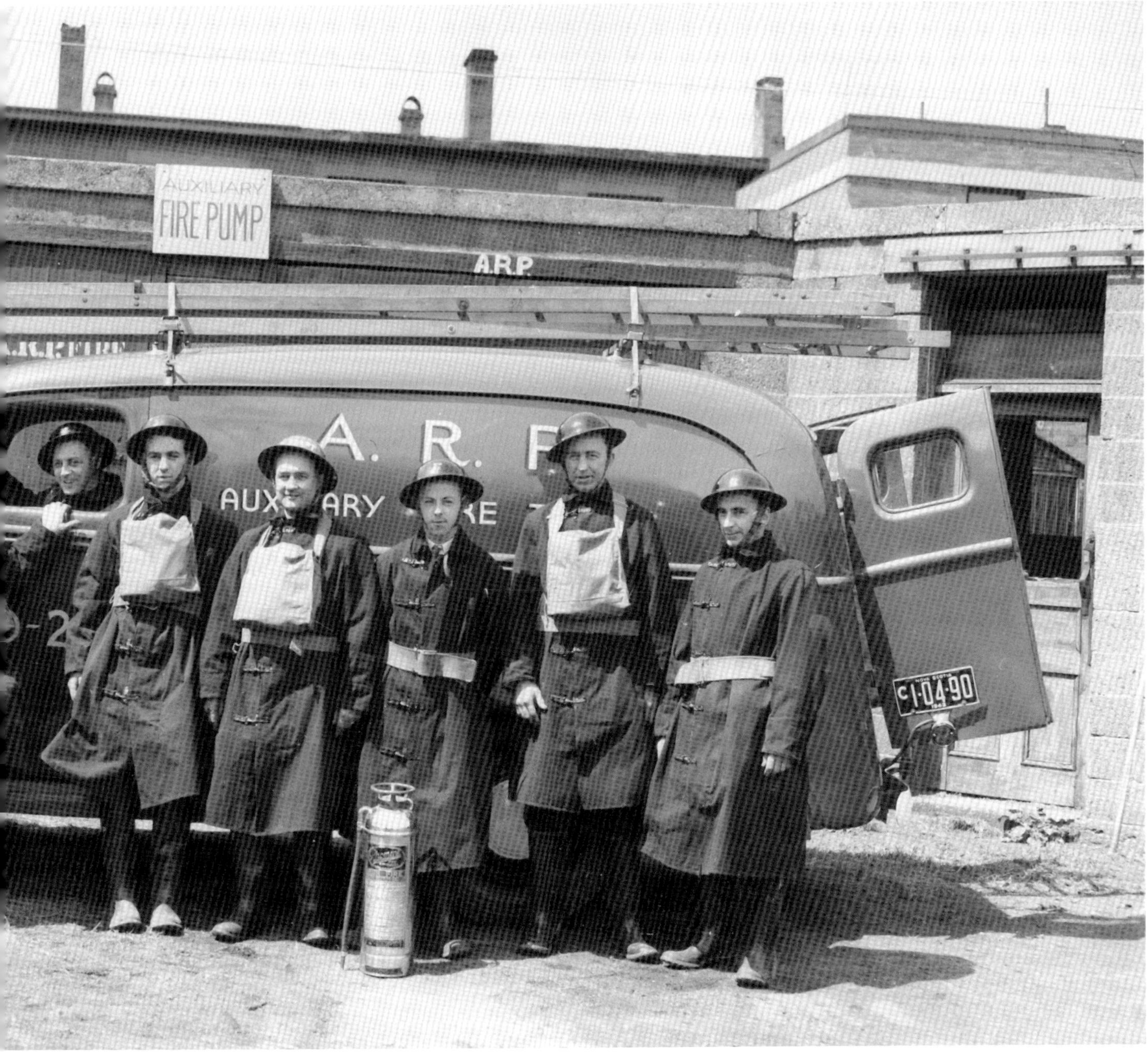
AUXILIARY
FIRE PUMP
A.R.P.
A. R. P.
C1-04-90

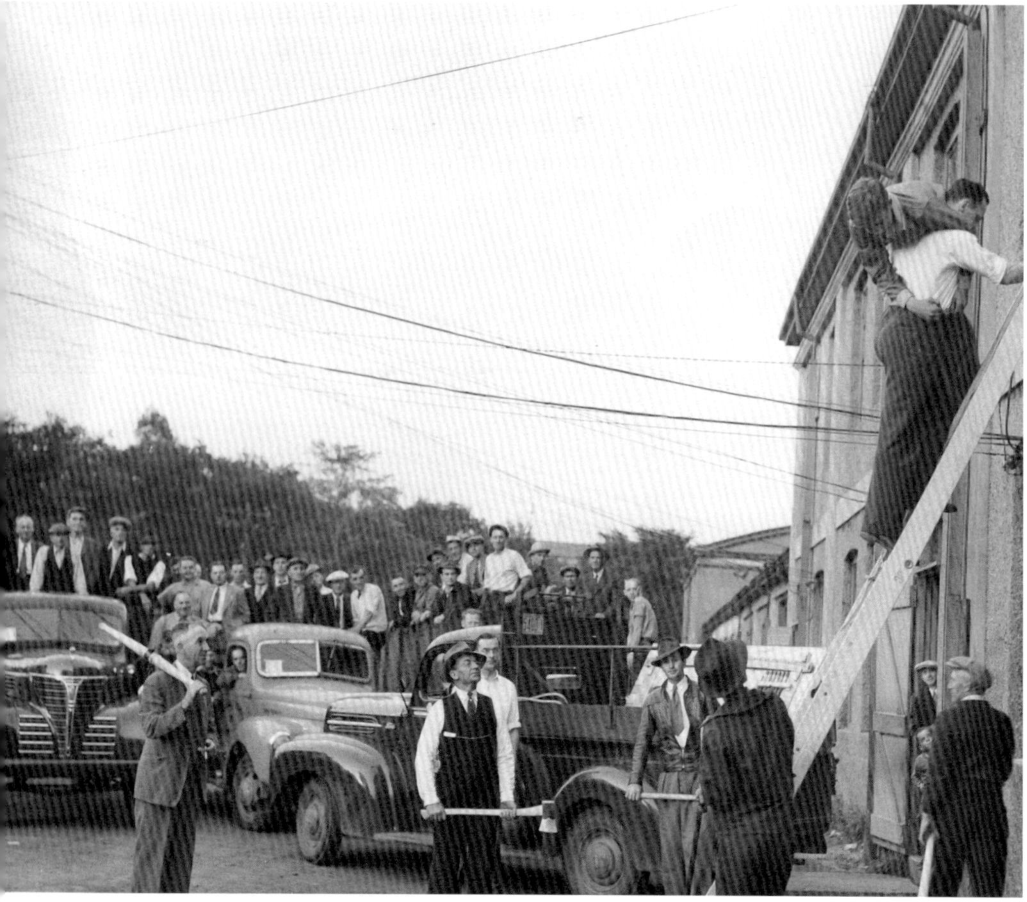

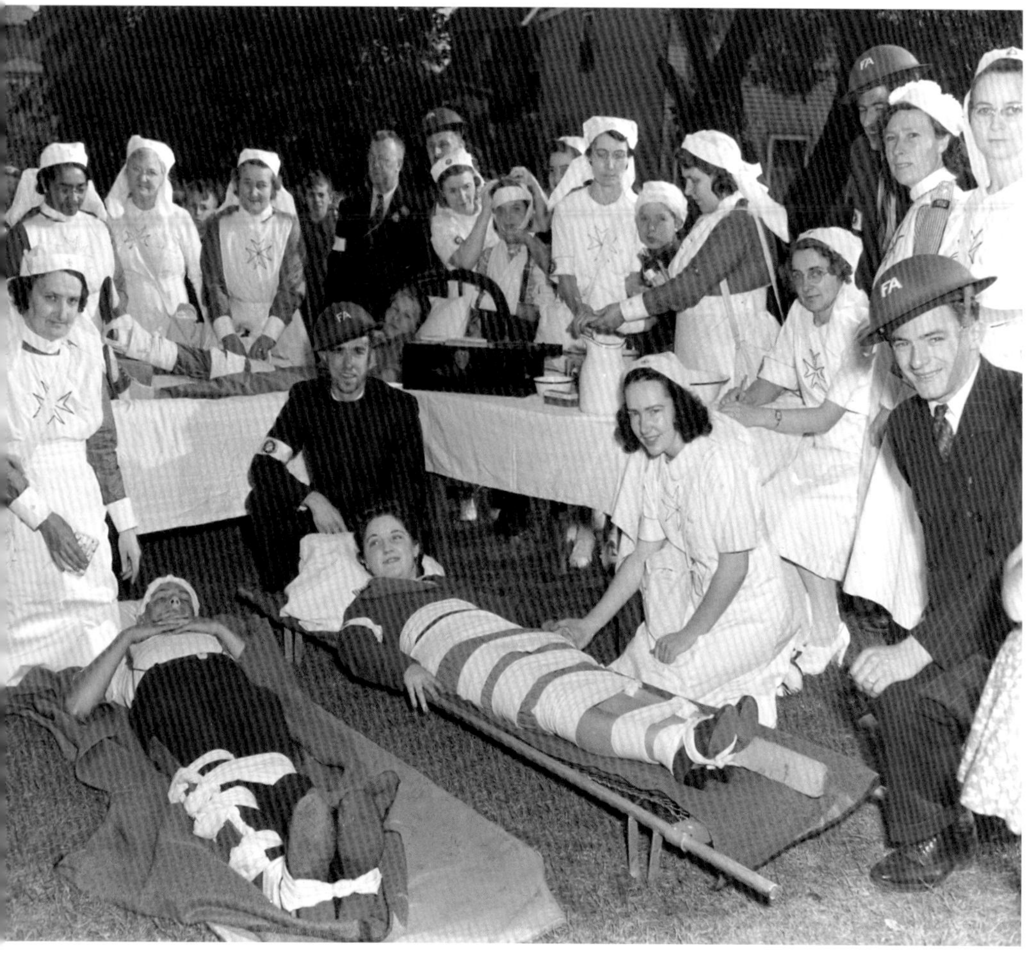

TOP: *Mock disasters such as the one shown here were intended to ensure that in the event of a German air raid comprehensive first aid training would protect and assist most if not all civilians, that communities would have the capacity to rescue survivors and deal with injuries until professional help came. During practice air raids, the Red Cross and St. John's Ambulance showed up at key designated locations in the community, which were staffed until the "all clear" sounded.*

BOTTOM: *Mock air raids were conducted with as much realism as possible, with exciting air battles, dummy bomb drops, and of course simulated carnage from which the dead and dying had to be extracted. Within two years of the war's start, the civilian population of the East Coast Port had every reason to feel that they were as much a part of the war effort as those in active service.*

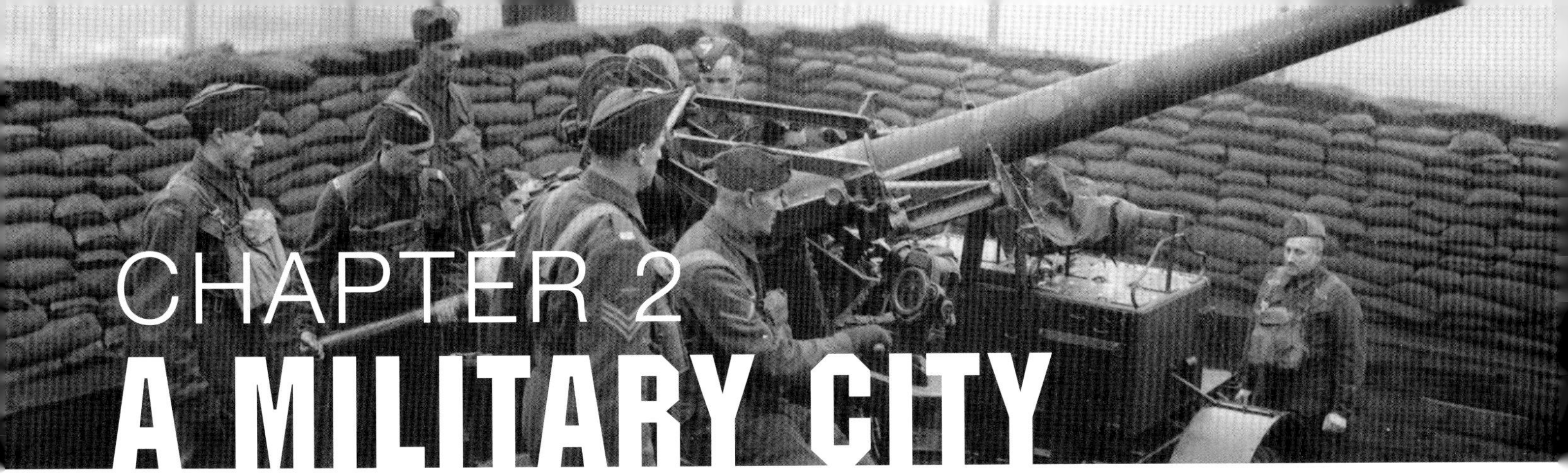

CHAPTER 2
A MILITARY CITY

In its role as the western anchor of the convoy lifeline to Britain, Halifax took on a very definitely military aura. At first it was tentative. Some of the ordnance and some of the uniforms were left over from World War I. All three services, the Royal Canadian Navy, the Army, and the Royal Canadian Air Force, underfunded orphans for two decades, struggled to cope with the sudden urgency of wartime roles. But once resources appeared, it was clear they all knew what they wanted and needed to do.

The 13 ships and 13,000 personnel of the Royal Canadian Navy were quite inadequate for their assigned role. Their Atlantic base was the picturesque but still nineteenth-century naval dockyard on the Halifax waterfront. In the autumn of 1939, the Royal Navy, under Admiral Stuart Bonham-Carter, reappeared in the harbour to provide stiffening, it operated out of a former motor yacht. In October 1941, the R.C.N. was well on its way to becoming the third-largest of the Allied navies, and Admiral Bonham-Carter headed home. By 1945, the R.C.N. had some 375 ships and 110,000 men and women in its ranks, and a proud and impressive record in the Battle of the Atlantic. HMC Dockyard, a crowded beehive of buildings and activity, scarcely resembled its antique self of six years before. Only in the last year of the war did it overcome a reluctance to invest in shore-based housing for its personnel, preferring instead to cast them upon an inadequate rental market. By then it was too little and too late and the consequences proved disastrous.

The Army had inherited from its Imperial predecessors an antique but more or less serviceable infrastructure. It was intended to defend the port and HMC Dockyard from nineteenth-century enemies, but the Army had a plan for the new realities, drawn up in 1936 by Major B.D. Treatt of the Royal Artillery. Though at a glacial pace, the Halifax defences were being upgraded. With the declaration of war, this work shifted into high gear. Some of the old harbour batteries were upgraded, such as Fort McNab; others were abandoned, such as George's Island; and brand new ones, such as Devil's and Chebucto Batteries, were quickly built. A spider's web of searchlights and anti-aircraft batteries protected the harbour from air attack. An Anti-Submarine Boom Defence and protective minefield backed up by an arc of searchlights and daily patrols by minesweepers guarded the port from the sea.

The vast majority of the Army personnel who came to Halifax during the war were on their way overseas to provide the human resources for the Normandy invasion, but a substantial garrison was needed to man the harbour defences and support the massive troop movements. For these, temporary barracks and office buildings sprang up everywhere, from downtown parks to isolated outposts.

The Royal Canadian Air Force did not even exist in World War I, but now a glamourous, technologically oriented newcomer appeared, liberated to some degree by its "new boy" from the venerable traditions which sometimes affected its sister services. For years the only local airport had been the grass runways of the Halifax Civic Airport in the open fields between Chebucto and Bayer's Roads on the Halifax peninsula. Adequate enough for the sturdy open cockpit biplanes of the post-World War I barnstormers, it had no future in the dramatic advances that occurred in aircraft technology, even in the straitened days of the Depression. Realizing this, the Canadian government began serious work on a new air base, RCAF Dartmouth, just inland of a location used by the United States Navy as a seaplane base in the closing days of World War I. Not quite complete when war was declared, the Halifax Civic Airport saw a few more weeks activity as home for a squadron of Wapiti bombers, rushed from their prairie base, until the runways were finished in November.

RCAF Dartmouth, with HMCS Shearwater in 1948, was the headquarters of Eastern Air Command, whose jurisdiction took in Canada's Atlantic coastline. It was a base for patrol aircraft, both land-based and amphibious, which kept an eye on coastal ship movements, patrolled for submarines, and escorted convoys as far as their range allowed. Eventually, the increasing range of patrol aircraft, based in Gander, Goose Bay and Iceland, in conjunction with British-based equivalents, provided an umbrella over the North Atlantic and significantly reduced the threat of the U-boat.

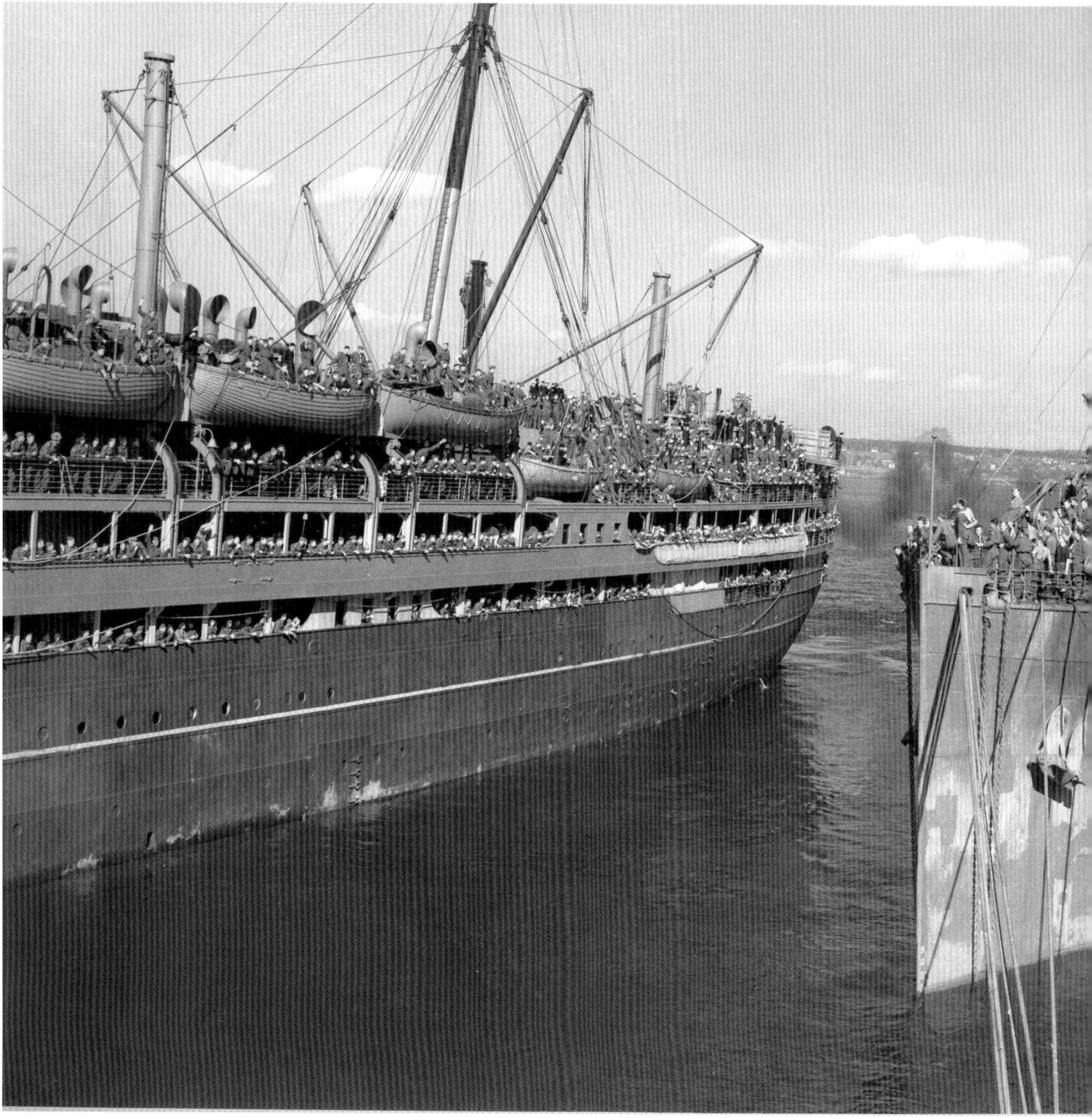

LEFT: *The build-up of troops heading to Britain began well in advance of D-Day on 6 June 1944. Passenger liners from all over the world, their peacetime purpose vanishing overnight, found a new lease on life as troop transports. Many, built for the sunny routes of the Caribbean or the South Pacific via the Suez Canal, found themselves battling the cold grey seas of the North Atlantic. For the initial voyages neither the crews nor the ships were equipped for such conditions. Sooner rather than later, however, the verandah lounges, swimming pools, and handsome dining salons disappeared under ranks of utilitarian bunks, the gleaming white paint was covered by dirty grey and rust, and the once-luxurious vessels merged into their new environment.*

ABOVE: *As the war got underway the "East Coast Port" communities witnessed the passage of tens of thousands of service personnel rolling in on long troop trains, coming from as close as the Annapolis Valley or Debert, others from the far reaches of a vast Dominion. It was possible for a soldier to see virtually nothing of the city if he arrived in the dark because blackout blinds sealed him off from the outside world as his train rolled right up to the dock, his only contact with Halifax the few hundred feet between the railway car and the gangplank of the troop ship from which he would next emerge in Liverpool or Glasgow. If a troop ship departed during the day, thousands of soldiers lined the sides waving to the hundreds of civilians who gathered to see such spectacles as these vessels laden with human cargo.*

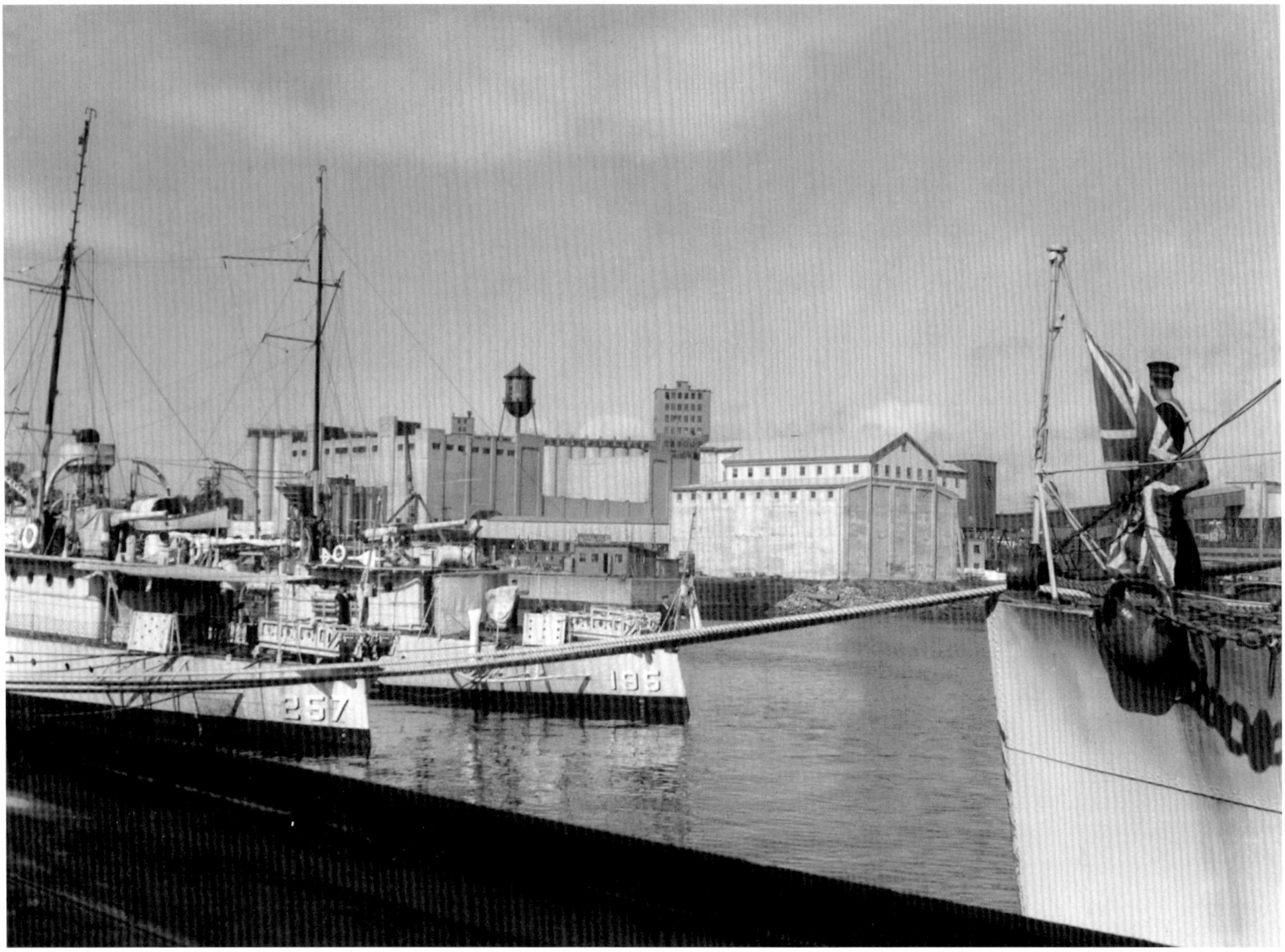
257

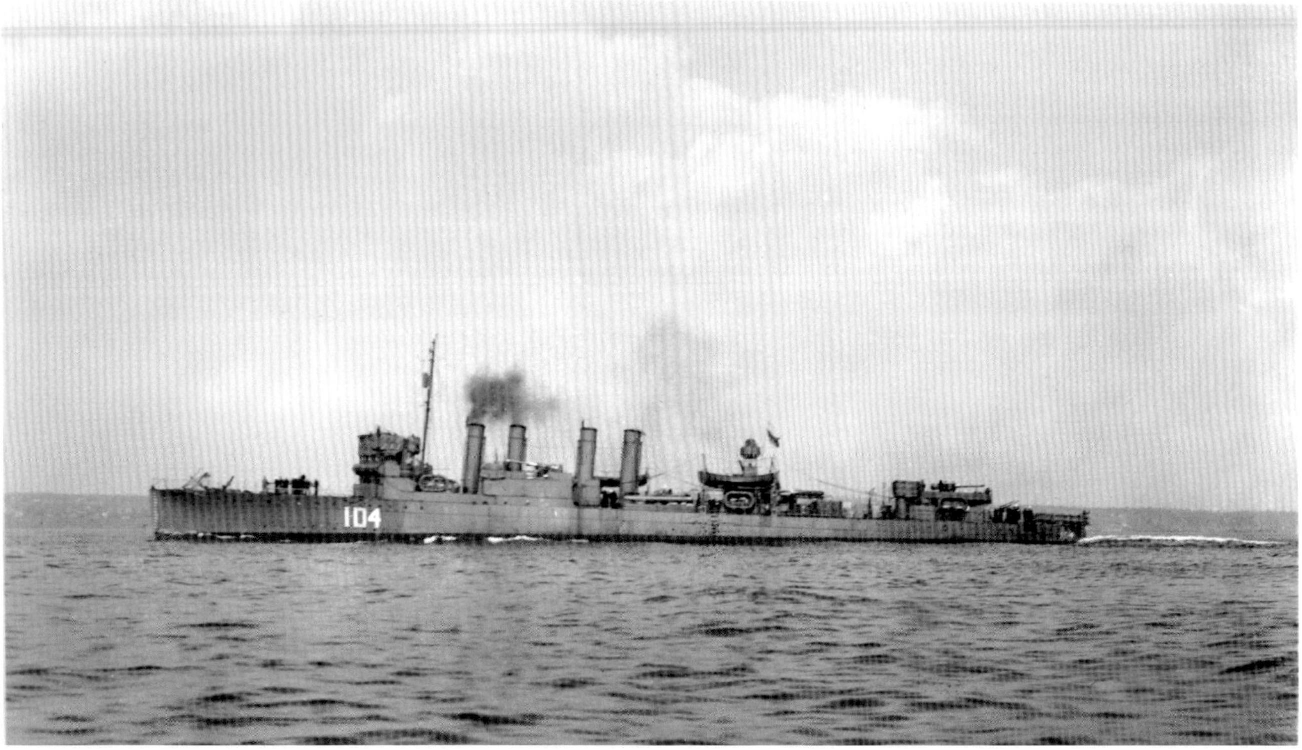
104

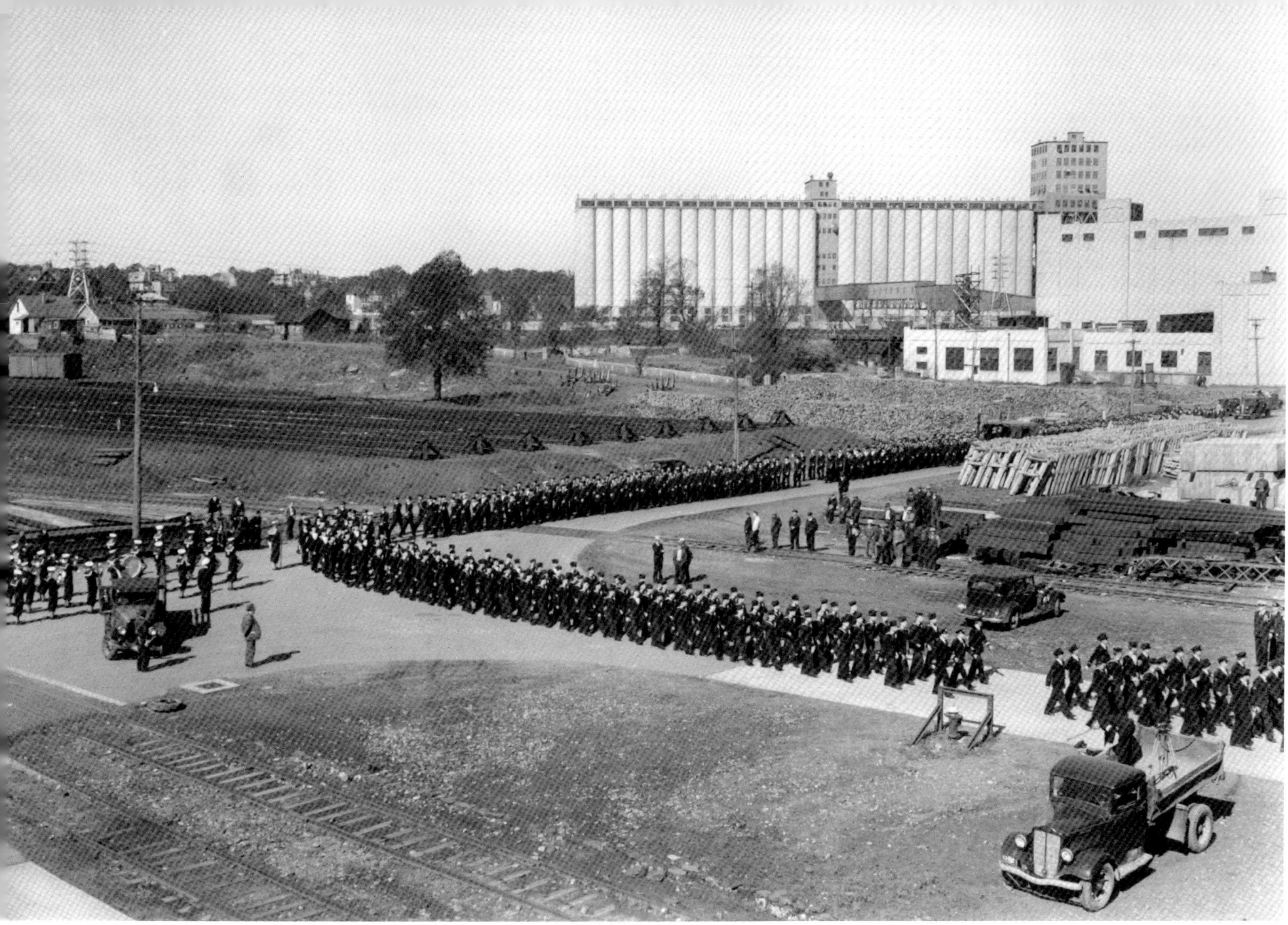

TOP LEFT: *Roosevelt and his advisers, in consultation with Winston Churchill, came up with the idea of lending destroyers in return for long-term leases of military bases in British colonies (the lend-lease programme). An example was the substantial American military presence in Argentia, Newfoundland, at the time a British Protectorate. There were others in Bermuda and the West Indies. Although most of the destroyers, 50 in the first batch, were of World War I vintage with four stacks, they became invaluable additions to the British and Canadian navies until industrial production was put on a full wartime footing. Here a sailor raises the Union Jack on one of the previously American ships.*

BOTTOM LEFT: *The careful maintenance of the fiction of American neutrality became unnecessary after Pearl Harbor brought the United States into the war without reservation. In the interim the form, if not the spirit, was carefully observed. American naval crews sailed the lend-lease ships into Halifax in September 1940, hauled down the American ensign, embarked on waiting trains, and departed. For a few hours on a sunny 24 September day, the stateless ships slumbered alone and deserted. Then the tramp of marching feet was heard and down the quay came squads of R.N. and R.C.N. sailors, each heading for one of the silent ships, six of which were designated for the R.C.N. The R.N. transferred two more later. Once on board, the white ensign was hauled up on the staff, allegiance switched from Franklin Roosevelt to George VI and a new navy was born.*

ABOVE: *R.C.N. crews march through the Ocean Terminals to board their "new to them" ships. These sailors, and thousands like them, made their home base in the harbour communities for the duration of the war, communities which had no idea what to do with them, or where to put them when ashore or on leave.*

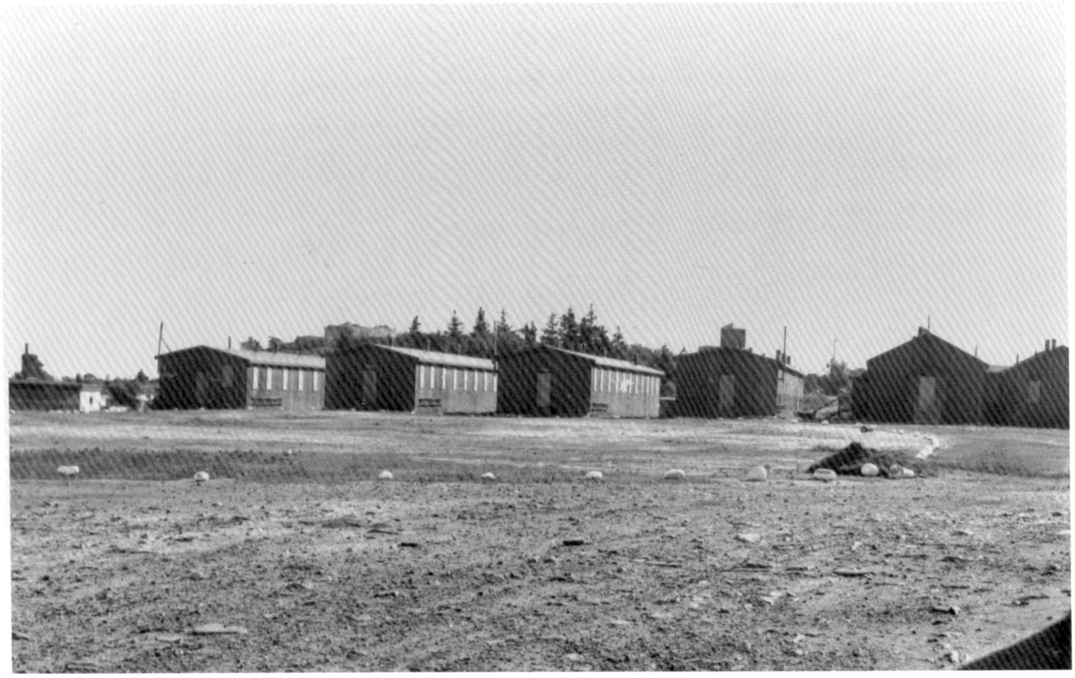

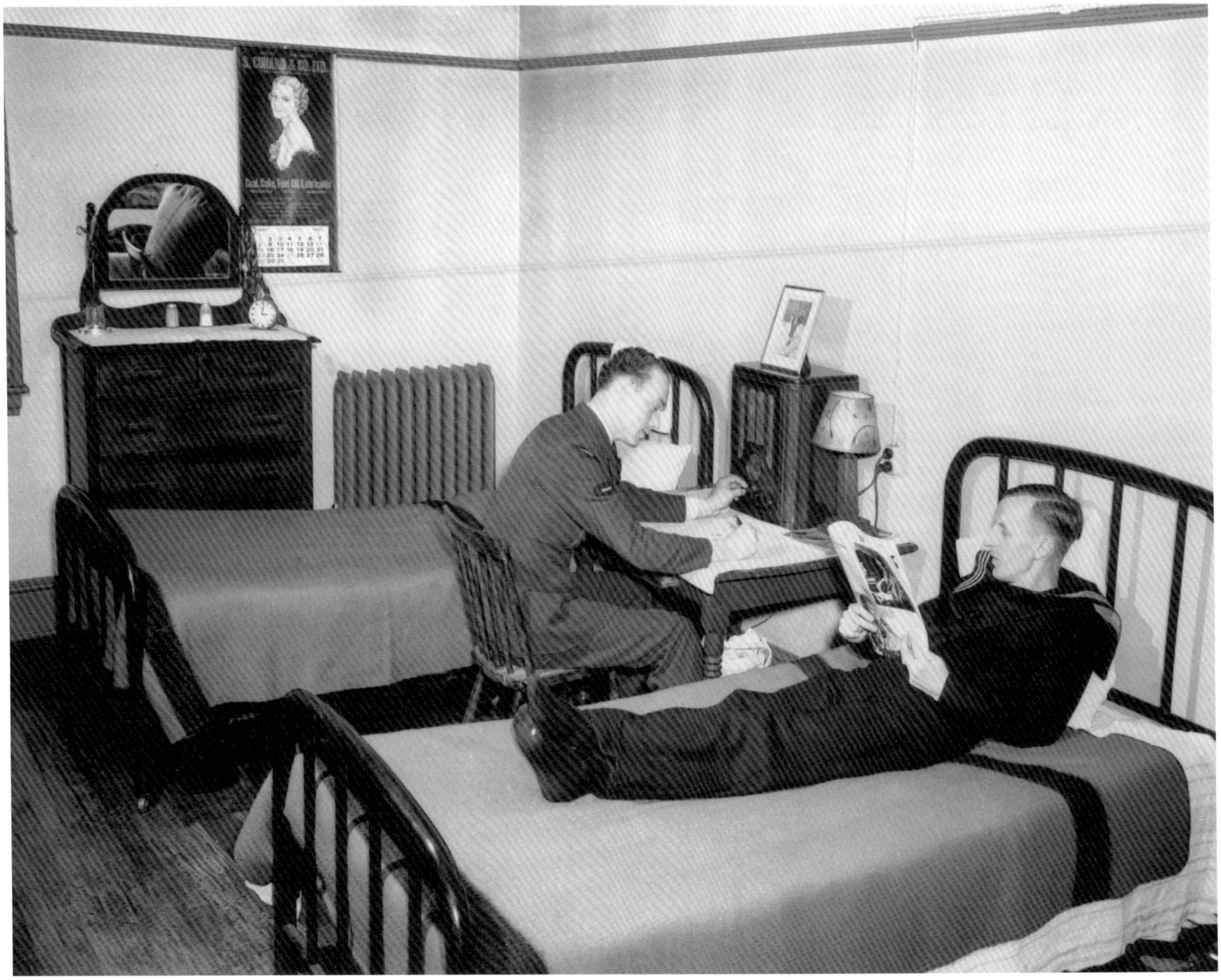
Coal, Coke, Fuel Oil, Lubricants

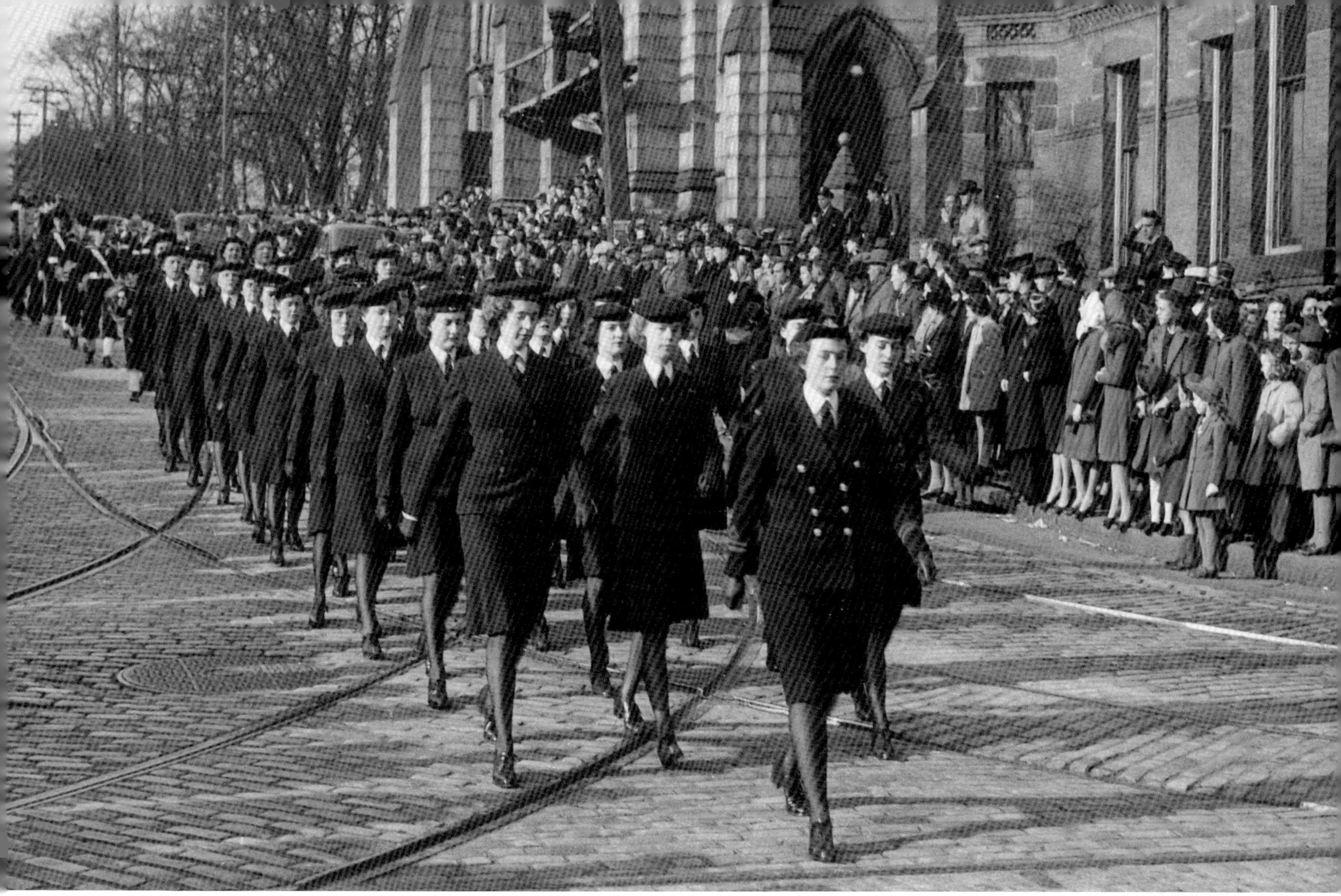

TOP LEFT: *While the Canadian Navy was expanding by hook or by crook, so too was the garrison designated to protect it. Although the R.C.N. only reluctantly came to accept a responsibility to house its shorebound personnel, the Army and the Air Force were prepared to do so from the beginning. This commitment did not mean that the housing was comfortable or attractive. These unlovely rows of hastily erected wooden barracks at York Redoubt, characterized by the liberal application of green coated tarpaper, were found at every outpost and on formerly vacant lands downtown.*

BOTTOM LEFT: *For the thousands of service men who came to the port of Halifax, the type of barrack shown here was a public relations fantasy. Even in the R.C.A.F., which had a somewhat more elite reputation, spacious and comfortable facilities were few and far between.*

ABOVE: *By 1941, it was becoming clear that Total War was inevitable. It was acknowledged that there would not enough men of military age to fight a long and demanding war without some rethinking of the established ways of doing things. One solution was to allow women to enlist, releasing men from administrative duties for active service. Perhaps only the crisis of war could have made such a dramatic social revolution possible because the concept that a woman's place was in the home was a deeply entrenched belief. This photograph shows a contingent of the Women's Royal Canadian Naval Service (W.R.C.N.S. though they were referred to, like their British counterparts, as W.R.E.N.S.) parading east on Spring Garden Road at the corner of Barrington Street. Saint Mary's Cathedral is on the right. Note the bricked road of "scoria blocks" and tram car trackage.*

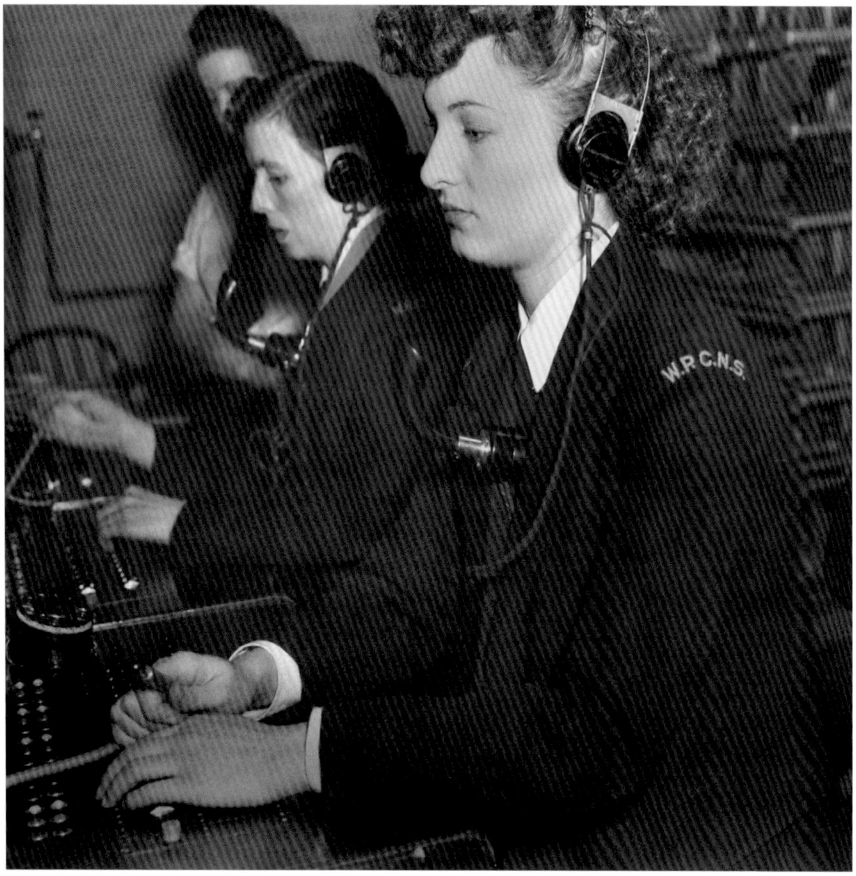

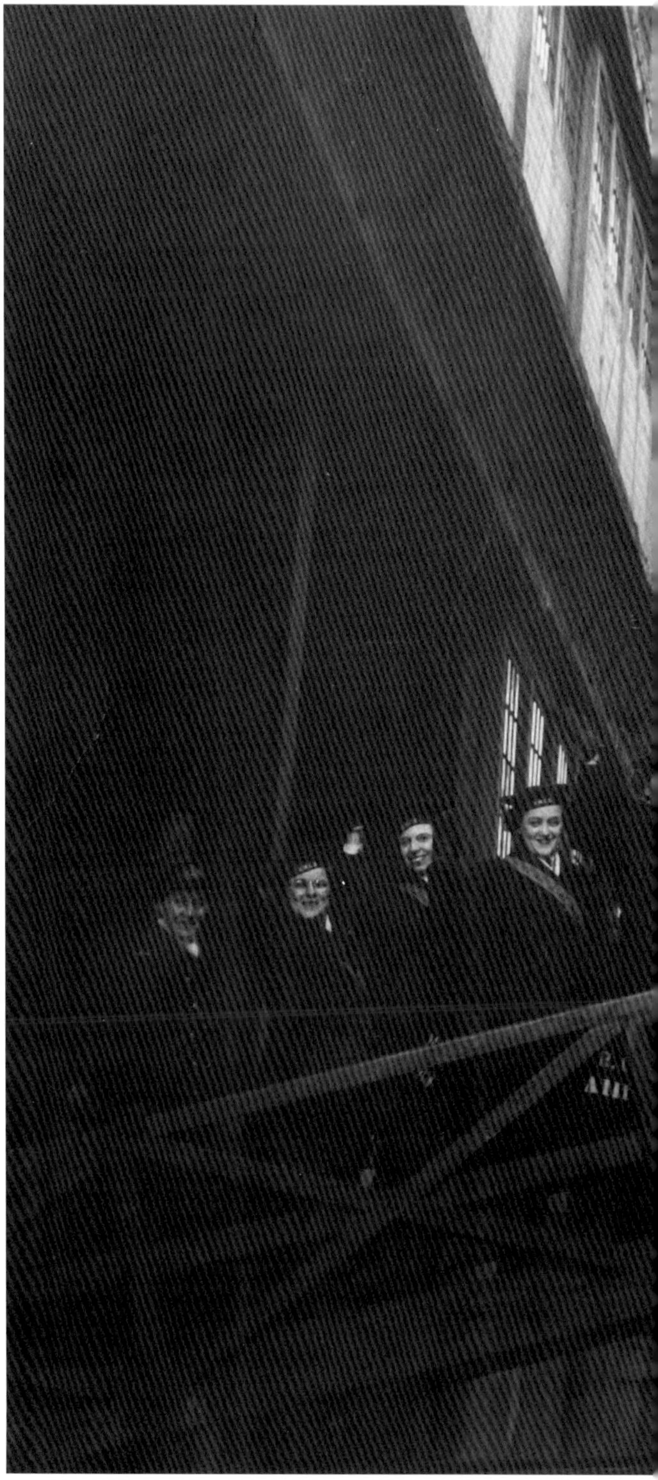

ABOVE: *Although strenuous arguments were made by women's groups from the beginning of the war that the armed forces should begin recruiting women, a process already underway in Britain, it was not until the summer of 1941 that old barriers began to fall. No one, not even the most committed advocates, argued that women should serve at the front. Their service would release men from routine administrative tasks, enabling them to head overseas. These W.R.C.N.S. are doing switchboard duty at HMCS Stadacona.*

RIGHT: *Eventually, the W.R.C.N.S., the Canadian Women's Army Corps, and the R.C.A.F. Women's Division did send personnel overseas; but whether at home or abroad, their role was to fill clerical positions, act as drivers, and sometimes serve as mechanics. Those women who got closest to the action were nurses serving behind the front lines after D-Day. Although the general and persistent view that a woman in the services was by definition "fast," for many young women whose only hope for independence from family was marriage, the war years were ones of liberation. This photo shows the first W.R.C.N.S. draft, commanded by Isabel McNeil, boarding ship for overseas at Pier 21 in August 1943.*

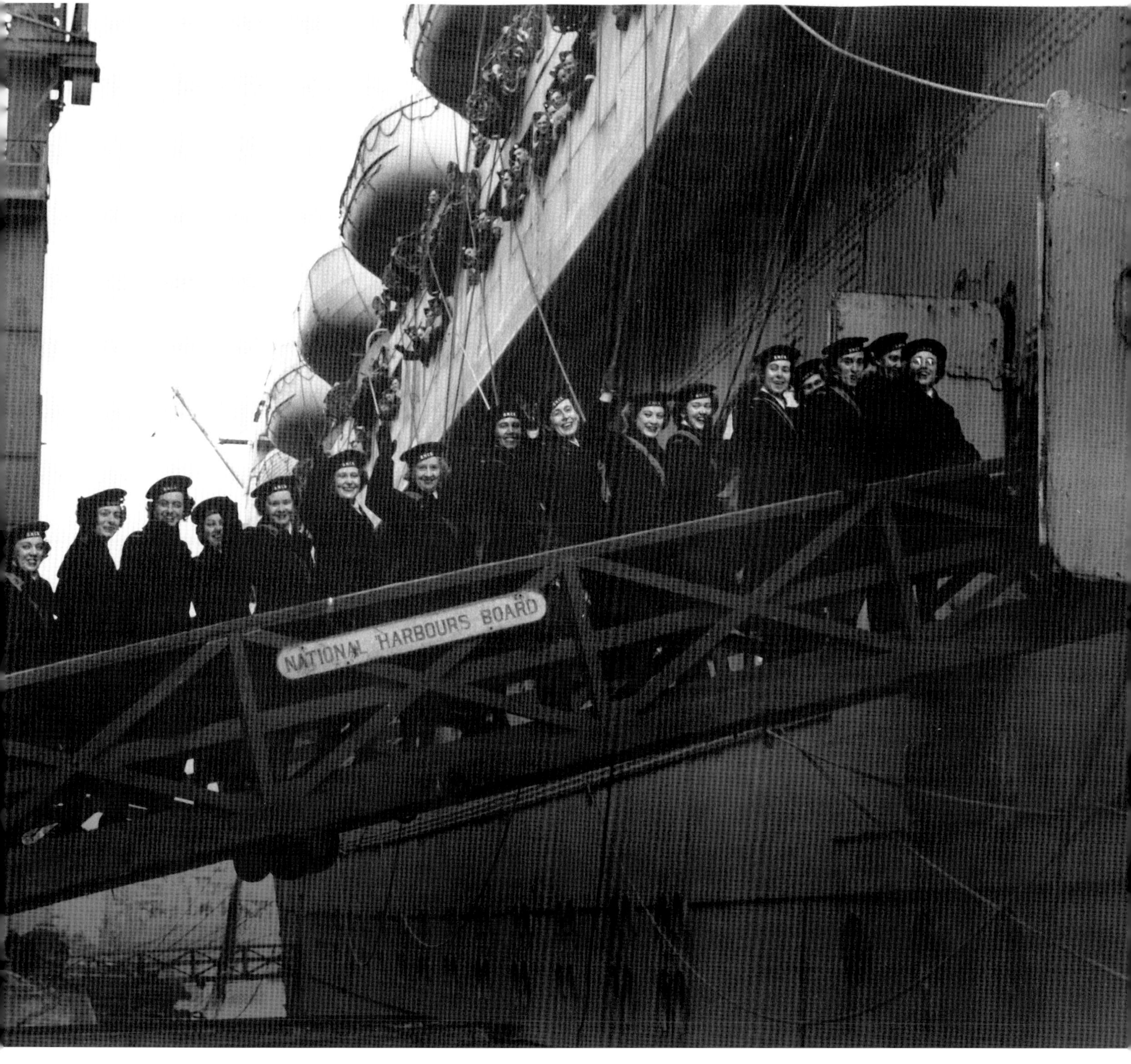
NATIONAL HARBOURS BOARD

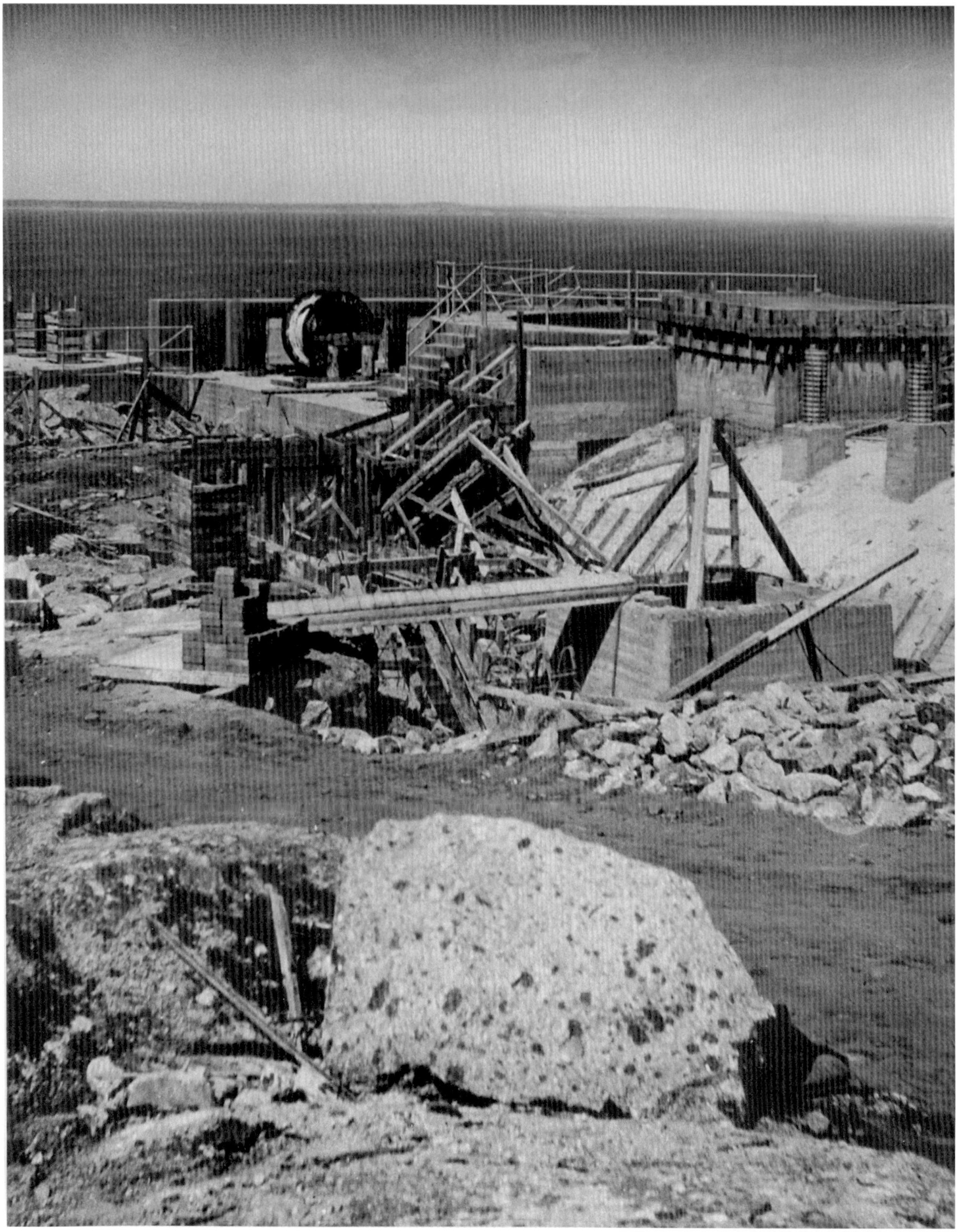

LEFT: *When the war began, the Halifax Harbour defences were essentially what had been built by the British beginning in the 18th century under Prince Edward, Duke of Kent. These installations had been upgraded and improved in the 1860s and 1890s, and some improvements had been made during World War I. In the new reality of the 20th century, following the 1936 recommendations of Major B.D. Treatt, R.A., some facilities, such as Fort Ives, Fort Hugonin, York Redoubt, and Point Pleasant, were abandoned as defensive works; others, such as Fort McNab, were upgraded. To push raiders or submarines as far as possible offshore, two massive new works were constructed at Chebucto Head and Devil's Battery overlooking Devil's Island.*

ABOVE: *Fort McNab on McNab's Island, directly opposite York Redoubt, was garrisoned by the 52nd Coastal Battery. Originally part of the British defences, it was manned during World War I and heavily upgraded in World War II. It became, with Chebucto Head and Devil's Island, one of the principal defences of the "East Coast Port".*

ABOVE: *Royal Canadian Artillery training on 3.7" anti-aircraft gun. Simulated air raids thrilled boys of all ages and kept up the pressure on the civilian population to maintain their vigilance. At other times, these and other ordnance around the harbour practiced on their own, punctuating the daily civilian routines with the distant boom of artillery. In 1941, there were four anti-aircraft batteries such as this one, but quickly the network expanded to seven heavy and 23 light AA batteries, with associated barracks.*

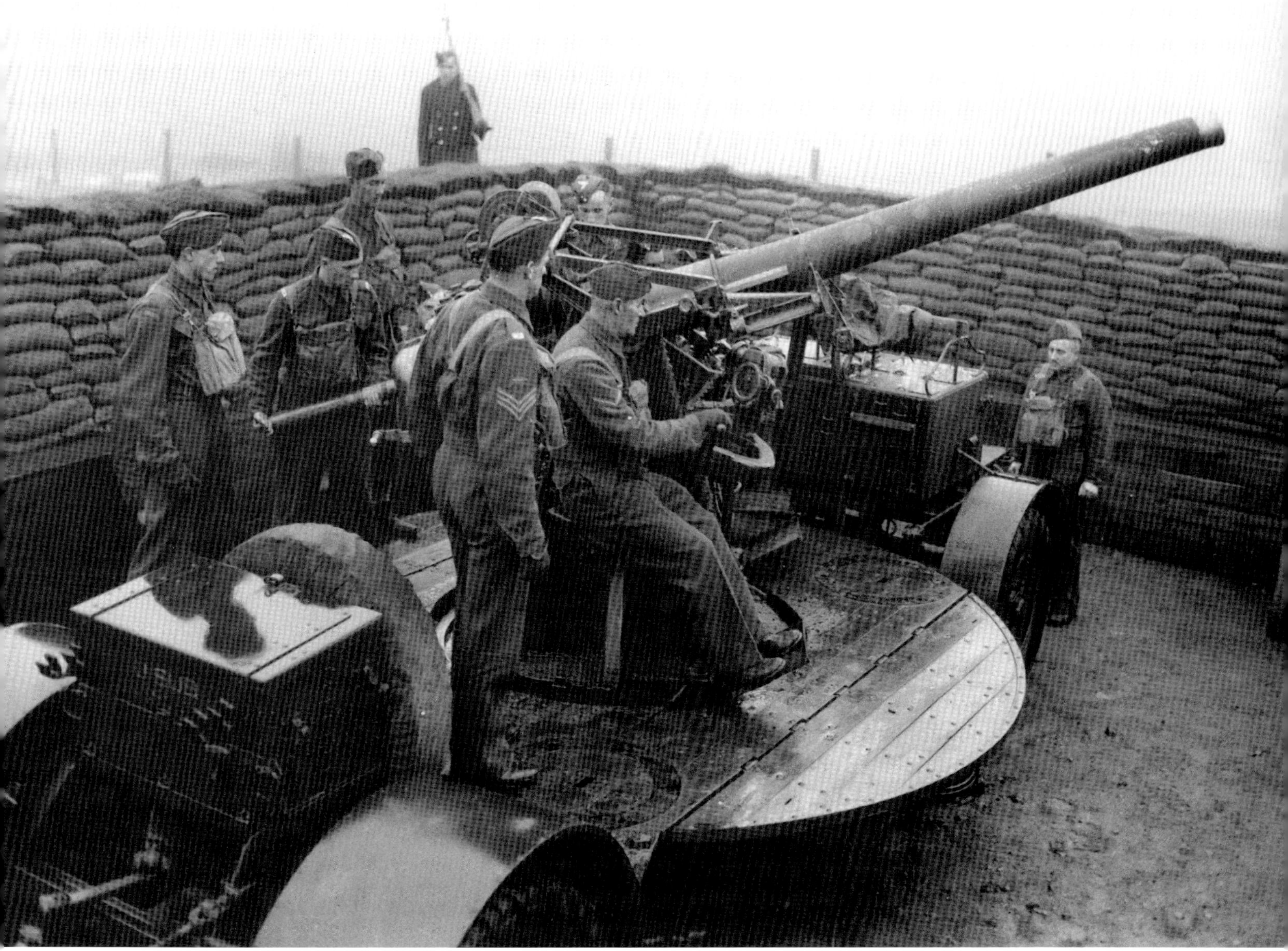

ABOVE: *Although the threat never materialized, Halifax Harbour, the convoy assembly in Bedford Basin, the Imperial Esso oil refinery, and its neighbour RCAF Dartmouth were protected by a web of anti-aircraft emplacements. This mobile 3.7" R.C.A. anti-aircraft gun was one of the first in what became a substantial network by war's end. In August 1939, the 4th Anti-Aircraft Battery, just winding up its annual practice at Picton, Ontario, was ordered to mobilize instead of going home. The gunners put their mobile AA guns on flatcars and headed for Halifax.*

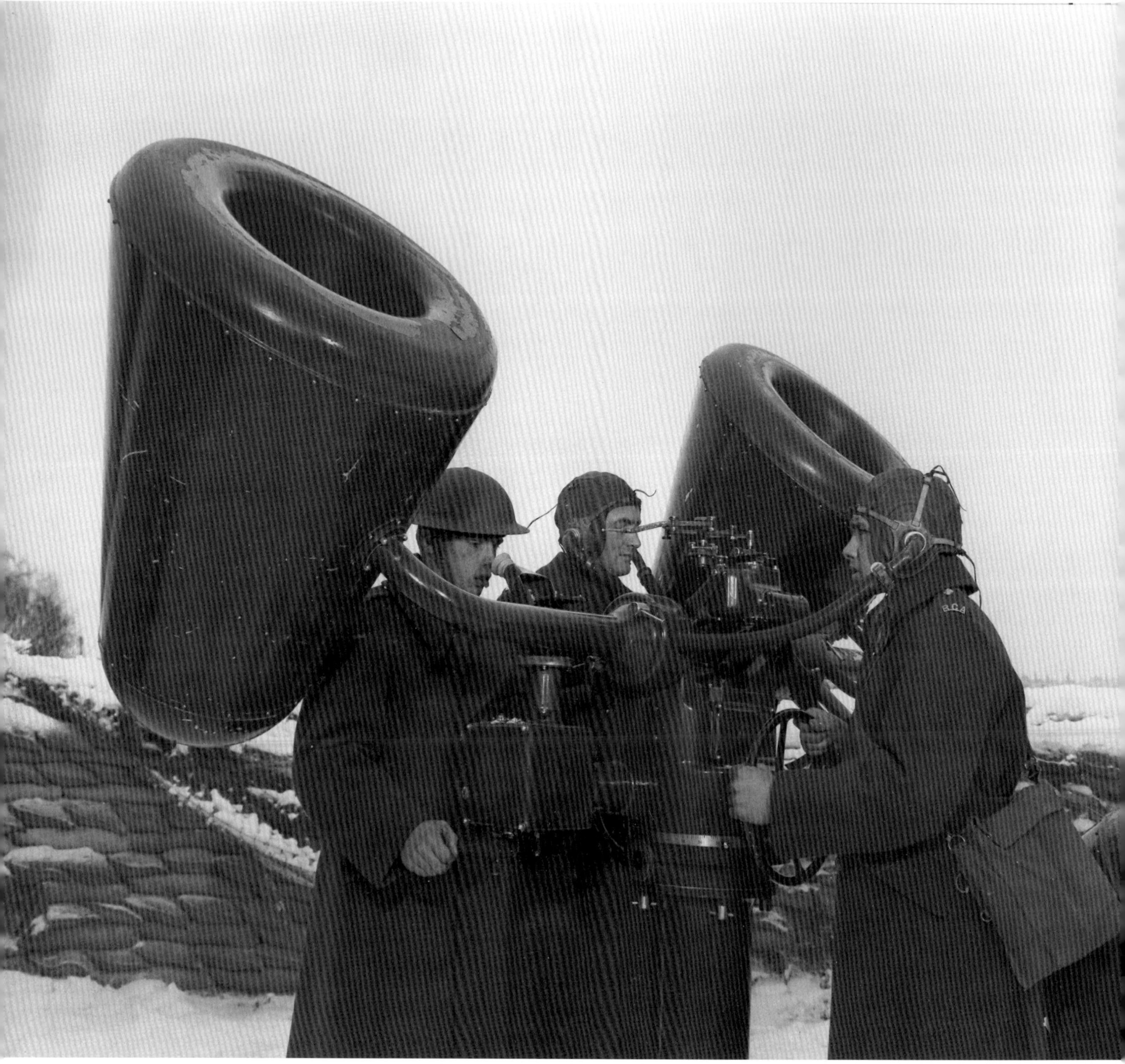

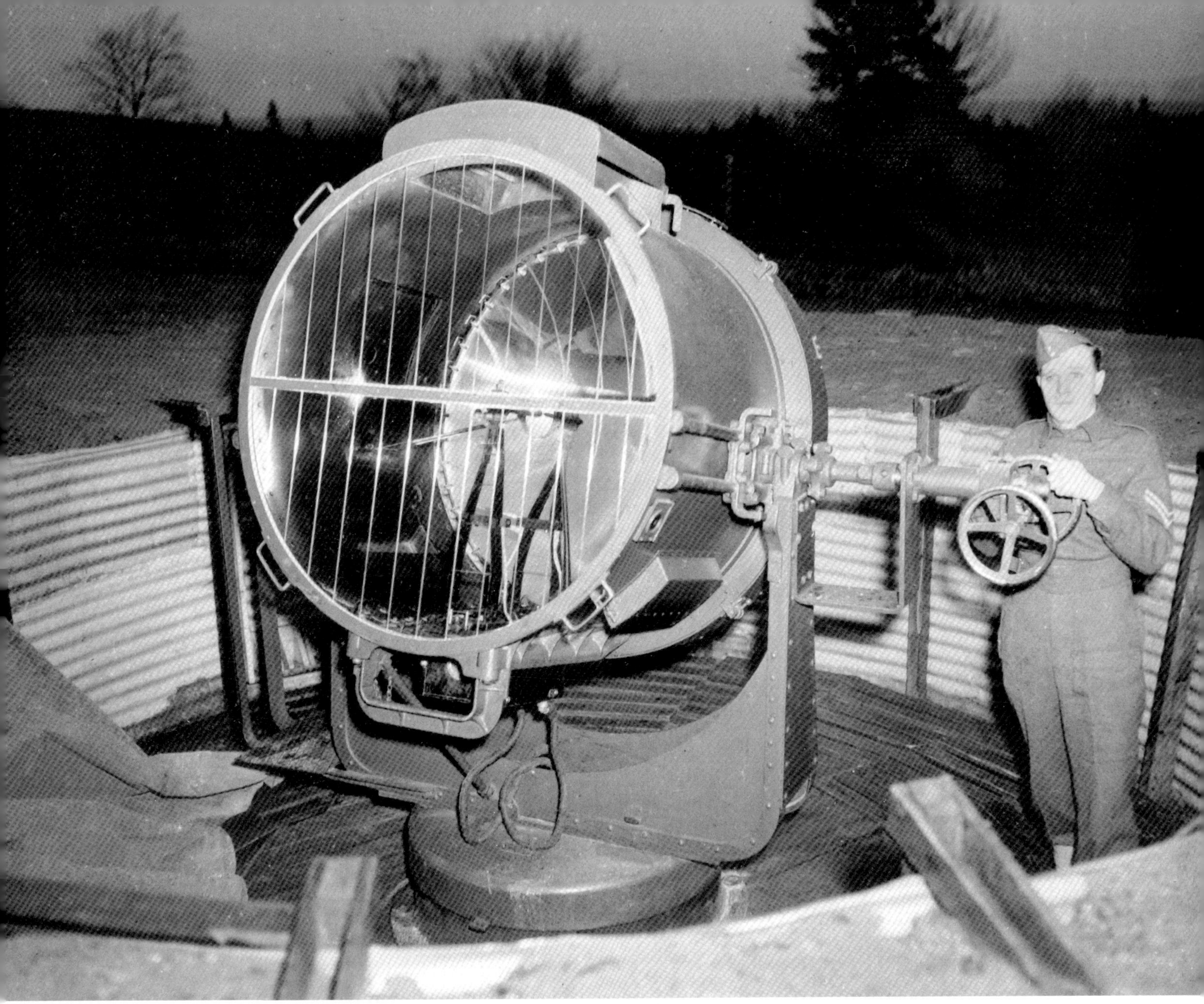

LEFT: *At the beginning of the war, gunners, whether heavy harbour ordnance or anti-aircraft, had only clear weather, binoculars, and a good pair of eyes during the day to aid their watch. At night, searchlights, such as the one seen here, and acoustic locators were added to the 24-hour watch to locate and protect against the enemy. Until late 1942, the aerial and sea threat from Germany was taken very seriously. By then the work of fortifying the harbour was well in hand, and soon the German war machine began showing signs of strain.*

ABOVE: *There were 17 harbour search lights in an arc from Chebucto Head to the southern tip of McNab's Island. In 1941 seven anti-aircraft searchlights were added to this network. Some of the harbour lights had dispersed beams, others, particularly the AA lights, had focussed pencil beams with a range of 30,000 feet. The searchlights were operated by the Royal Canadian Engineers.*

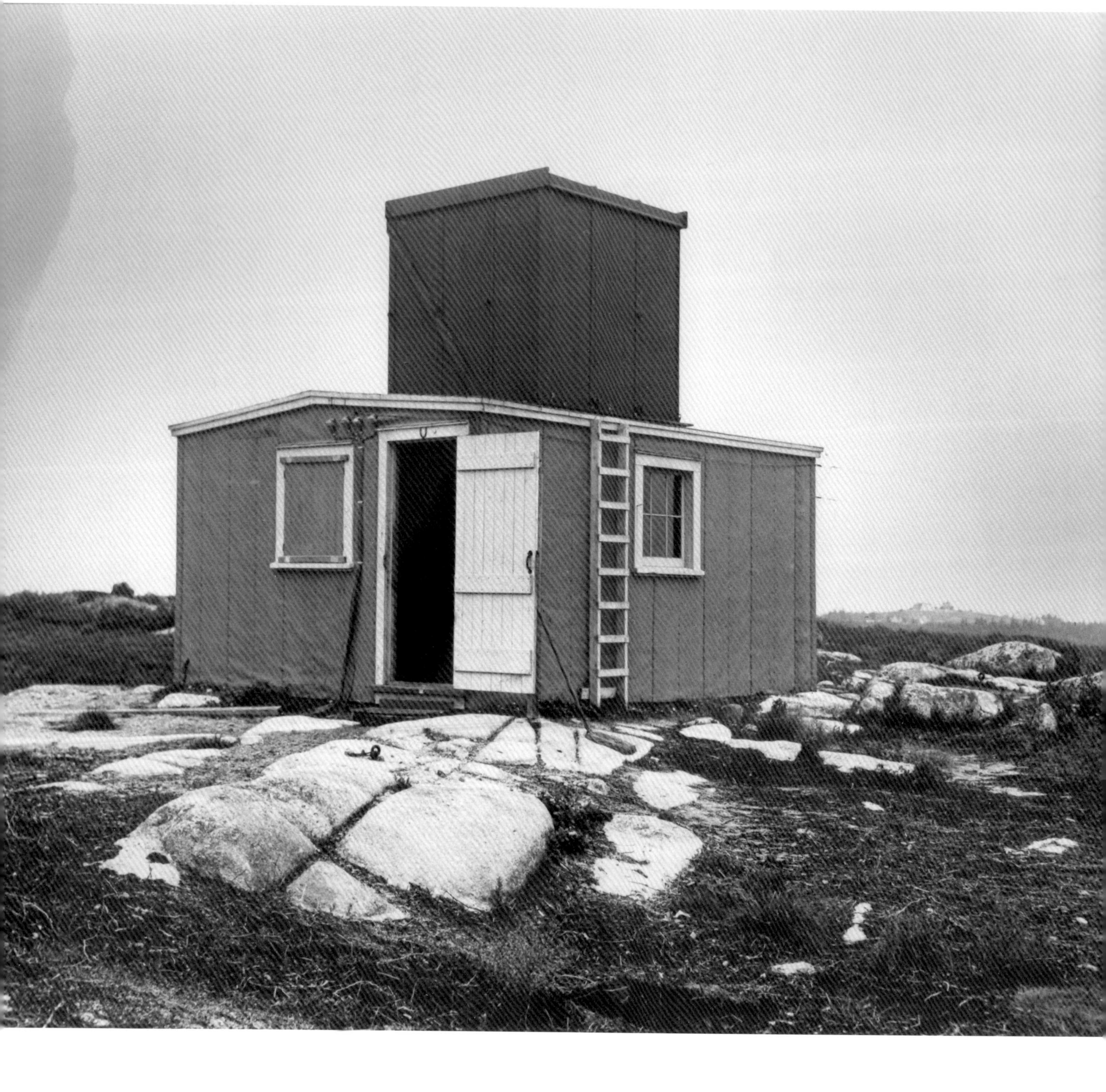

LEFT: *Radar, a system of broadcasting pulses of radio energy which reflect off surfaces in such a way as to produce a visible signal, was developed as a practical means of identifying moving airborne targets early enough to be of valuable assistance to the R.A.F. in the Battle of Britain. Although the early versions, both British and Canadian, were fussy, the technology evolved rapidly and spread quickly both on land and sea. Some of the earliest Canadian installations were here in Halifax and provided information to RCAF Dartmouth. The installation seen in this photograph at Chebucto Battery, CDX model radar, No. 1, MK 5, provided information for the Fire Command Post at York Redoubt.*

RIGHT: *Such was the secrecy surrounding the very existence of radar that the general public was not aware of this technology until the end of the war. All publicity photographs, such as this of one of HMC ships, were not released until the radar gear had been censored out.*

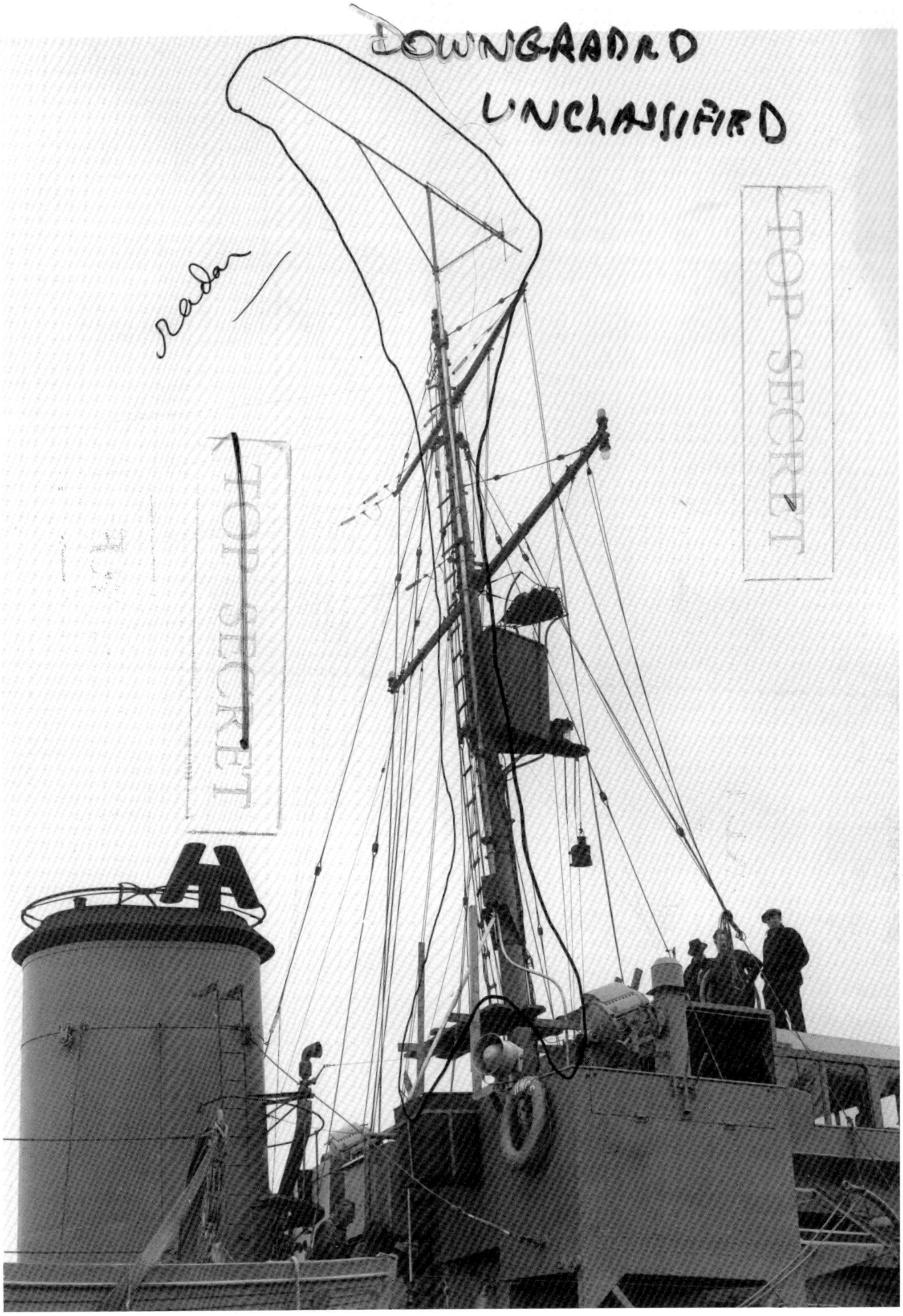
DOWNGRADED
UNCLASSIFIED
Radar
TOP SECRET
TOP SECRET

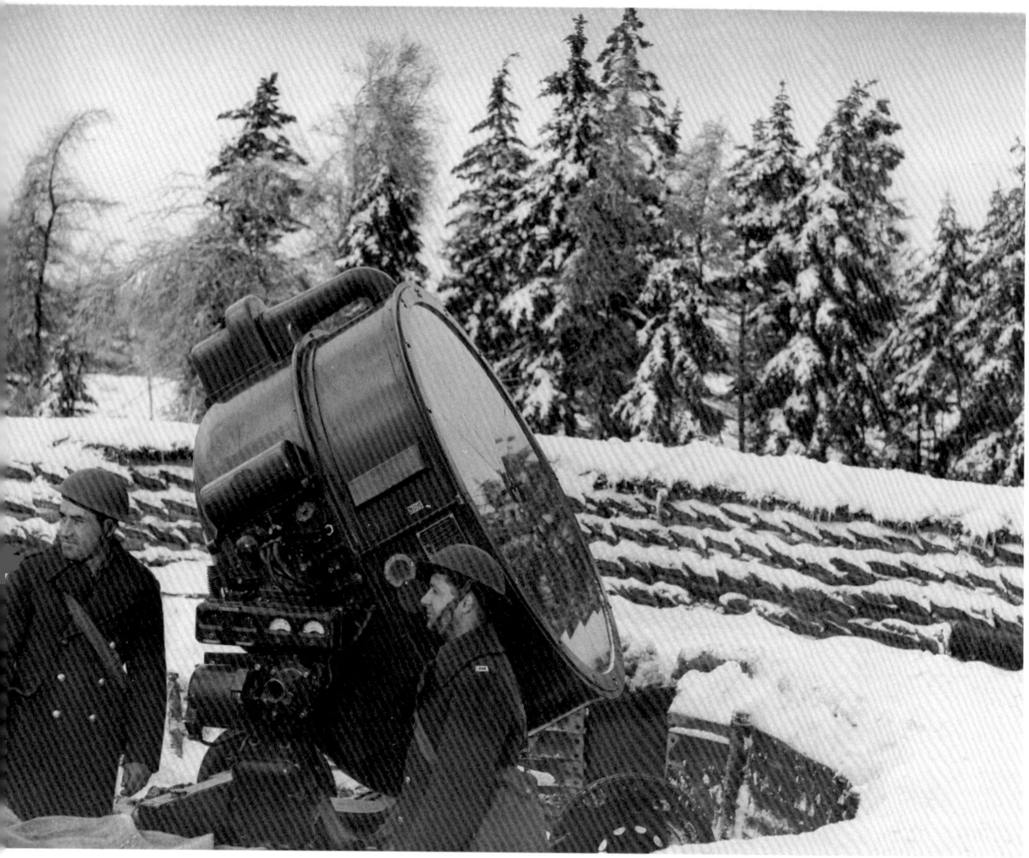

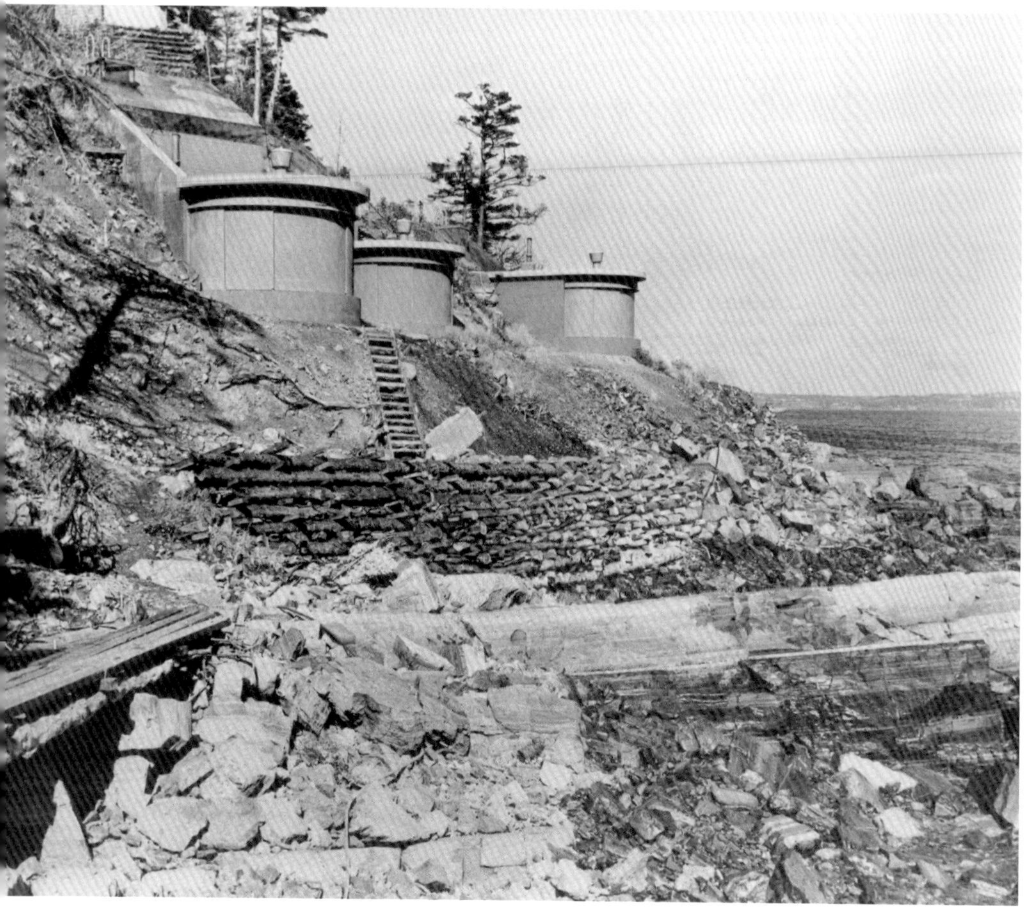

TOP: *A key component of the port's defences, radar or no, were the extensive network of searchlights. Boer War–era searchlights installed by the British were still functioning dependably in 1939, but time and technology had marched on and they were rapidly replaced. These original installations were expanded to cover the harbour approaches and, of course, the threat from the air, unknown at the century's beginning. From time to time the Civil Defence organization staged practice air raids, one of whose dramatic and arresting features was the searchlights probing the night sky for "enemy" aircraft. This photograph is of one of the anti-aircraft defence lights.*

BOTTOM: *Not all the searchlights probed the skies or the distant horizon. The lights at York Shore, below York Redoubt, were focussed on the Anti-Submarine Boom Defence, which stretched across the harbour mouth to McNab's Island, and any ships or submarines that approached it. During World War I, the searchlights had initially been kept on all night, every night; but eventually this practice was deemed too much of a good thing and they were only lit when necessary. In World War II, although the lights illuminating the net and examination area were kept on, the rest stayed off until an alarm was given, or for the Fire Commander's surprise alerts that were intended to keep the harbour defenders on their toes.*

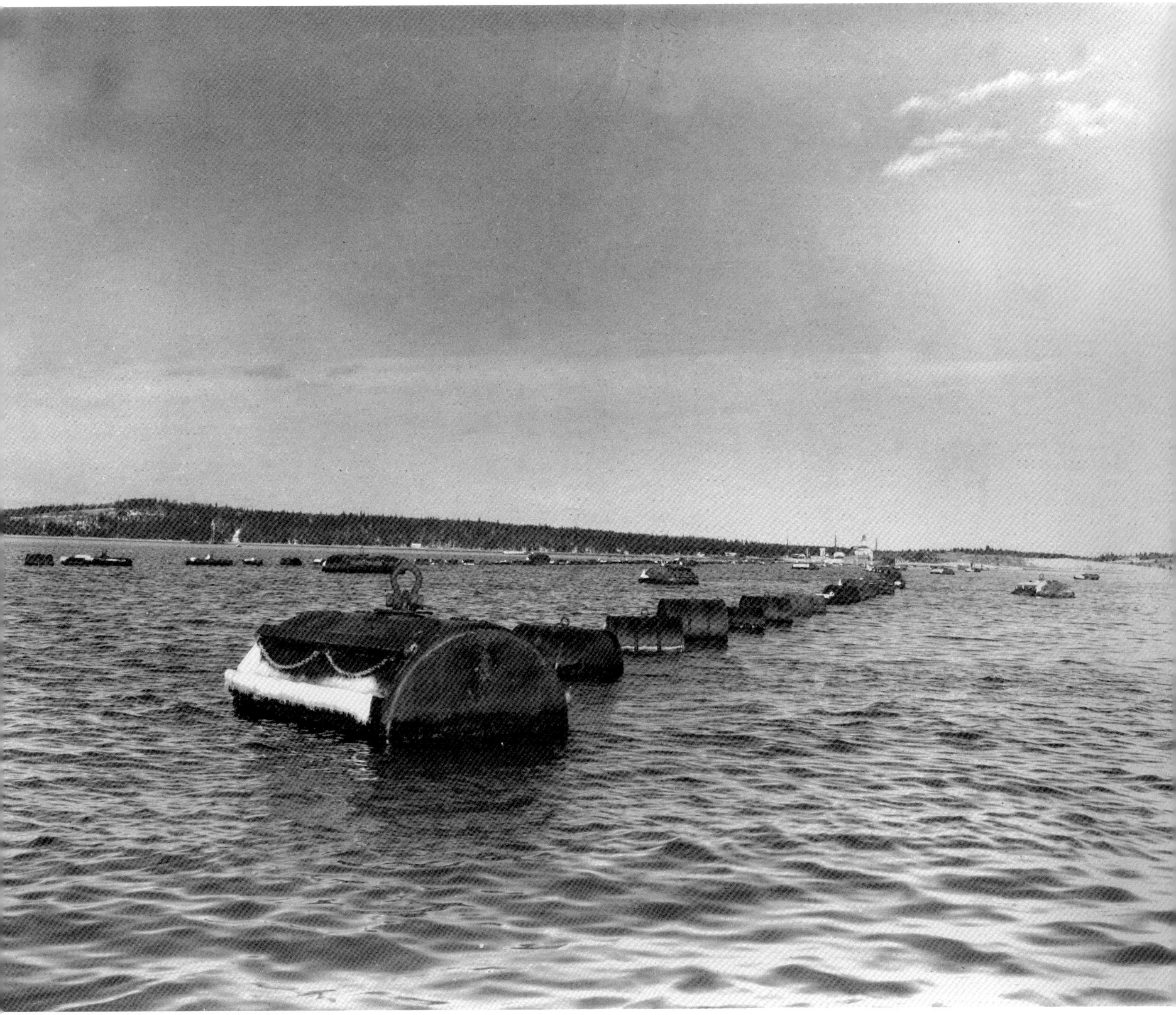

ABOVE: *The Anti-Submarine Boom Defence was an effective means of keeping out submarines which, without it, could have sunk ships at critical locations and closed the harbour for weeks or months with a couple of well-placed torpedoes. Getting in or out, however, was a tedious procedure, as it took time for the identification process and for the gate vessels to open the entrance. Smaller vessels, therefore, from time to time, took the chance of a shot across the bow by scooting across the top of the net which hung a few feet below the surface. The ends of the net were far enough from the shore to allow fishing boats to come and go without problems.*

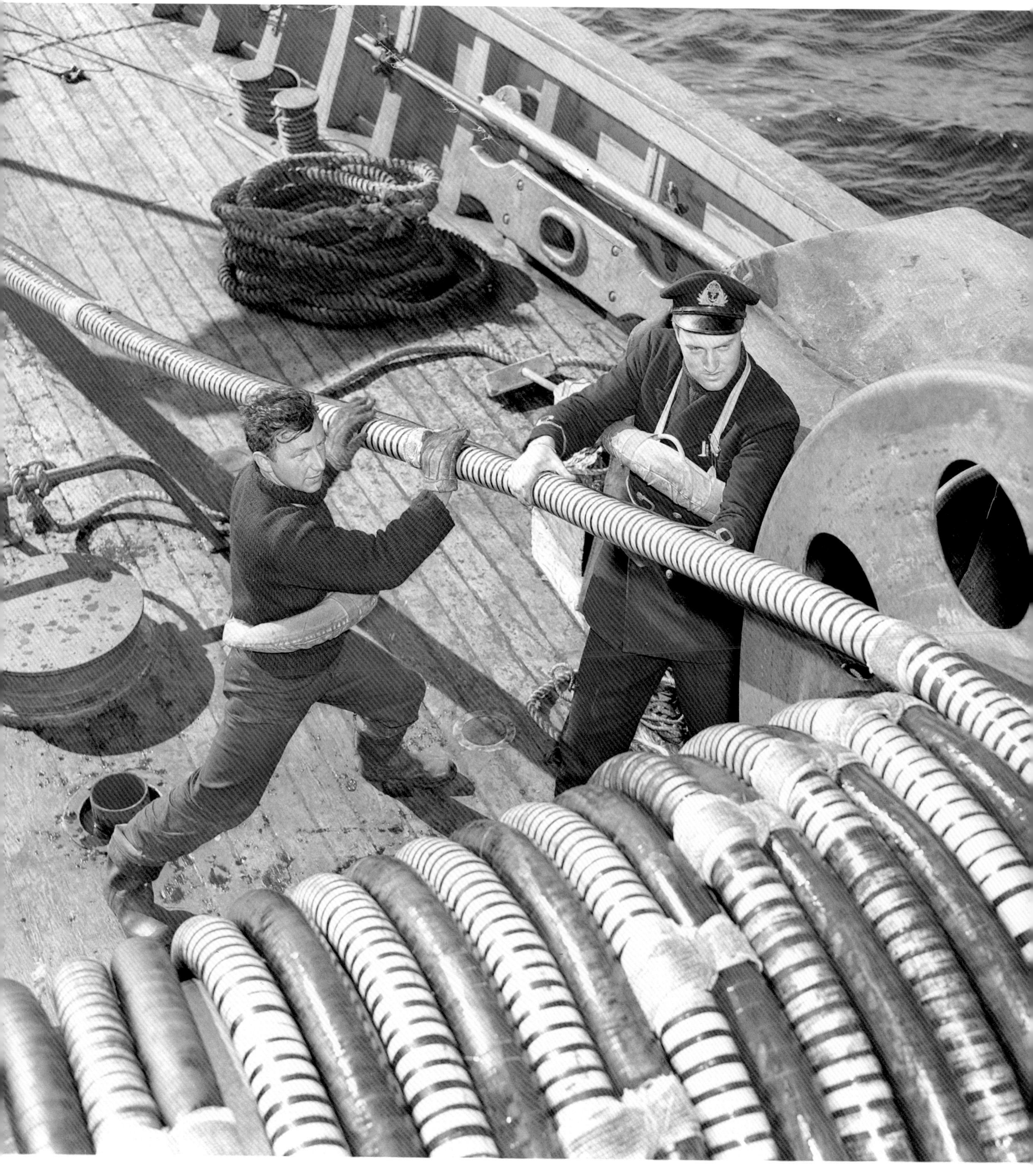

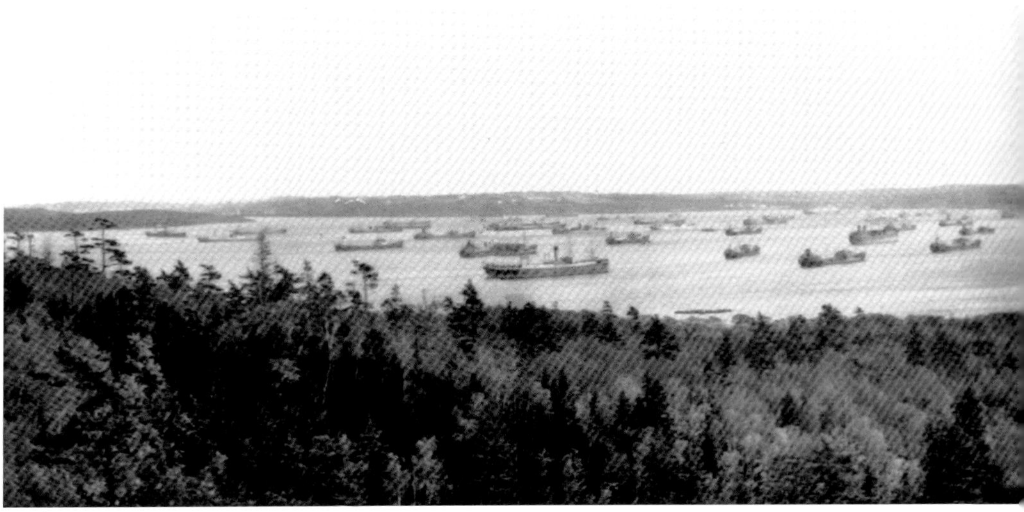

LEFT: *The minesweeper* Lloyd George *seen off Halifax Harbour. It was a two-way street, of course, as combatants could and did mine each other's harbours. Probably to the disappointment of the daily, often monotonous minesweeping patrols, only once did the Germans try to close off Halifax in this manner, when in June 1943 U-119 laid an arc of 66 mines across the harbour mouth. They were quickly discovered and detonated.*

ABOVE: *When America was still neutral, the sight of convoys coming or going was a tourist attraction. However impressive to view from a distance, in this case at Admiral Rock near Bedford, the ships were not careful with their leavings and the waters and shores of Bedford Basin and Halifax Harbour became a reeking stew of garbage, oil, and general filth.*

RIGHT: *Even the most blasé observers were fascinated by the massing of ships filling Bedford Basin then, seen or unseen at night, slipping out of the harbour in line and disappearing over the horizon leaving, for a few days, empty waters. The location of Halifax right on the trans-Atlantic sea lanes, its splendid harbour and basin, and access to the continental railway system, made it a focal point for supplying Britain with foodstuffs and for the build-up of the allied war machine for the invasion of Europe. With the entry of the United States into the war in December 1941, Halifax lost its absolute primacy to ports on the American Eastern Seaboard, but even so the pace rarely slackened.*

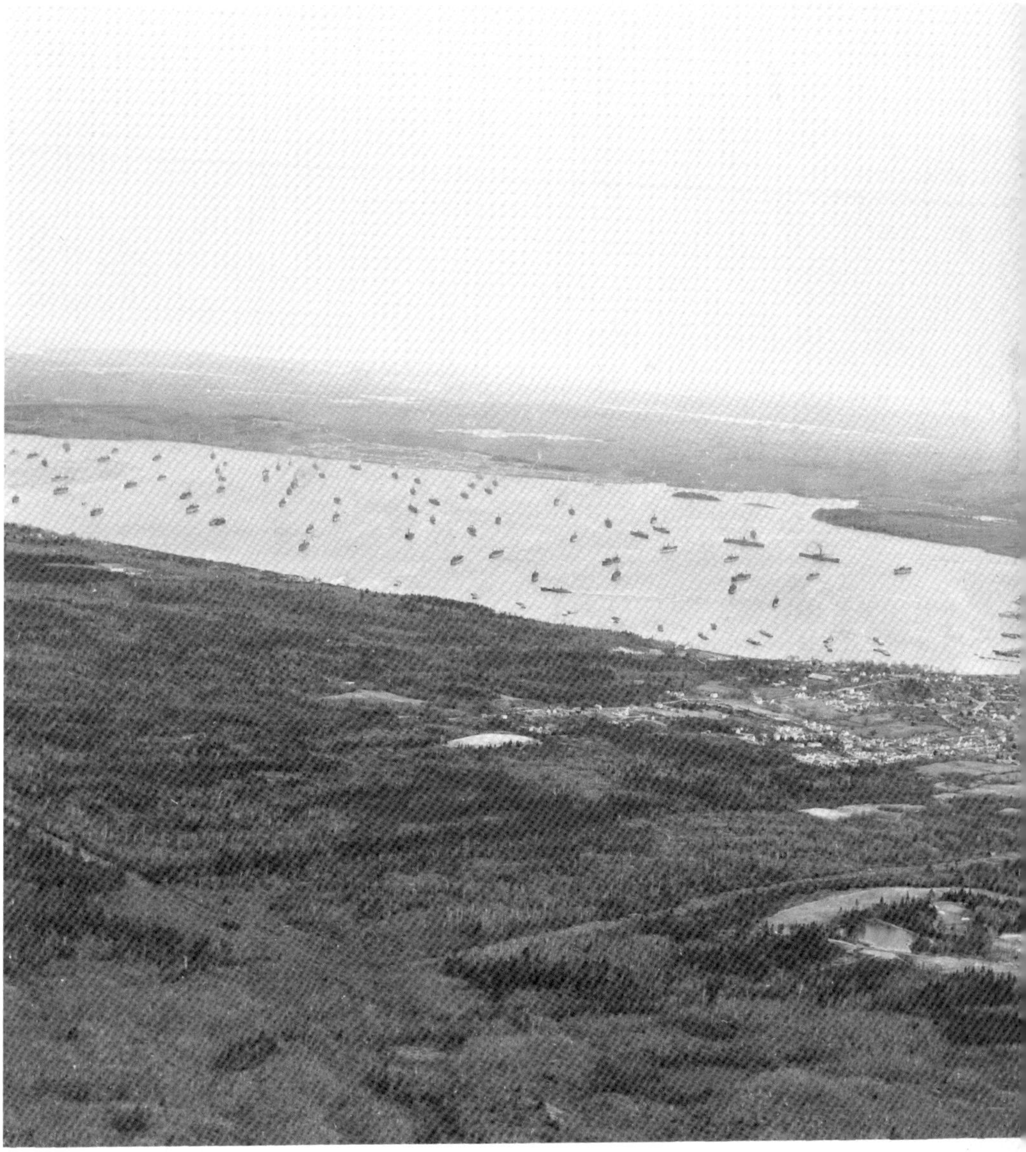

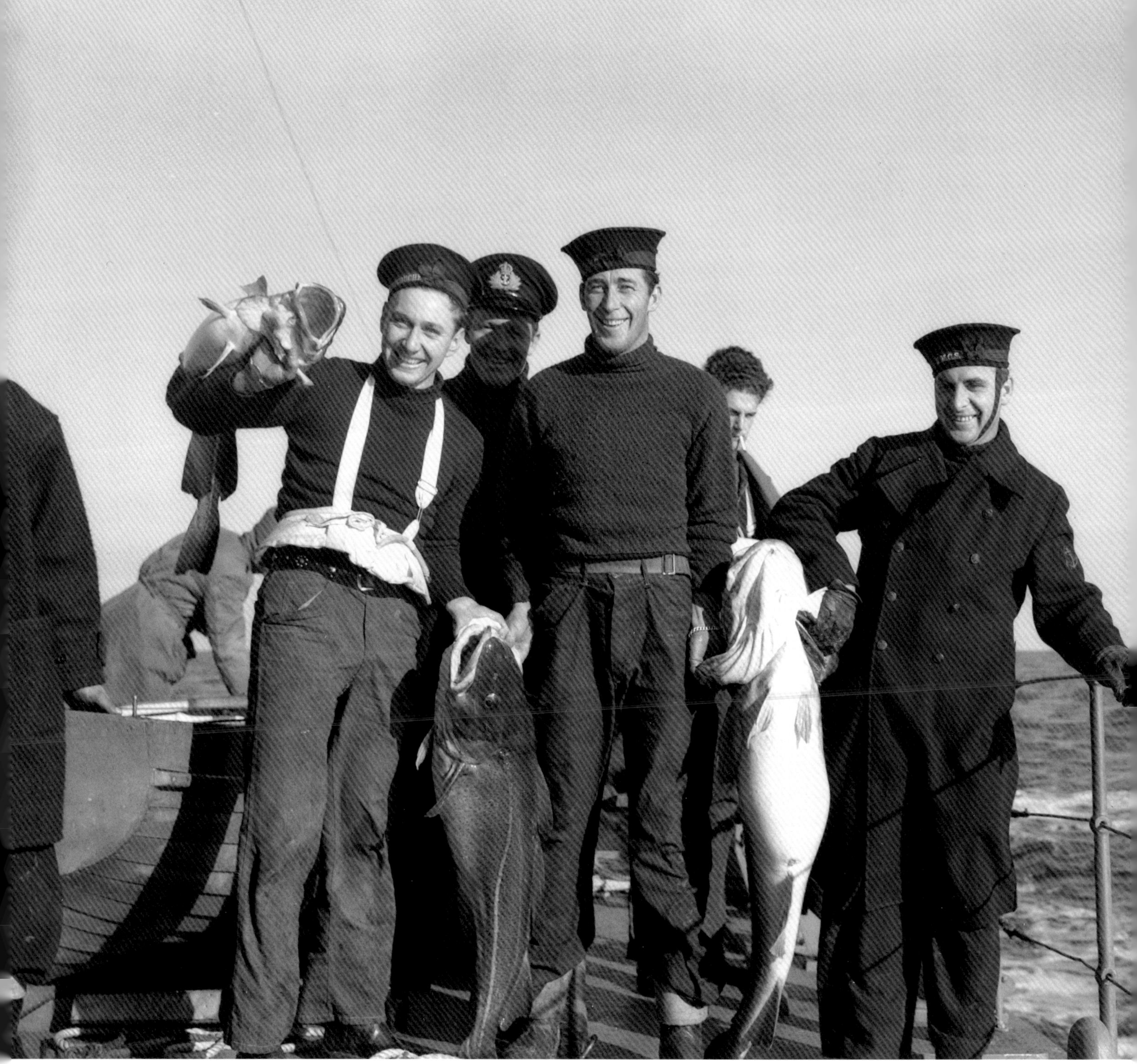

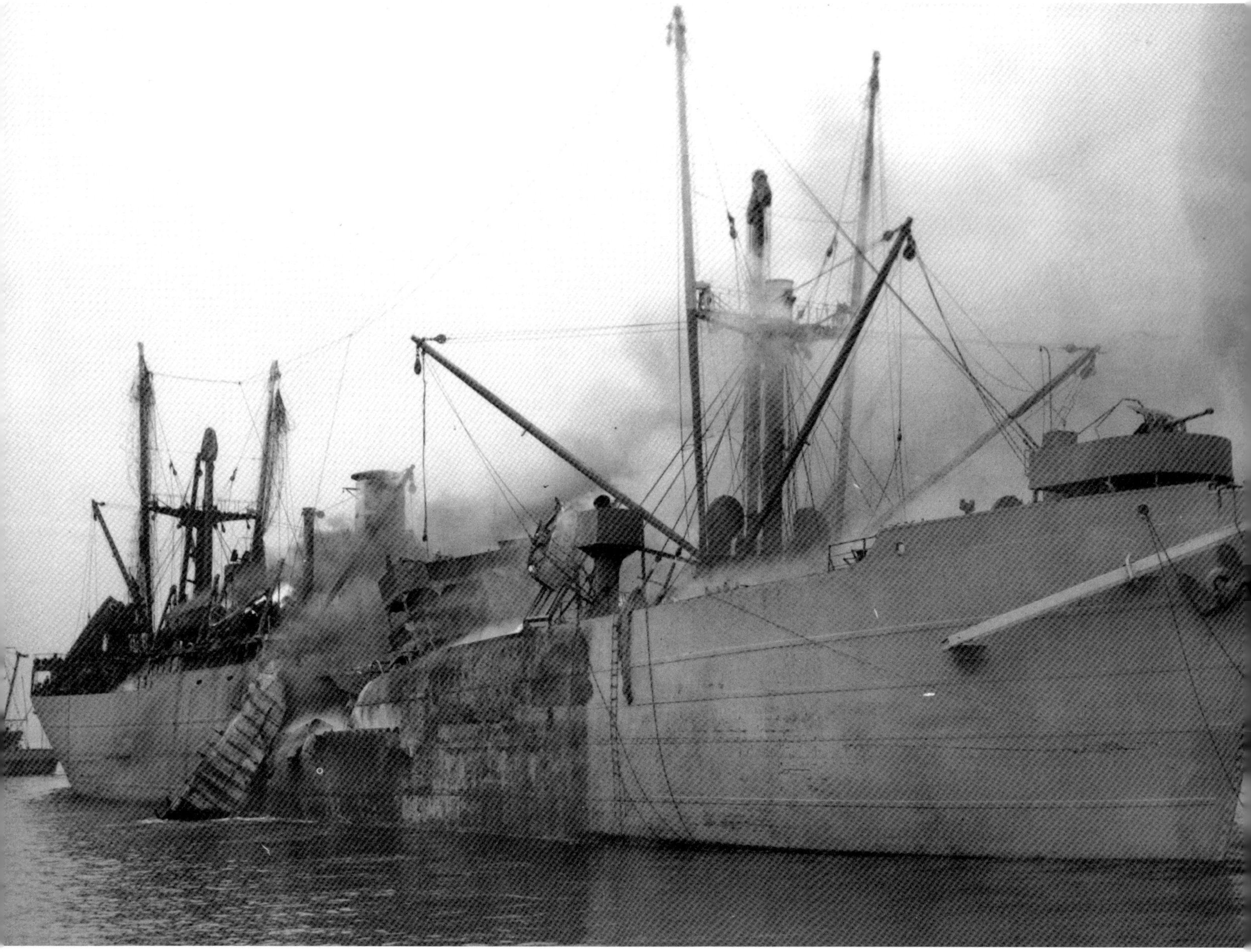

LEFT: *Sometimes the harbour defenders, intentionally or not, found other targets. Naval ratings hold up codfish killed by the explosion of depth charges dropped by the Fairmile motor launch ML 052 of the R.C.N. off Halifax Harbour, an addition to the evening's mess.*

ABOVE: *Not all torpedoed ships went to the bottom. Some survived to limp into port, such as this Canadian "Park" ship torpedoed and on fire at a National Harbours Board pier. Since every cargo ship was vital, even seriously damaged ships were repaired and sent back to sea. 7,145 ships went through the Halifax Shipyards, not all of course in this condition. Some jobs might be minor, such as the installation of the small armament seen at the bow of this freighter, which in theory allowed it to put up some sort of (usually futile) defence against a surfaced U-boat.*

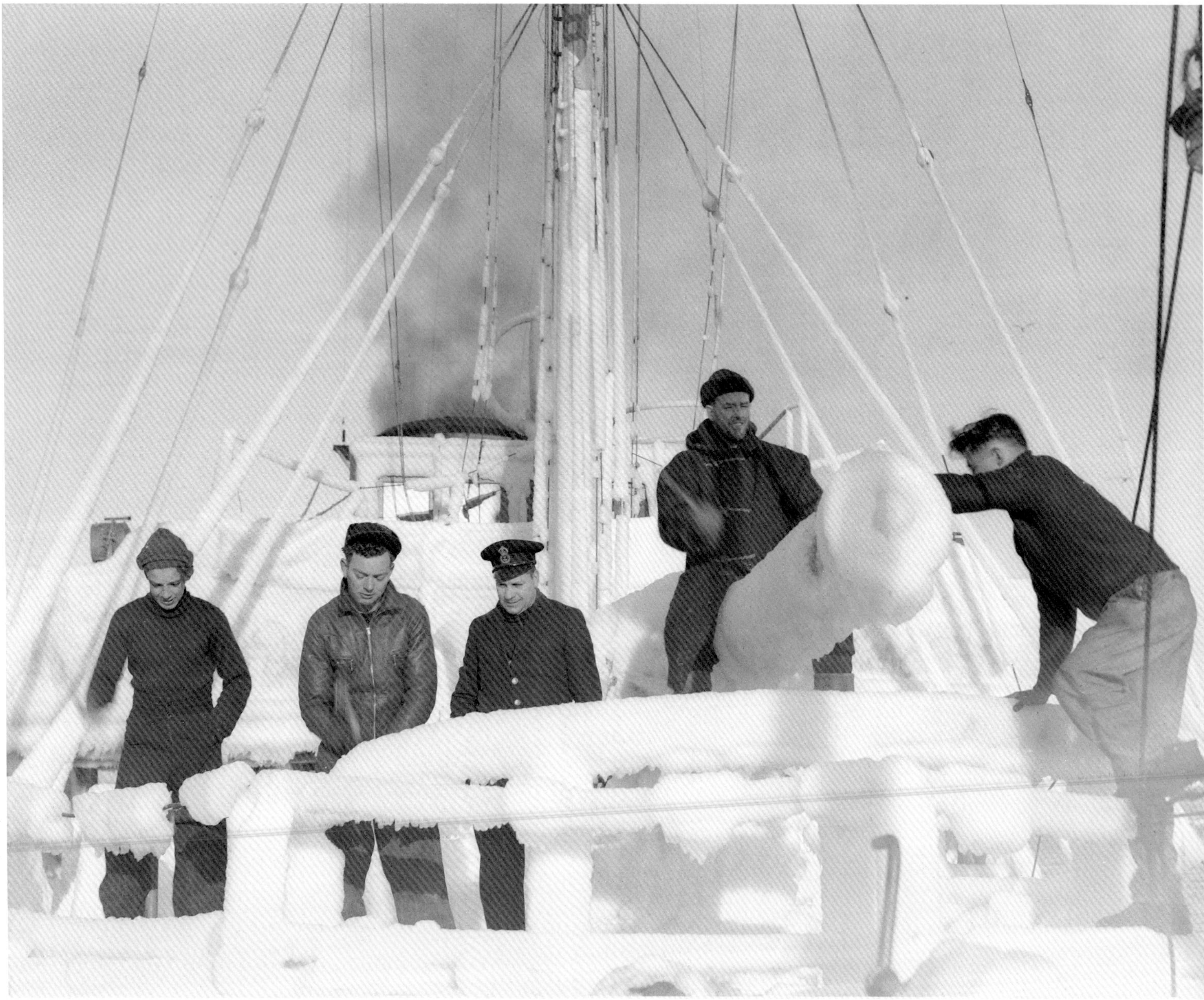

ABOVE: *Convoys travelled in all weather and under often-appalling conditions. Weather was often as much of a menace as the U-boat. The naval escorts never rested and never relaxed regardless of the circumstances. Here ratings clear ice from the forecastle of* HMCS Lunenburg *in January 1942, a serious winter danger caused by freezing spray, which could capsize a ship.*

RIGHT: *As early as 1941, HMC Dockyard in the foreground, which had plenty of space a couple of years earlier, was rapidly filling up. An establishment that had a definite eighteenth-century appearance at war's start, rapidly evolved during the war as ancient buildings were swept away to meet new realities. From left to right, the Nova Scotia Hospital, the Acadia Sugar Refinery with its smoke stack, and the Imperoyal refinery can be seen on the Dartmouth side of the harbour.*

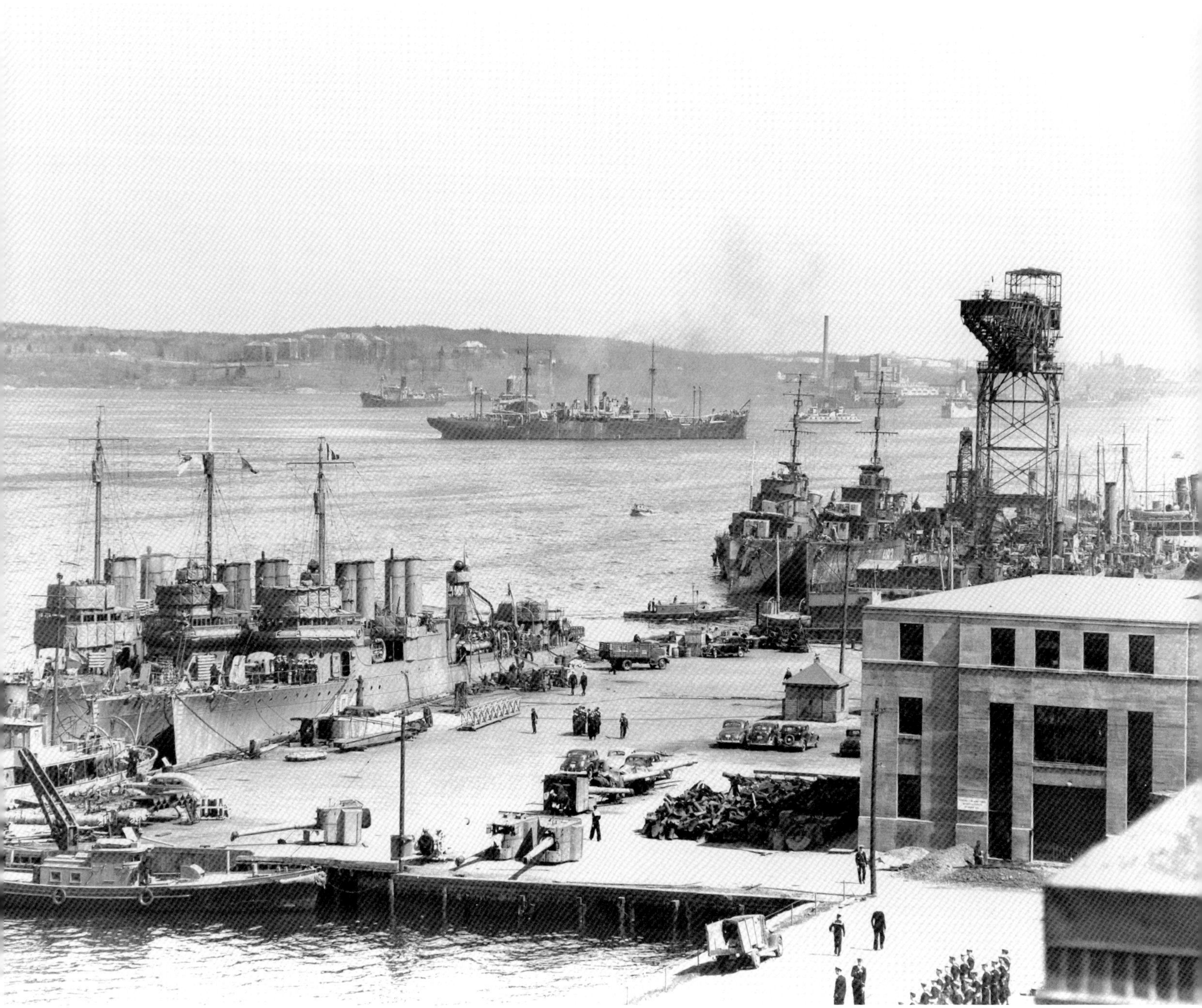

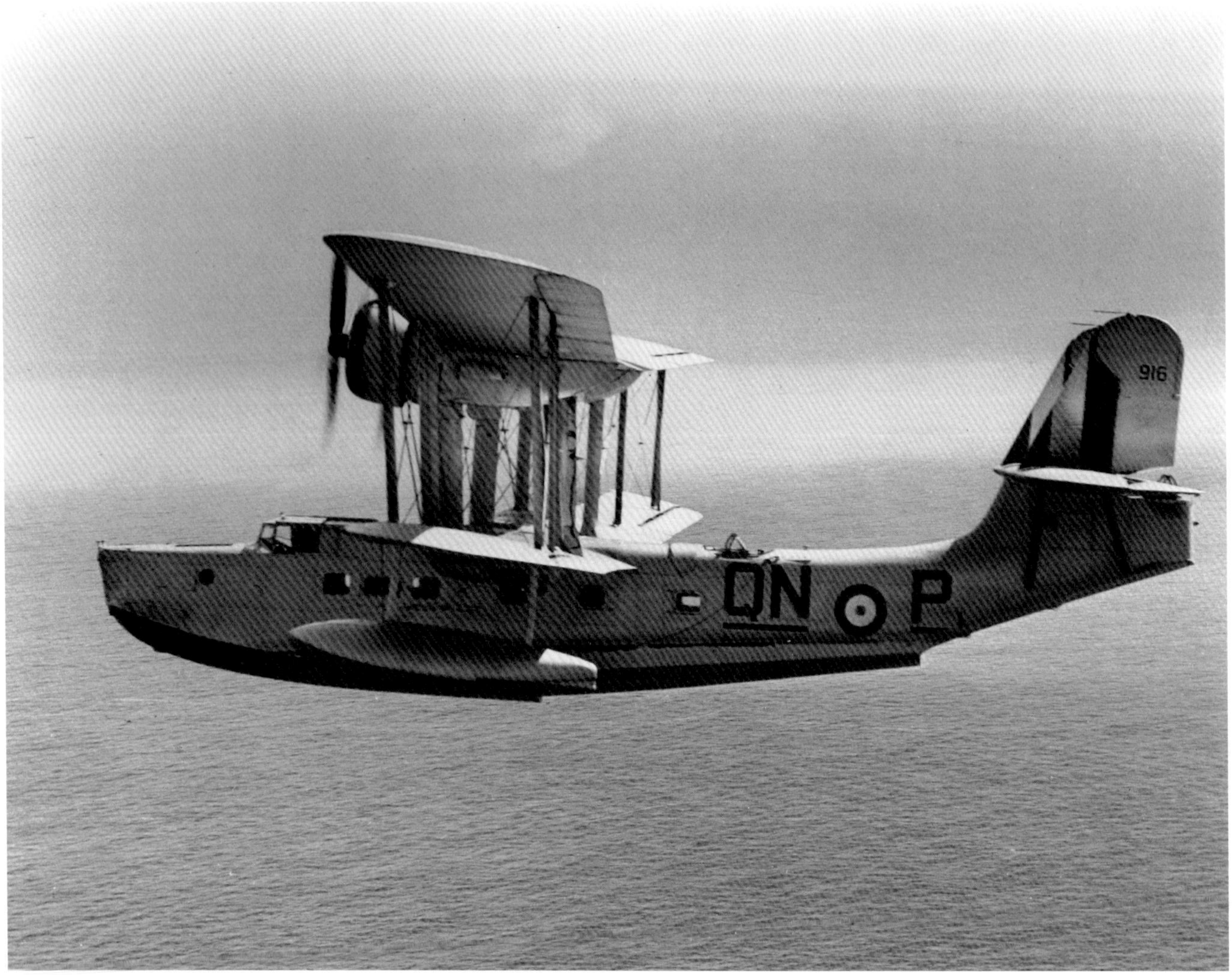
916
QN P

ABOVE: *This impressive aircraft, a Stranraer, patrolled the offshore coastal waters and escorted convoys to the limit of its range, about 1,000 miles. These aircraft carried a crew of six and were armed with two Lewis machine guns, one of which was mounted in an open cockpit in the bow. The machine gunner stood there in the open as the pilot veered down to demand identification from suspicious vessels. From time to time, in good weather a Stranraer on patrol extended its range by landing on the lake on Sable Island rather than returning to base.*

TOP RIGHT: *The Stranraer was replaced by the American Consolidated Catalina PBY 5. Although not as seaworthy in rough weather, its range of 2,500 miles made it much more useful for coastal patrol and escort duties.*

BOTTOM RIGHT: *The Liberator shown here was a long-range bomber which extended the airborne coverage of and reconnaissance for convoys. By the end of the war, Liberators were based in Nova Scotia, Newfoundland, Iceland, and Britain, providing virtually complete protection of the North Atlantic.*

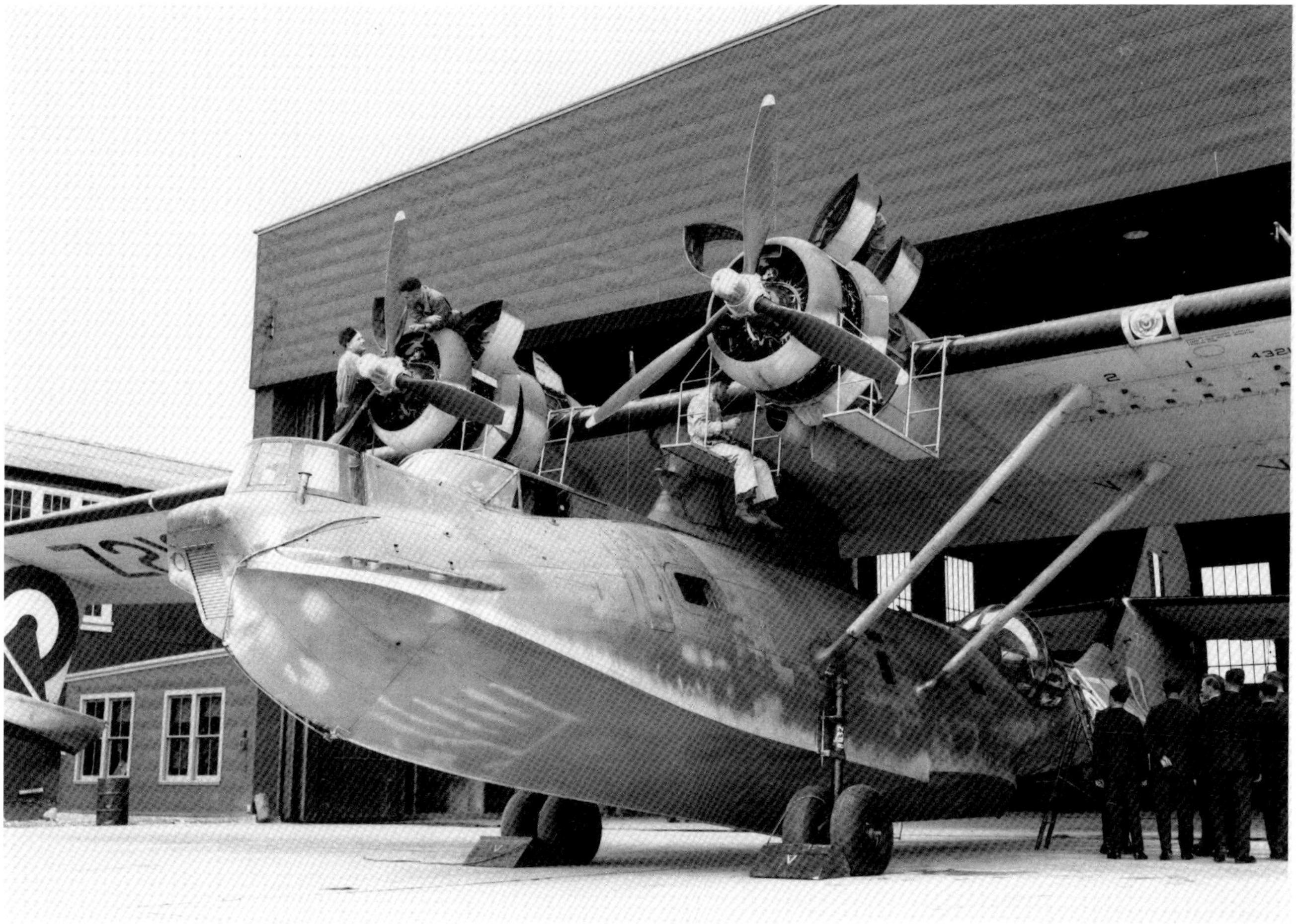

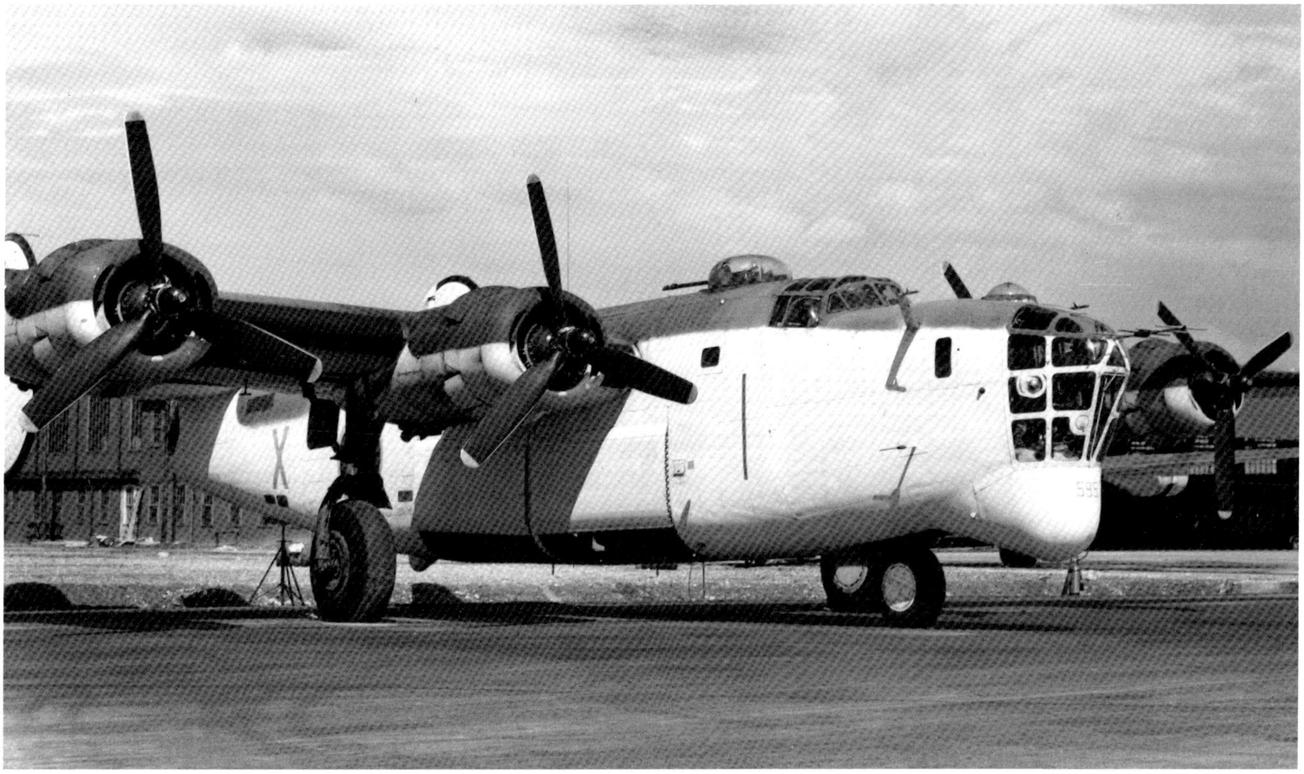

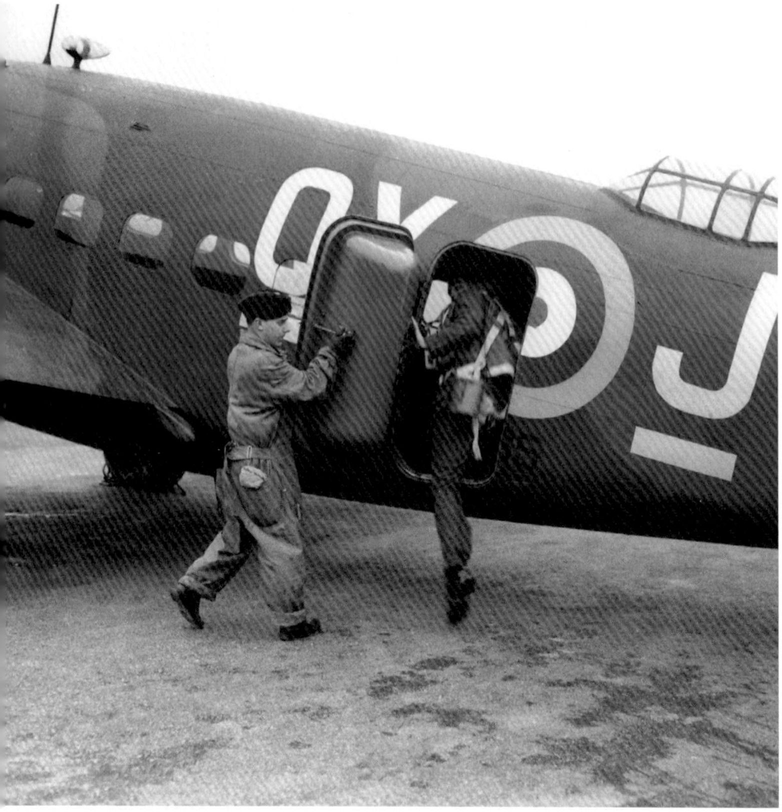

ABOVE: *R.C.A.F. crew training with a Lockheed Hudson bomber based at RCAF Dartmouth (present-day Shearwater). The station was home base for the Eastern Air Command, whose jurisdiction included Canada's Atlantic Coast. Somewhat isolated from Dartmouth and Halifax, an effort was made to provide complete services for its thousands of personnel, so that it was a town in all but name.*

RIGHT: *The Lockheed Hudson was another coastal reconnaissance aircraft, as well as a light bomber. Although American-built, most of these aircraft served in the Royal Air Force and the Royal Canadian Air Force. Shown here, Hudson 625 of Eastern Air Command based in Yarmouth sank U-754 on 31 July 1942.*

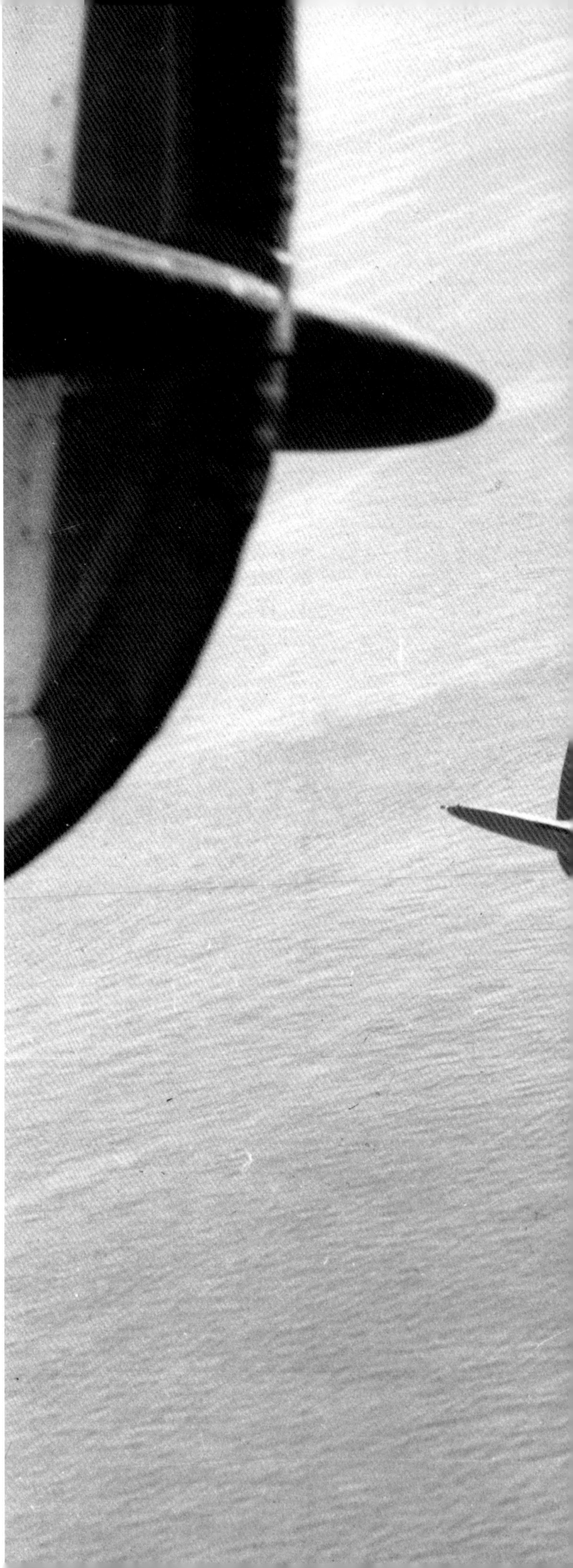

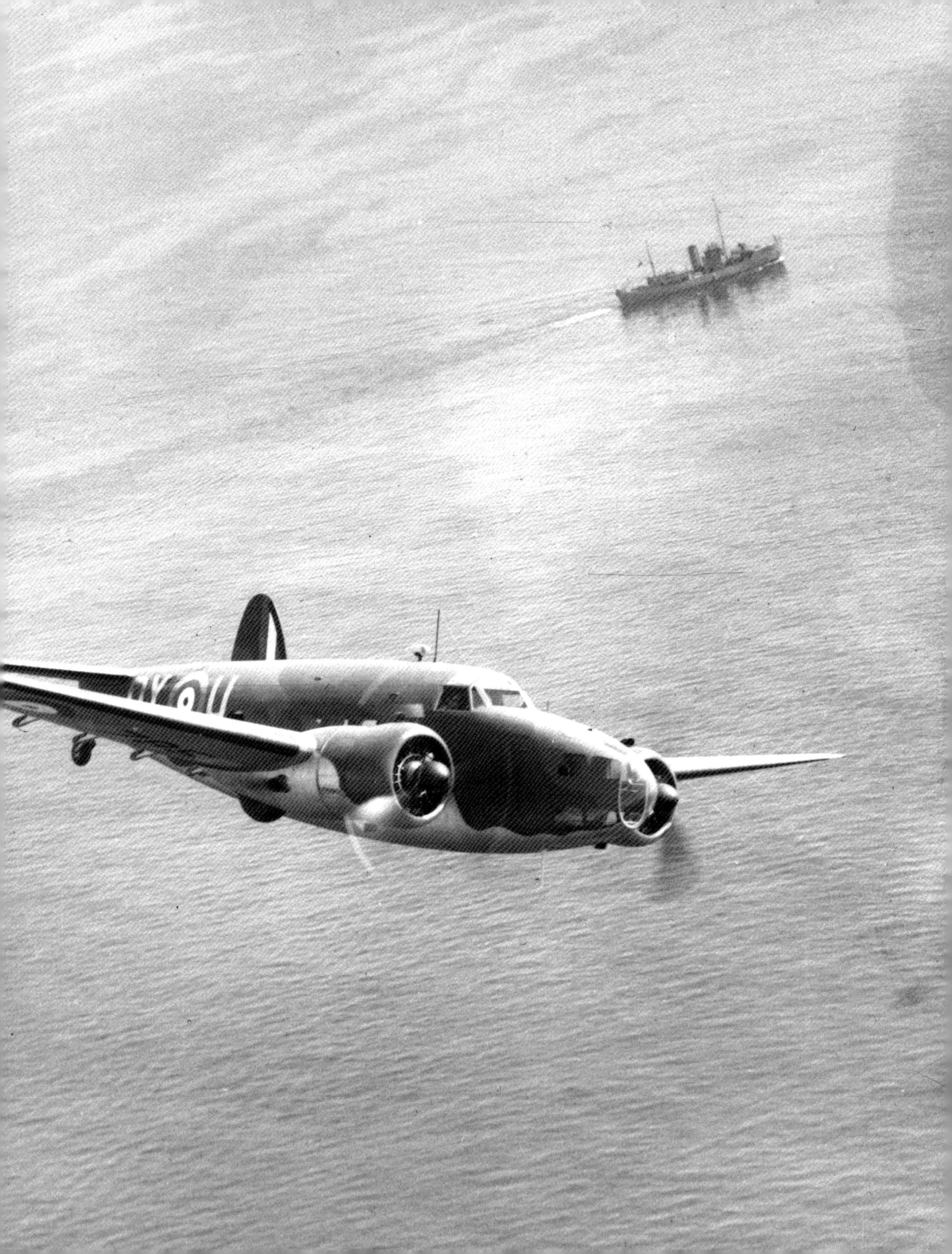

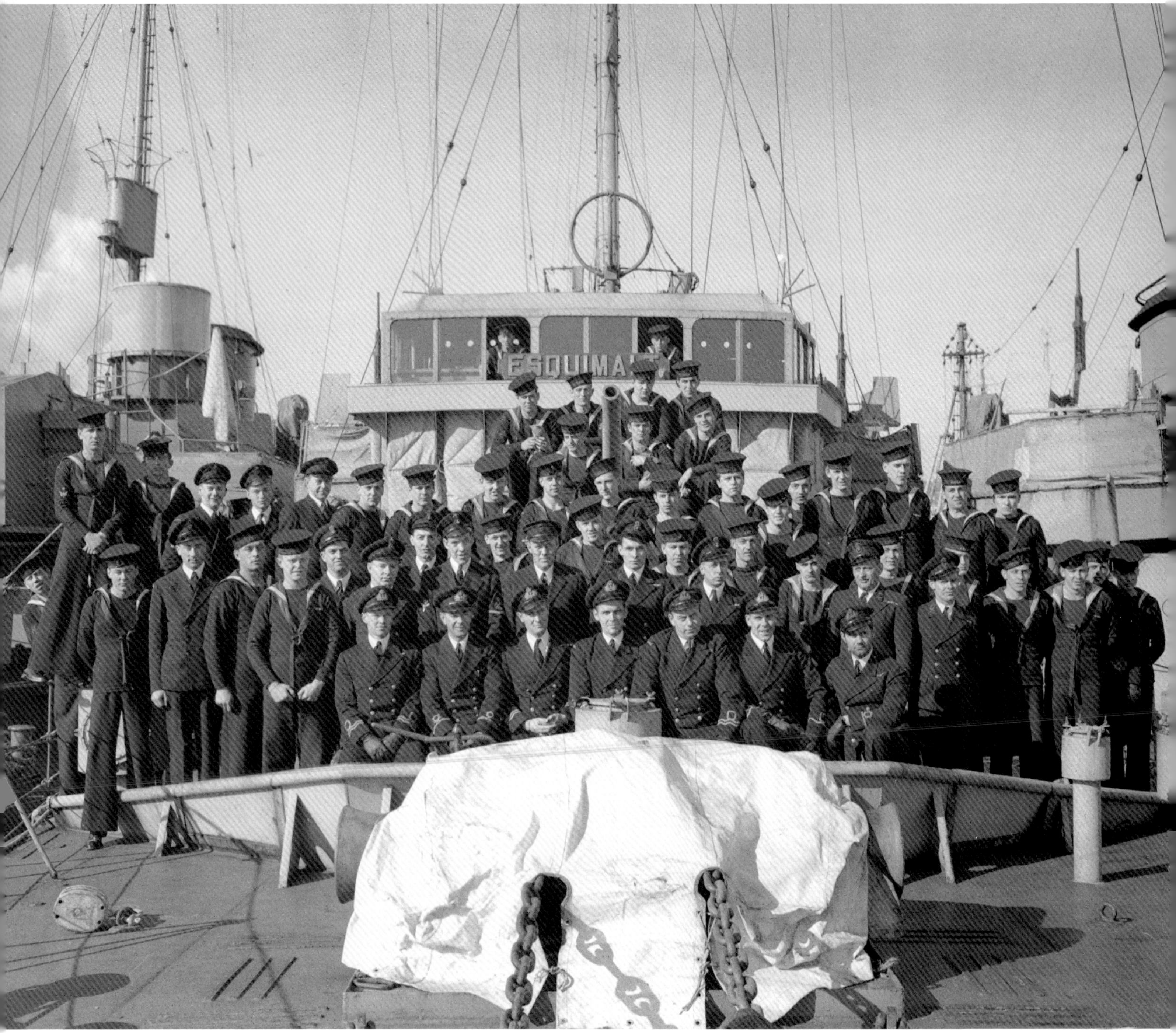

ABOVE: *The final word of this chapter is owed to HMCS* Esquimault *whose ship's company is shown here. While on patrol at the mouth of the harbour on 19 April 1945, just weeks before the end of the war, it was sunk by a torpedo from U-190. So rapidly did it go down that only 46 of the crew of 70, some of them only in their underwear, made it to the lifeboats. There had been no opportunity to send a radio message. Hours later, by chance, HMCS* Sarnia *came upon the survivors, reduced by then to 26 owing to the frigid weather. U-190 surrendered at Bay Bulls, Newfoundland, and was sent to Halifax to be used for training. It was sunk by gunfire at the site of the* Esquimault's *watery grave on Trafalgar Day, 21 October 1947.*

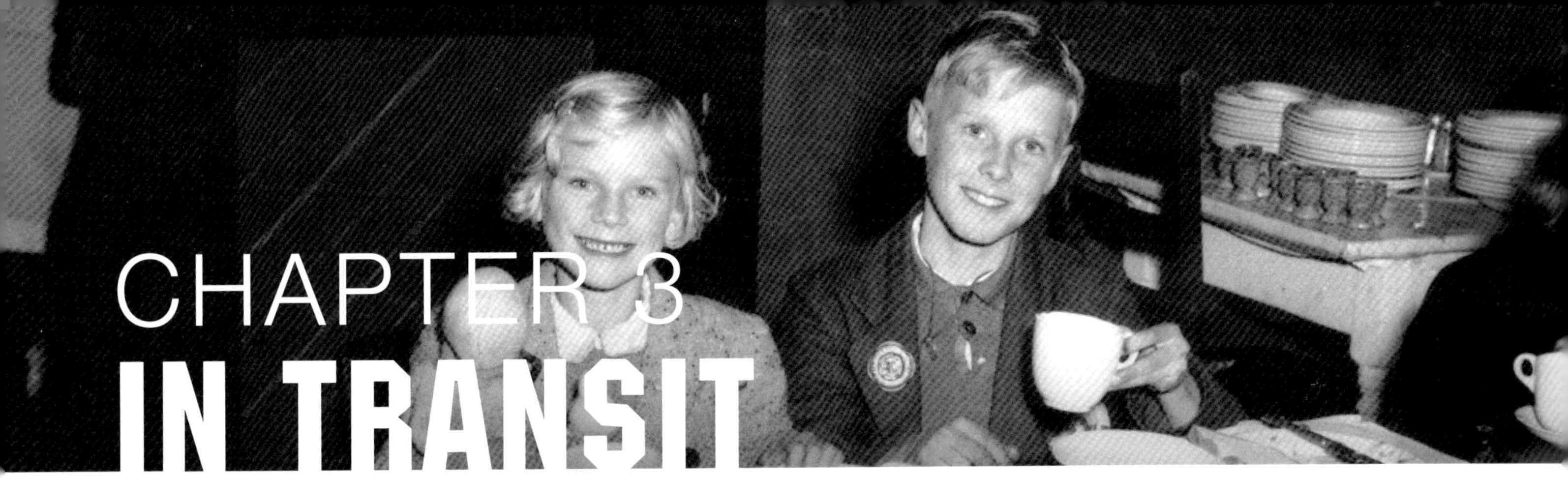

CHAPTER 3
IN TRANSIT

For six years, the port of Halifax was host to thousands of visitors who in peacetime might scarcely have been aware of its existence. The bulk of these people were the tens of thousands of troops heading to Britain, beginning with the 1st Division in December 1939. Troop trains made up of every kind of passenger car that could be scrounged, from main-line trains to scrap lines on forgotten sidings, were marshalled from as far away as the Pacific coast, or from just up the line at the training camps of Aldershot and Debert. If a train came in at night, troops would see nothing. Windows were blacked out as the train rolled into town and right onto a siding on a pier. Here a ship waited with gangplanks ready only a few hundred feet away. Some troops probably had no idea where they were or where Halifax was, but observers comment on what an impressive and moving sight it was to see one of the big ocean liners heading out to sea, troops lining the rails and singing and waving to those on shore. Between June 1945 and April 1946, the lucky ones came back again, perhaps on the very same liner, but to a world that was very different from the one they left. Perhaps this time they noticed Halifax, or perhaps their eyes were solely focused on the future.

There were others, the great and the near-great, who came and went. Princess Juliana, Crown Princess of the Netherlands, arrived in June 1940, heading into Ottawa exile with her two children. She returned from time to time to visit her compatriots stationed in Halifax. Norway supplied a whole community of exiles from its naval, mercantile, and fishing fleets stranded when the Nazis invaded their homeland in April and May 1940. Crown Prince Olav and Princess Martha visited their local establishments in Halifax and Lunenburg from time to time. Many other personages—film stars, military officers, bureaucrats, and Winston Churchill, twice, on his way to Quebec City to meet with President Roosevelt in August 1943, and again in September 1944. In spite of efforts to maintain secrecy around his visit, word leaked out, crowds gathered and the great man, who could not resist a crowd, led them in song in 1944.

There were others who came and went. One group was the British "Guest Children," refugees from the German Blitz of British cities. It was still possible, other priorities being filled, to buy passage on a ship and many British families, in fact, whole schools, took the opportunity to send their children out of danger. Since it was something only the well-to-do could afford, it became a political issue and a Children's Overseas Reception Board was established to enable and coordinate a wider evacuation. For a variety of reasons the British and Canadian governments were cool to the idea, but the public was not. The children who arrived at the Ocean Terminals during the summer of 1940 were welcomed by large and enthusiastic crowds. In the Battle of the Atlantic, however, no quarter was asked and none was given. Eighty-three of the 90 children on board the *City of Benares* perished when it was torpedoed on 16 September and the shock effectively ended the evacuation.

Others who came included German prisoners of war surprised that they had made it alive. The U-boats, they had been assured by Dr. Goebbels, had the Atlantic in a death grip. They were even more surprised at the quantities of food issued them on their trips inland to the prison camps that became their home. A few tried to escape, even in Halifax, but only one ever made it home. The rest sat out the war in isolated bush camps and with varying emotions watched as the Thousand Year Reich disintegrated.

Some visitors, survivors of torpedoed ships, probably did not care where they were so long as it was on dry land. Stories abound of epic survivals in lifeboats, and were it not for the constant R.C.A.F. coastal patrols there would have been far fewer happy endings. Not all of these stories began on the high seas; some, just as dramatic, began within sight of Chebucto Head where the iron grip of the North Atlantic could be as fierce as a thousand miles out in mid-ocean.

Cargo, of course, in both directions, was part of the rationale for Halifax Harbour's vital contribution to the war. Convoy after convoy kept Britain fed while building up the war machine that would lead to invasion of Europe on 6 June 1944, and eleven hard-fought months later, victory in Europe. Although not so overwhelming, cargo did travel in a westward direction, as some of Britain's export industries still functioned, distilling, for example, which provided vital foreign exchange.

At the beginning of the war one of the most astonishing

imports to flow through the port, in utter secrecy, were the hundreds of millions (billions in today's values) of dollars of gold in bullion and coinage forming the gold reserves of Britain and France, plus some rescued from the German advance into Norway. Landed on the docks in Halifax from battleships or fast liners, it was loaded into C.N.R. express cars, made up into what were called "fish trains," and sent to vaults in Ottawa and New York. The movement was initially intended to reassure America, which was bankrolling war matériel on a for-sale basis; but Germany's advance through Europe and the very real threat of an invasion of Britain lent sudden urgency to the need to empty the vaults of the state banks lest captured gold further fund the German war machine.

High drama, all unknown until after the war, unwound in Halifax Harbour after the French cruiser *Émile Bertin* arrived 18 June 1940, with some 245 tons of gold on board, only to find France's final collapse before the German advance just hours away. A tense waiting game ensued while the French weighed their options and the Royal Navy and Canadian officials waited like cats at a mouse hole. On 21 June, the *Émile Bertin* was allowed to sail with its gold, but only on condition that it and its cargo wait out the war in exile in Martinique. The British transfer was less remarkable for its drama, but not its quantity, and in no case was even a penny lost in transit. Like the soldiers who travelled in the opposite direction, once the war was over, the gold turned around and went back home the way it had come.

ABOVE: *Although the British government disapproved — "Wars are not won by evacuation," Churchill declared of Dunkirk, and the Royal Family made it clear they were not budging — at the beginning of the war many considered leaving Britain. The advent of the Blitz, the attempt by the Germans to break British morale by the wholesale bombing of its cities, did not in the long run have that effect; but it prompted an effort to move children out of danger. Most, in the end, simply went into the English countryside away from known Luftwaffe routes and billeted with families there; but there also developed a movement to send as many as possible far from the danger of invasion, to the safety of the British Dominions. Canada, being the closest Dominion, was a favourite destination and Canadians responded enthusiastically. The evacuation of British "Guest Children" began in the summer of 1940. Guest Children are shown here arriving in Halifax.*

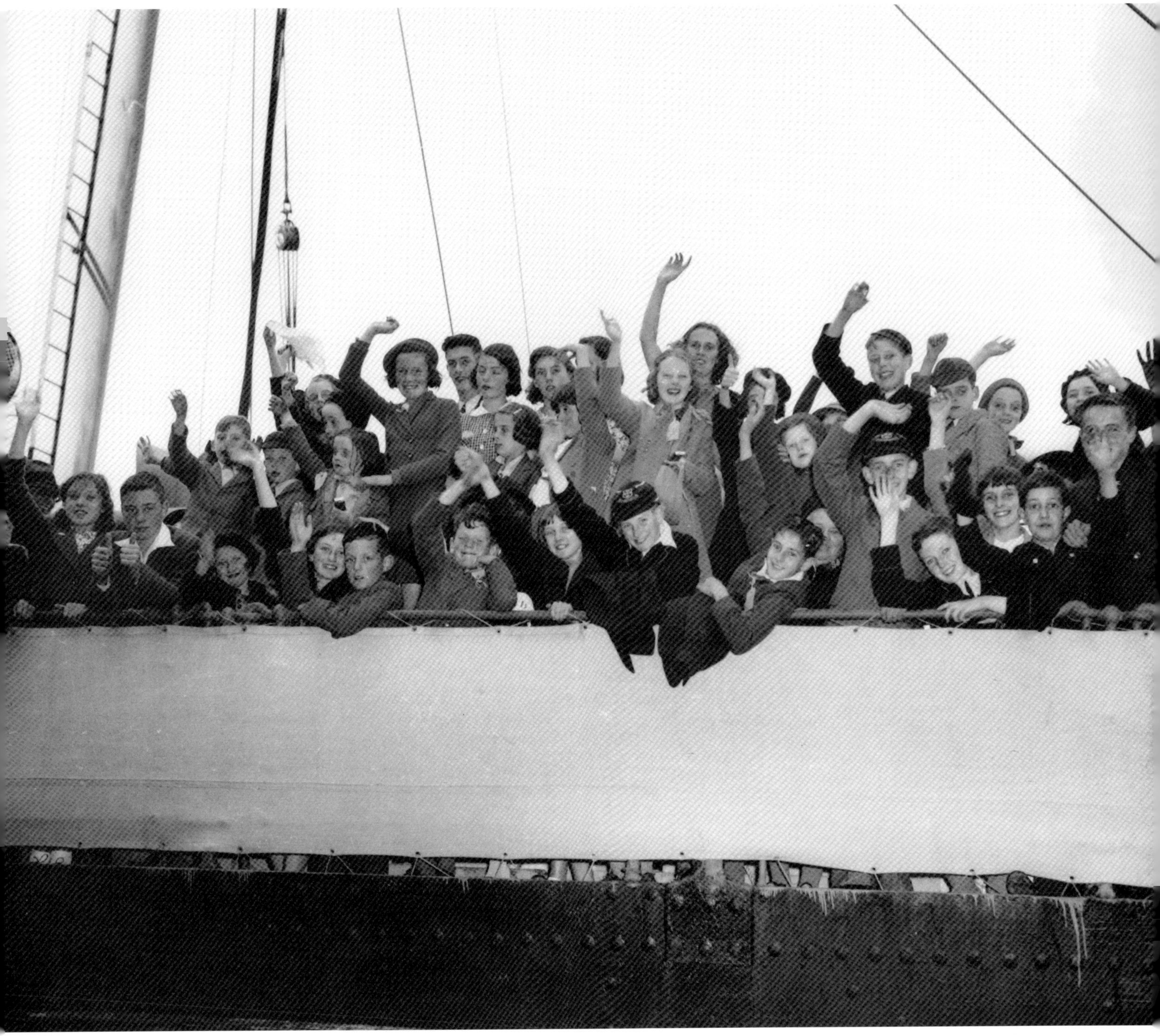

ABOVE: *Thousands of British families signed up to send their children to safety and thousands of Canadians signed up to give them homes. The first few transfers went well and this photograph shows the excitement and anticipation of the youngsters participating in the great adventure as they arrive at Pier 21. When their ships docked at the Seawall they were greeted by enthusiastic crowds and the youngsters responded in kind, singing songs and, most of all, scanning the dockside for their first sign of a red-coated Mountie. When, however, a torpedo sent the* City of Benares *to the bottom in September 1940 with the loss of 83 of the 90 children on board, the cold reality of Total War sank in and the transfer came to a sudden and permanent halt.*

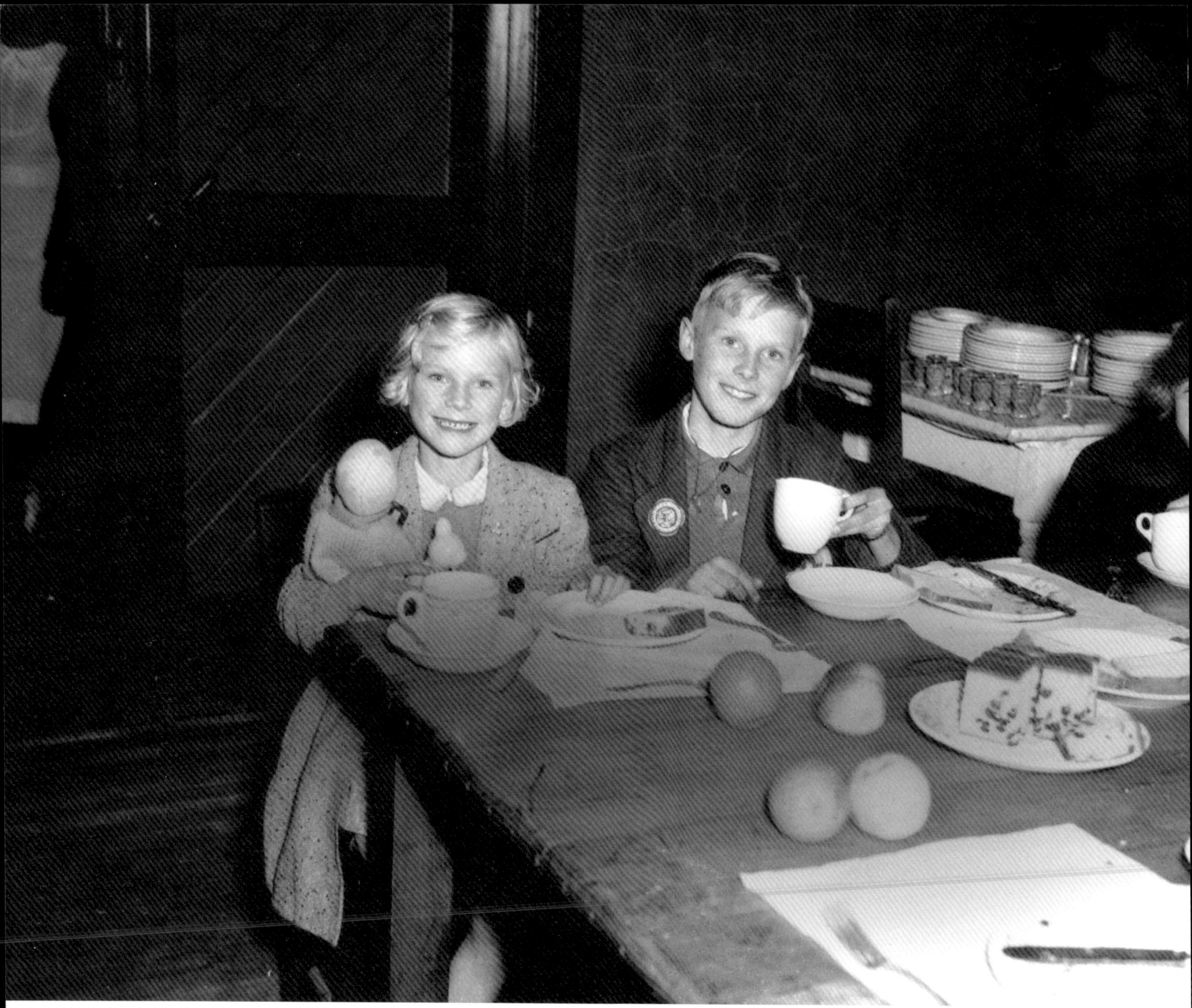

ABOVE: *The war brought many visitors to Halifax, most of them transient, who in more peaceful times would have travelled through more high-profile ports. If not bumped by those with higher priority, anyone with the fare and a convincing reason could travel back and forth across the Atlantic, such as these two Canadian children coming home to join their parents. These youngsters travelled with a group of British Guest Children who were part of a brief phenomenon of evacuation in the first year of the war.*

RIGHT: *The most obvious visitors, and the most transient, were the troops who rolled into town on long trains and marched aboard troop ships, often with barely a chance to glance around. Here the* Ile de France *casts off from the Ocean Terminals laden with departing troops.*

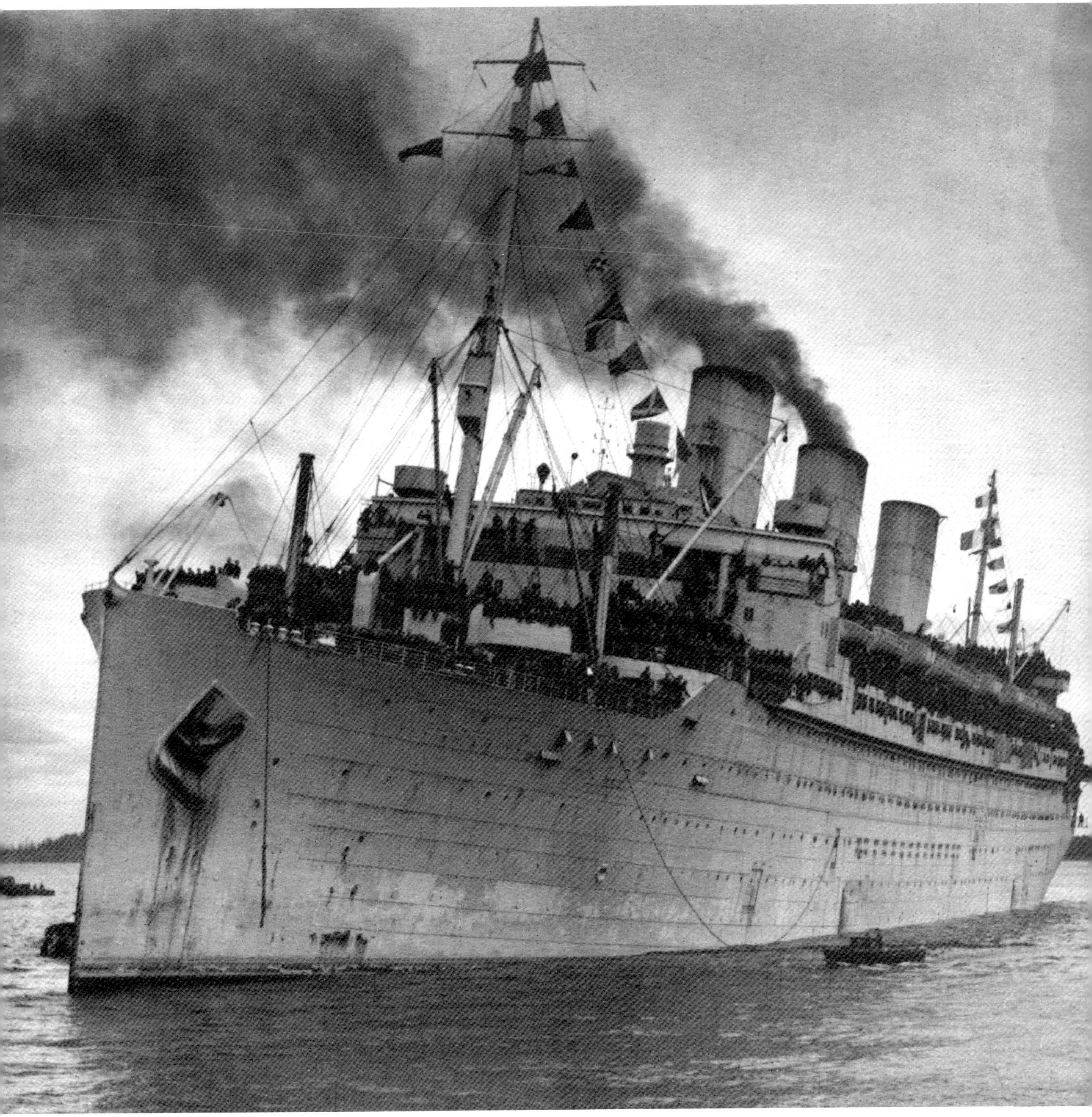

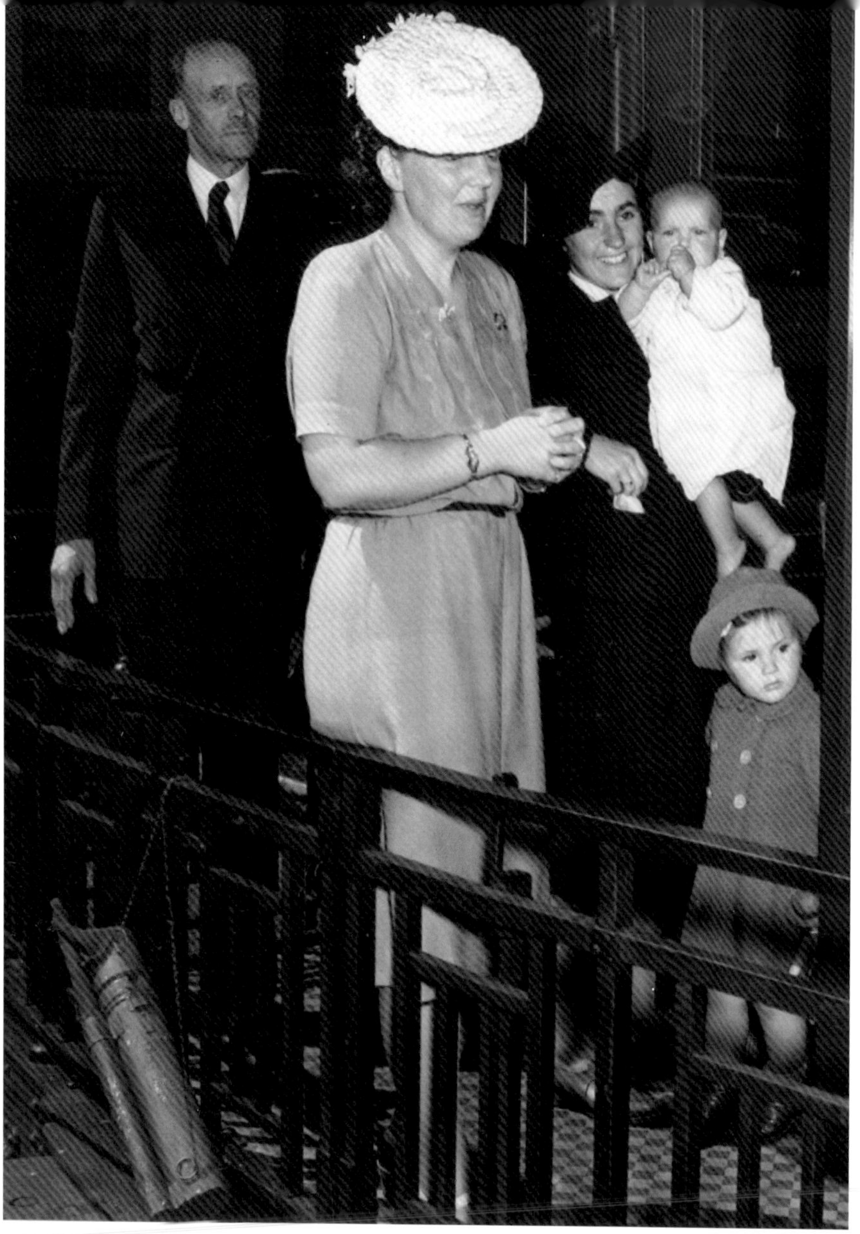

TOP: *After the relative calm of the winter of 1939–1940, the "phoney war," Germany swept through the rest of Europe in the spring, with the exception of Sweden and Switzerland. Among the refugees from Europe was the heiress to the Dutch throne Princess Juliana who, being on the Gestapo hit list, had to be sent to safety. That June she arrived in port aboard a Dutch naval vessel with other refugees and boarded a railway car that took her to wartime exile in Ottawa. She was accompanied by her two daughters, including Beatrix, the eldest who succeeded her mother as Queen of the Netherlands in 1980. Princess Juliana returned to Halifax from time to time to visit the large contingent of Dutch stationed and living in the city.*

BOTTOM: *The Dutch cruiser HNMS* Sumatra, *which brought Princess Juliana and her daughters to Canada.*

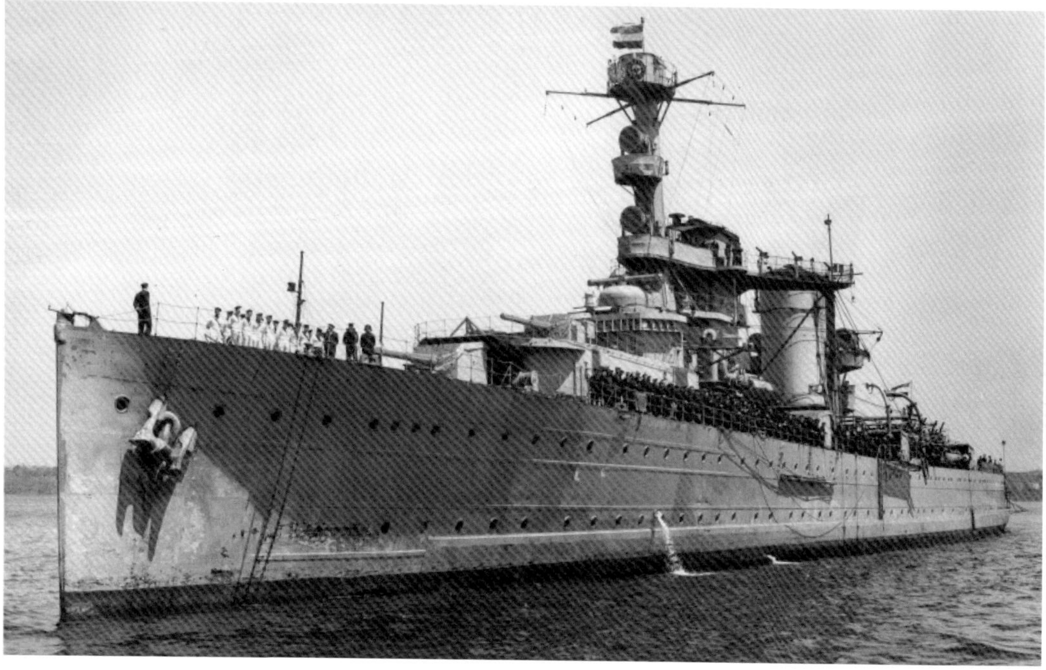

RIGHT: *Drawing by Robert Chambers of Winston Churchill, his wife Clementine, and daughter Sarah talking with a soldier on Citadel Hill. They visited Halifax briefly in August 1943 en route to the Quebec Conference with President Roosevelt. Chambers was editorial cartoonist for the* Halifax Herald *and the* Halifax Mail, *and their post-war successors. This drawing is one of a series published that year as "Halifax in Wartime."*

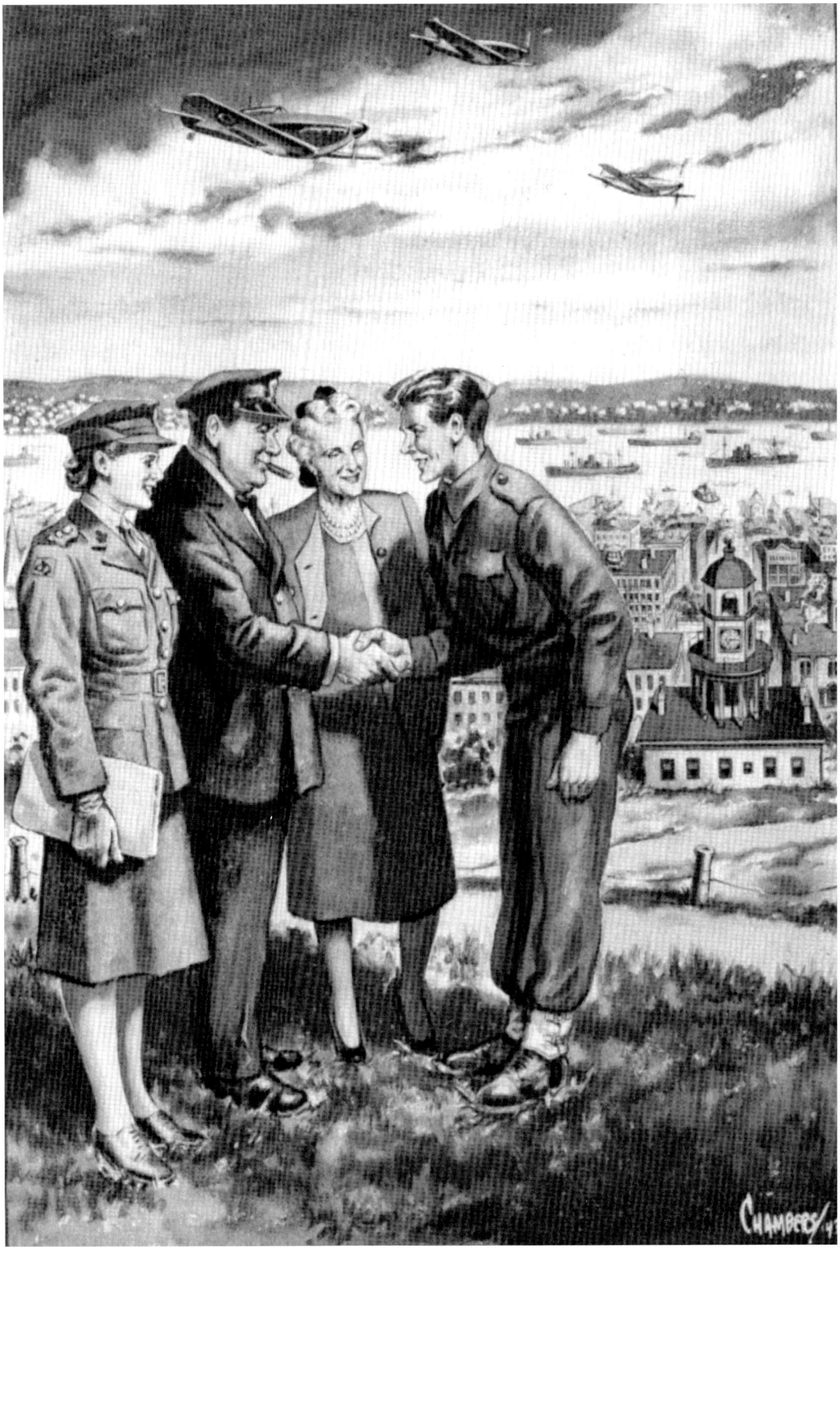

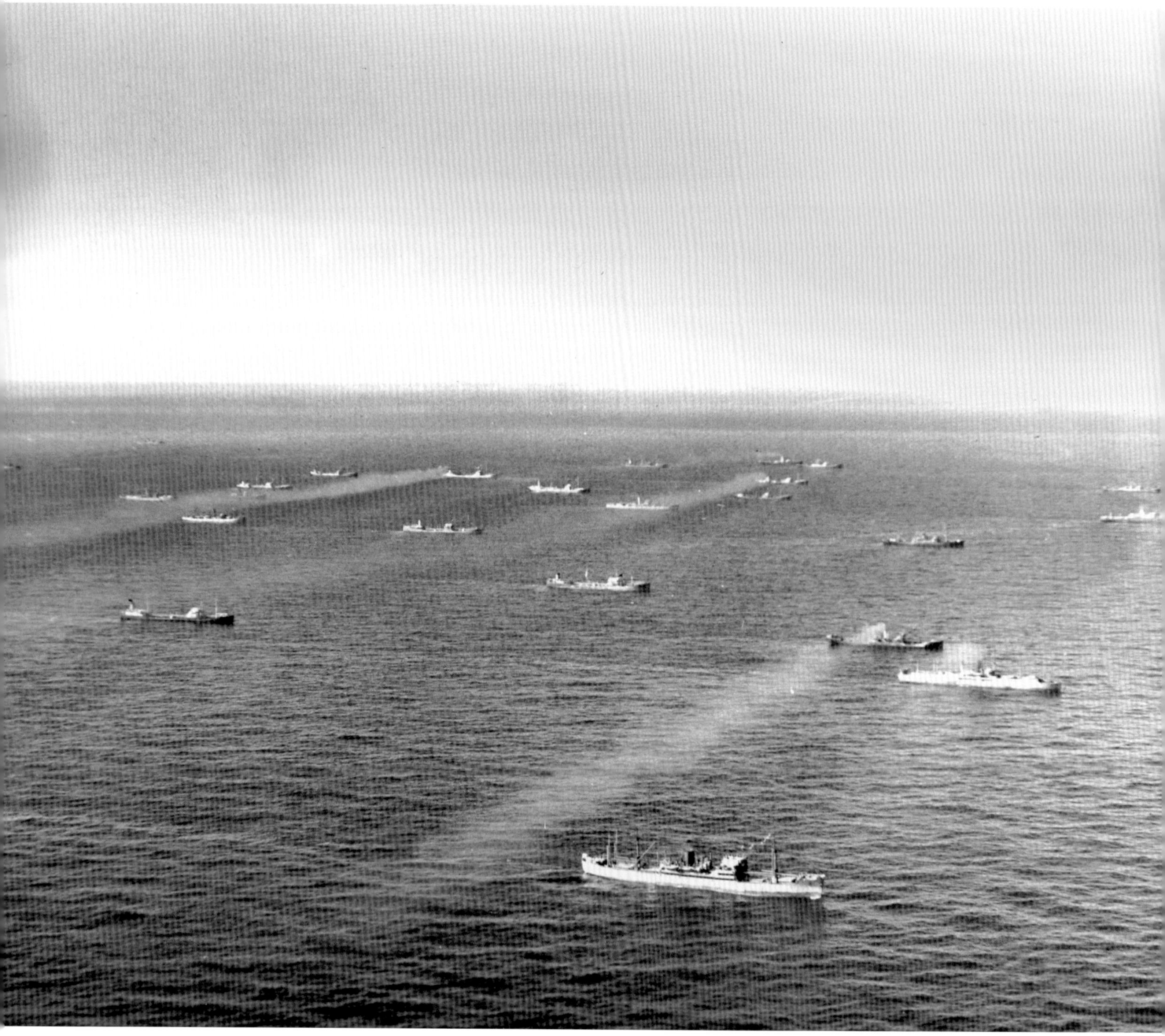

ABOVE: *Even though transient, like their merchant seaman and navy crews, convoys had a major impact on the Halifax. They had to be supplied with vast quantities of food and water and had priority over the local population. They had no qualms about dumping their waste into the waters of the basin and harbour while they waited to head out to sea. At Mulgrave Park, on lands in the north end of the peninsula "cleared" by the Halifax Explosion of 1917, barracks and dining facilities were erected to accommodate merchant seamen who were between ships. A Manning Pool was part of the complex and it found them new berths. Merchant seamen looking for a place to relax found it on Hollis Street in the extensive facilities of the Merchant Navy hostel.*

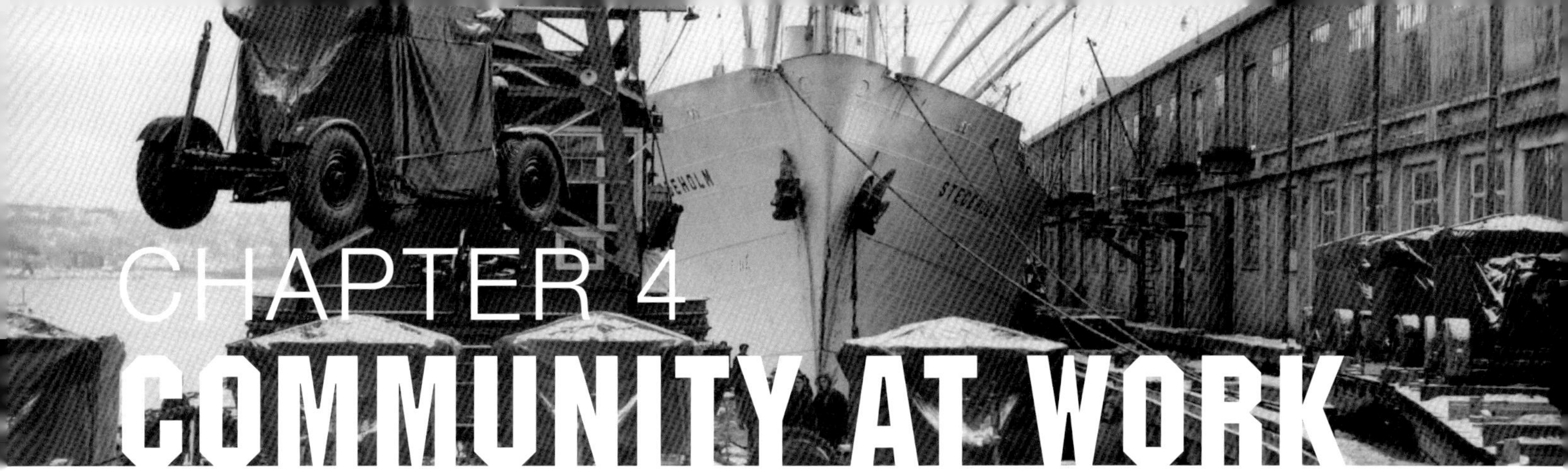

CHAPTER 4
COMMUNITY AT WORK

The war was good to existing Halifax industries, for most thrived in the hothouse atmosphere of wartime spending, even if it brought in its wake a serious level of government control. It may or may not have been a good thing that war did not bring to the city new industries to boost the post-war economy, and there seems to have been a government policy resisting this kind of development. Aircraft-based industries, very much a symbol of World War II elsewhere, barely appeared. Only one, Clark-Ruse, based in RCAF Dartmouth, was brought into the area. It was largely focussed on aircraft maintenance work from the base and as the war wound down it did so too. It re-opened in 1948 as Fairey Aviation and continues as IMP. As a new industry, it differed from more established businesses by having less baggage around the role of women in the workforce, and women were hired as a matter of course without publicity.

Chief among the old-line industries which thrived in wartime was, as may be imagined, the Halifax Shipyards, with two plants, one on the north boundary of HMC Dockyard, the other at Dartmouth Marine Slips, across the harbour in Dartmouth Cove. Over 7,000 ships passed through one or the other of the plants. For whatever reason, Canadian government policy discouraged the yard from developing into an important shipbuilder. To do so would have meant developing new facilities because the existing ones were stretched to the limit simply to accommodate repairs from enemy action, from convoy collisions, and from perhaps the worst enemy of all, the North Atlantic gale. During wartime, overall direction of the operations fell under a national Director General of Shipbuilding, but the local management remained in place. Miracles were routinely accomplished, as the yards operated flat out and men and equipment travelled to any part of the harbour inside and outside the yards to get a ship seaworthy and ready for its assigned convoy. Its male employees were exempt from registering for military service, but as a concession to labour shortages, Halifax Shipyards trained and employed a token complement of five women welders in 1943. They remembered their experience fondly, but in retrospect it was a token action because their duties were carefully circumscribed. As soon as the war was over, they were let go to re-employ returning veterans.

A multitude of other small, specialized ship repair facilities dotted the waterfront and industrial areas of the city, along with machine shops involved in more general work. Another associated industry was the substantial plant of the Dartmouth Ropeworks, operated by the Plymouth Cordage Company. Like many wartime industries, it found that former sources of supply, in this case manilla and sisal, disappeared behind enemy lines and they had to scramble to find alternative sources or substitutes.

Just as vital to the war effort as the shipyards were the operations of Imperial Oil, whose local roots went back to the 1880s, and whose operations at Eastern Passage in the "company town" of Imperoyal went back to 1918. During the war it was an important trans-shipment point for oil supplied from fields in Mexico, Venezuela and the United States, as well as supplying local civilian and military needs. Initially, unable or unwilling to grasp the concept of the convoy after they entered the war, American authorities left their coastal tanker fleet to make their own way up the Atlantic coast, to the great profit of U-boat captains. In February 1942, 23 tankers heading up the Eastern Seaboard were lost. This U-boat success had serious effects on supply. Since the R.C.N. and R.C.A.F. had absolute priority, civilians suffered, no matter what their ration coupons said. To ensure continuity of supply, Britain built a vast tank farm behind the refinery and production was increased from just under 4,000,000 barrels a year in 1939, to just under 7,000,000 barrels a year six years later. It accomplished this increase by shifting to 24-hour-a-day operations, and expanding refining facilities onto the property formerly occupied by the then-obsolete Fort Clarence. On a more mundane level, the company bunkered some 10,500 ships that passed through the harbour, an operation that never stopped.

On another level, the war brought an unexpected business opportunity to the Nova Scotia Light & Power Company. Asked to supervise the installation of degaussing systems on shipping, which rendered ships somewhat immune to the magnetic mine developed by Germany, the company found that if it did not do the work itself the work did not get done. Already busy, company engineers were seconded to a newly formed Marine Division, which ensured that every ship, naval or merchant, that left the harbour had the degaussing equipment installed. Since everything was a priority, it meant long days for everyone. As fleets were gradually equipped, the work of the Marine Division shifted to the installation of still top-secret radar, gyro compasses, generators and routine marine electrical work.

Moirs Limited, which supplied a nationally known brand of chocolates, "Pot of Gold", from its downtown Halifax plant, was another manufacturer that kept up production, deemed vital for civilian and military morale. It scrambled to find new sources of raw materials after the Japanese overran southeast Asia. Chocolate bars became a special treat for children at home, but millions flowed overseas to gladden the hearts and tastebuds of the boys on the front lines.

Clothing factories, Clayton's and Murphy's, shifted overnight from a struggle to cope with economic depression to a struggle to cope with the demand for armed forces uniforms. The Kempt Road paintworks of Brandram and Henderson also experienced the same kind of shift and increased demand from the armed forces for its products.

None of these firms were new. They were all, in fact, survivals of a brief Victorian industrial renaissance at the end of the nineteenth century. They all benefitted from government investment in aging infrastructure and provided sterling service during the war. It must be said, however, that for most of them, Halifax Shipyards excluded, the war only postponed the inevitable. The continental economy that boomed after the war had little room for small local industries on its periphery. Even if the government had invested heavily in new industries, it is doubtful if they would have survived any better than did those established with government support in the post-war years. In spite of government investment in existing plants and equipment, one by one they and their blue-collar jobs disappeared, replaced by new service industries foreshadowed during the war: government, health care and education bureaucracies.

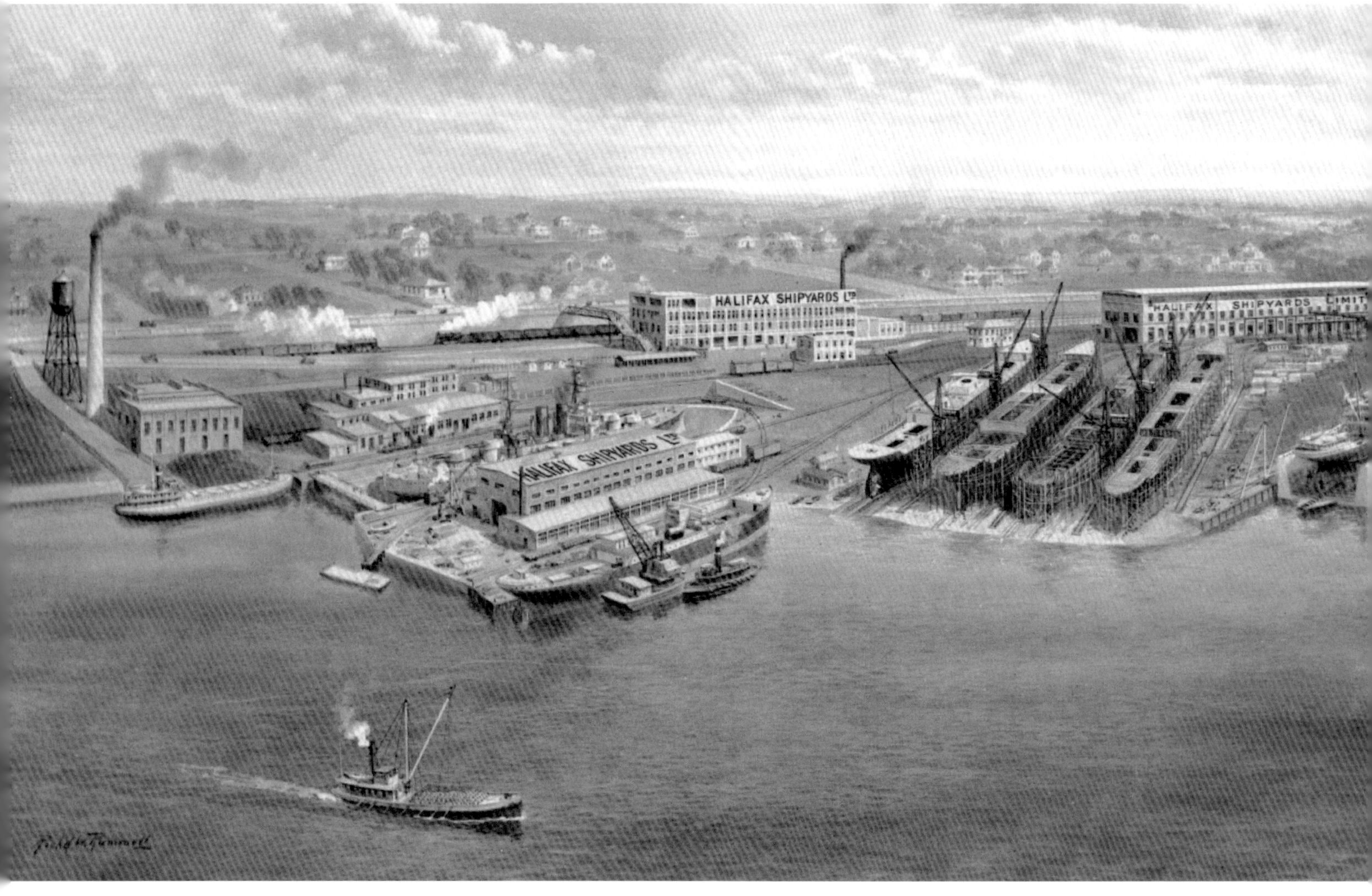
HALIFAX SHIPYARDS LTD
HALIFAX SHIPYARDS LTD
HALIFAX SHIPYARDS LIMIT

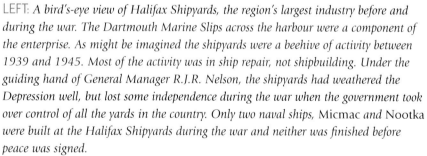

LEFT: *A bird's-eye view of Halifax Shipyards, the region's largest industry before and during the war. The Dartmouth Marine Slips across the harbour were a component of the enterprise. As might be imagined the shipyards were a beehive of activity between 1939 and 1945. Most of the activity was in ship repair, not shipbuilding. Under the guiding hand of General Manager R.J.R. Nelson, the shipyards had weathered the Depression well, but lost some independence during the war when the government took over control of all the yards in the country. Only two naval ships, Micmac and Nootka were built at the Halifax Shipyards during the war and neither was finished before peace was signed.*

ABOVE: *The Halifax Shipyards was a priority industry and in spite of the reluctance of the Canadian government to invest in it as a centre of shipbuilding, its repair facilities were vastly improved. The skilled tradesmen seen here, because of the importance of their work, were exempt from military service. Indeed, they would not have been allowed to join up if they had wanted to.*

ABOVE: *In the early years of the war, before navies got up to strength, much of the work of the Halifax and other shipyards involved turning peacetime ships into combatants. Usually this meant adding some kind of ordnance to a merchant or passenger ship so that it could put up some kind of fight and help out the initially inadequate naval escorts, or at the very least draw off an attacking submarine or surface ship. More ambitiously, some ships, such as Catapult Freighters, had aircraft catapults added which allowed them to launch a fighter plane, as seen in this photograph of a Hawker Hurricane, known in this configuration as a Sea Hurricane. Unlike the less glamorous but more amphibian*

Corsair, a Hurricane could not land on the water. Unless it was within reach of land when its mission was over, it must crash into the ocean and, with luck, its pilot rescued.

RIGHT: *Less ambitious modifications allowed for "Defensively Equipped Merchant Ships," D.E.M.S., to fire two-inch anti-aircraft rocket projectiles, demonstrated here in June 1941 by a naval rating in Halifax. These rockets trailed behind them a long thin wire which, with luck, would entangle an attacking aircraft's propeller, bringing it down.*

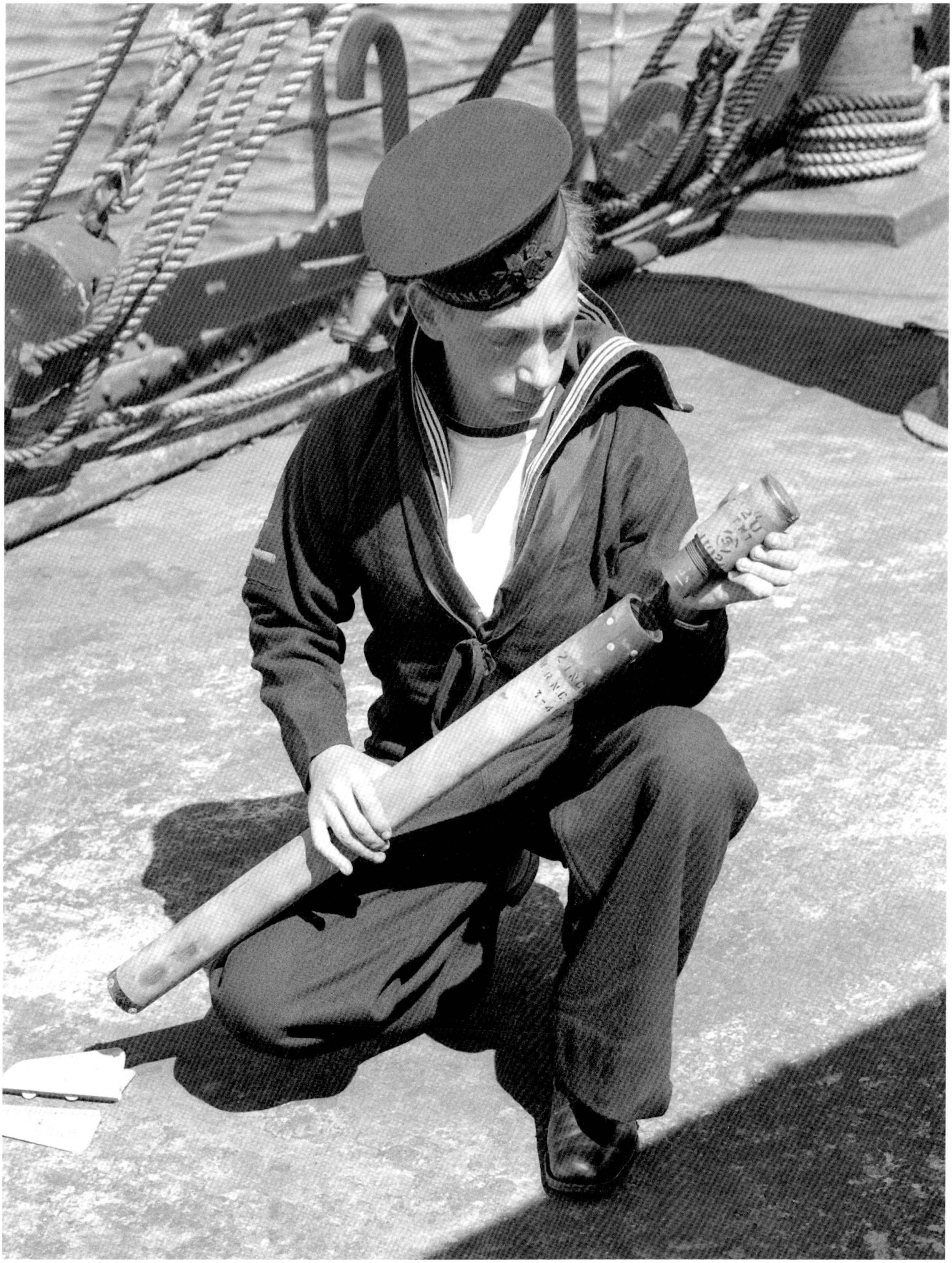

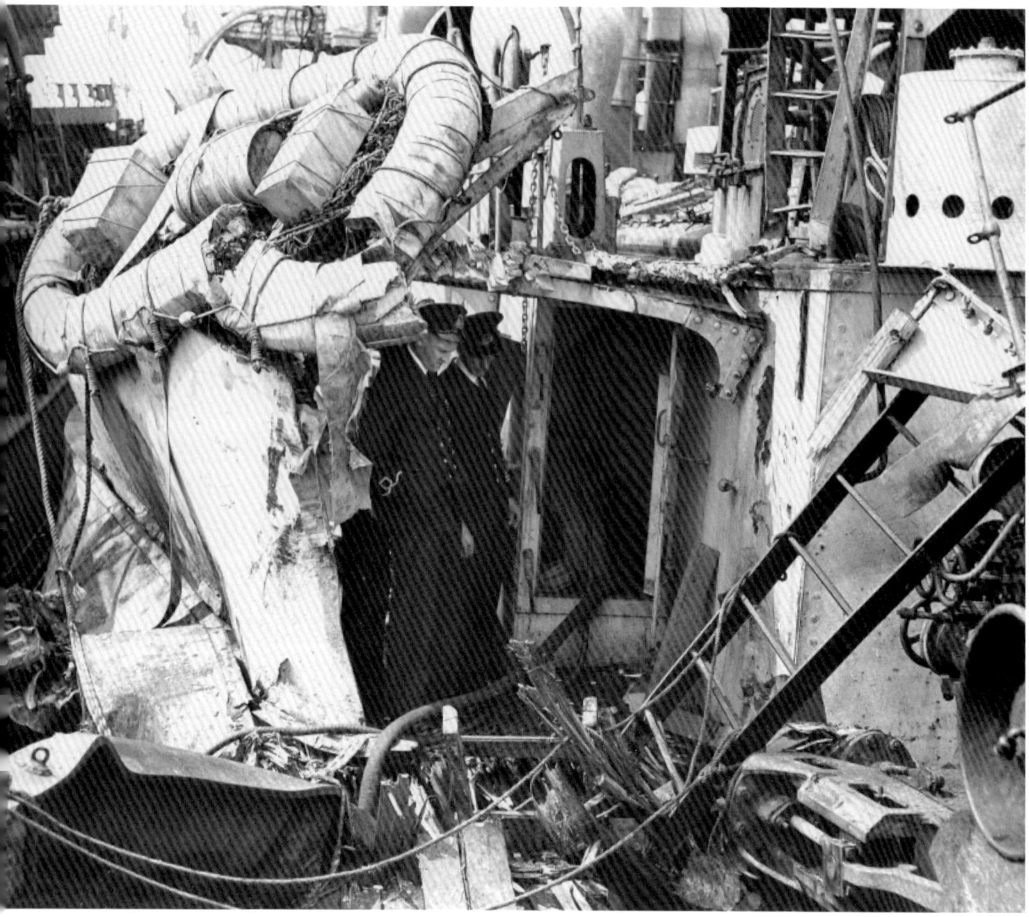

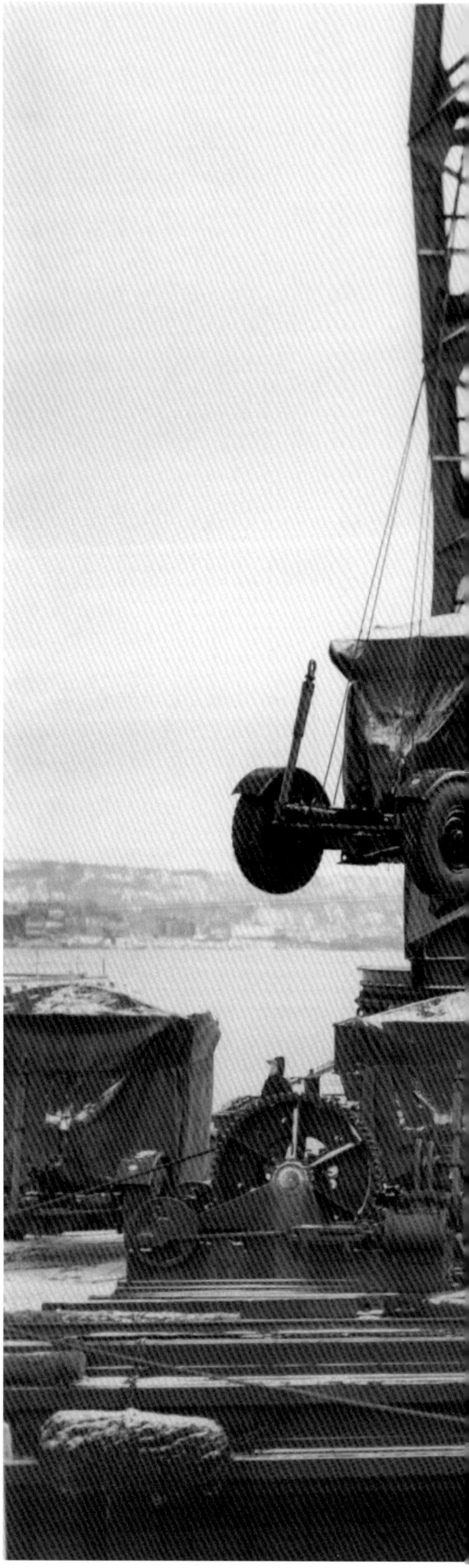

ABOVE: *HMCS* Moncton *collided with the merchant ship* Jamaica Producer *on 28 July 1943. The* Moncton, *shown here, was sent to the Dartmouth Marine Slips to have the damage repaired.*

RIGHT: *In its fixed plants, the Halifax Shipyards included heavy repair facilities such as a fixed graving dock and a floating drydock on the Halifax side of the harbour. At the Dartmouth Marine Slips, by war's end, five marine railways existed capable of dealing with surprisingly large ships. Not all of the work required haulouts, however, and as long as a ship could float, work might be carried on while at anchor or docked at a pier. A key component of this mobile work was a floating steam crane, Halcrane, shown here unloading military vehicles. It could be towed anywhere in the harbour that could float its bulk. Shipyard work crews could go to the job rather than have the job go to them, freeing fixed shipyard facilities for the truly disabled.*

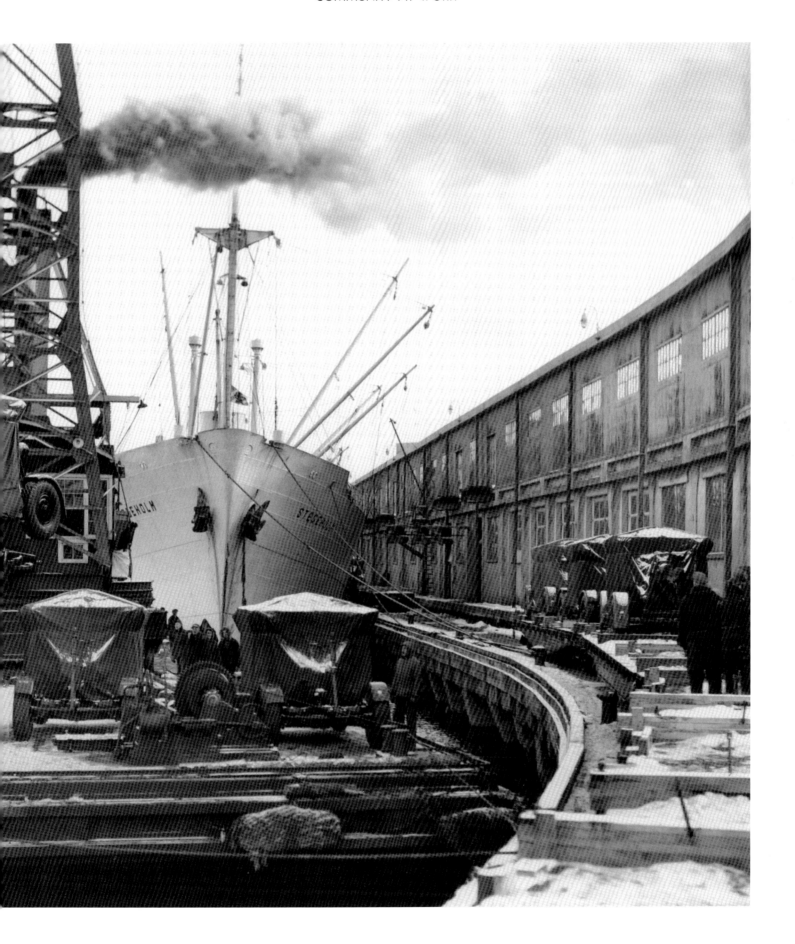

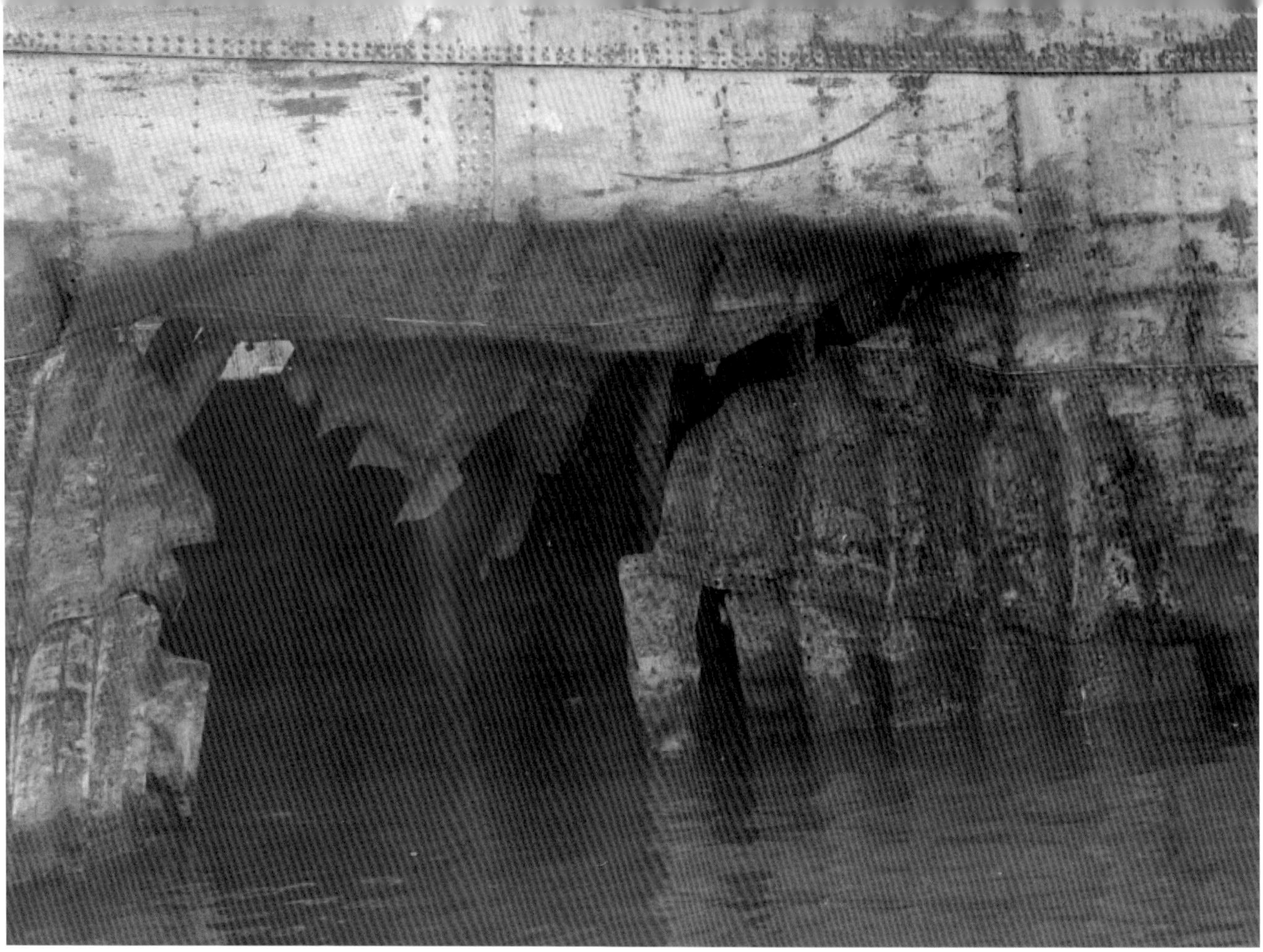

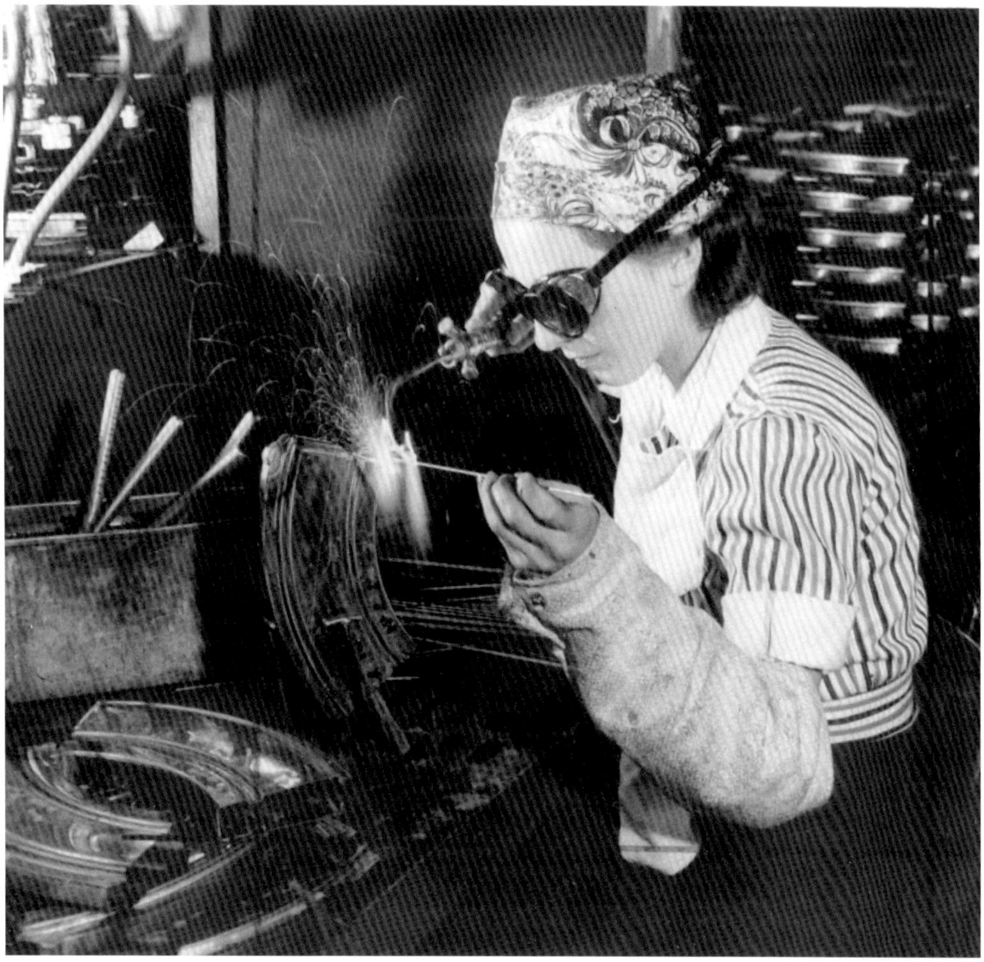

ABOVE: *Dramatic torpedo damage to an unidentified ship. Some vessels survived the most astonishing damage and were able to make it into port either on their own or under tow from the* Foundation Franklin, *whose record as an ocean tug and salvage vessel operating out of Halifax Harbour was unparalleled.*

LEFT: *Surprisingly enough, the shipyards, responding to a shortage of labour and political pressure, trained and employed female welders. In spite of the very traditional, exclusively male-dominated nature of ship repair, the women were well received by their male colleagues. Perhaps because their conditions of employment were sufficiently hedged with conditions, women were not perceived as a threat. The instant the war was over they were out of work. Still, the women enjoyed the experience and the substantial salary that went with it, and appeared to have no expectations that their employment was anything more than a response to wartime emergency.*

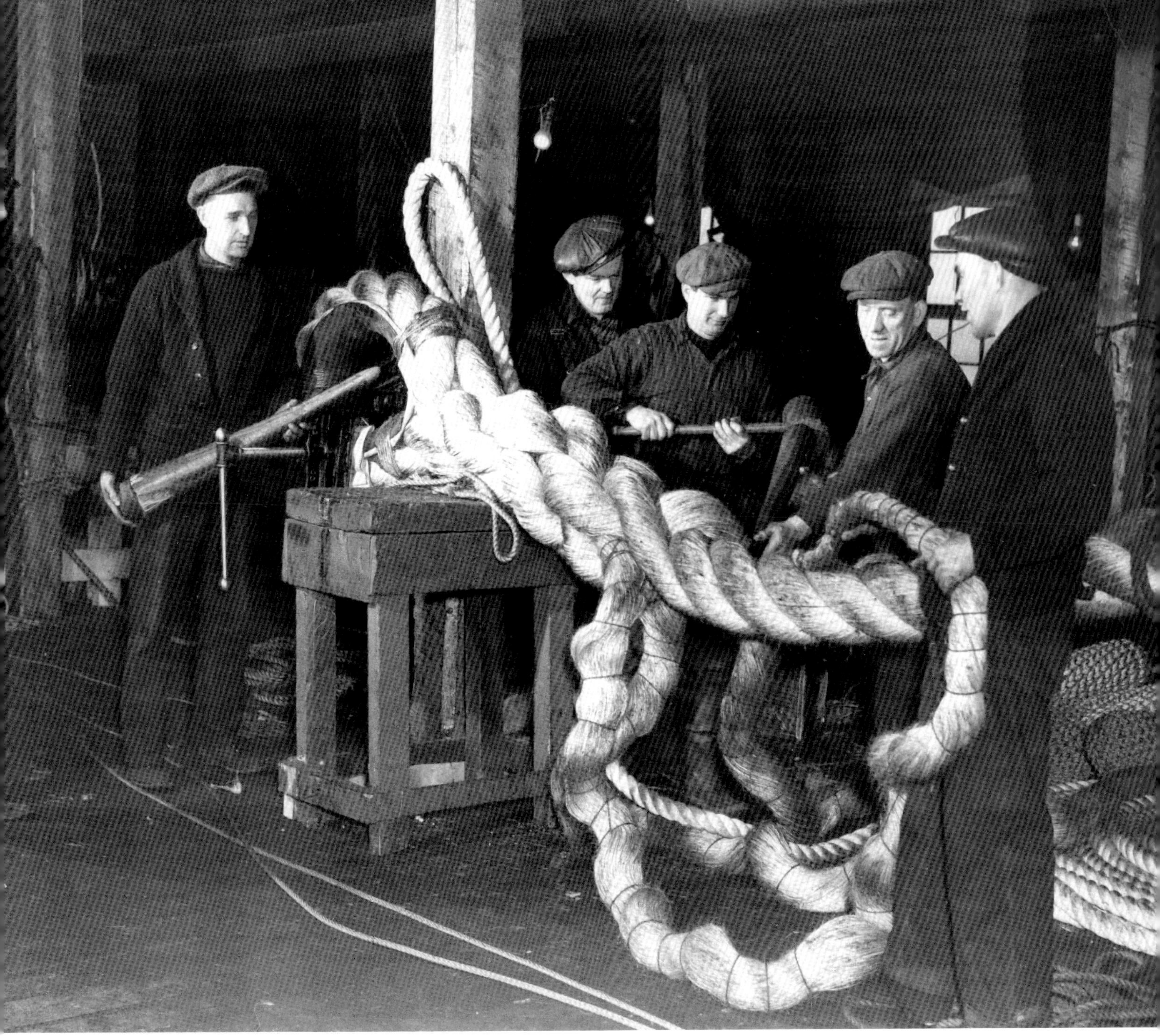

ABOVE: *The shipyards housed within its confines many specializations. One of the world's largest galvanizing plants co-existed with more traditional skills such as splicing rope as seen here.*

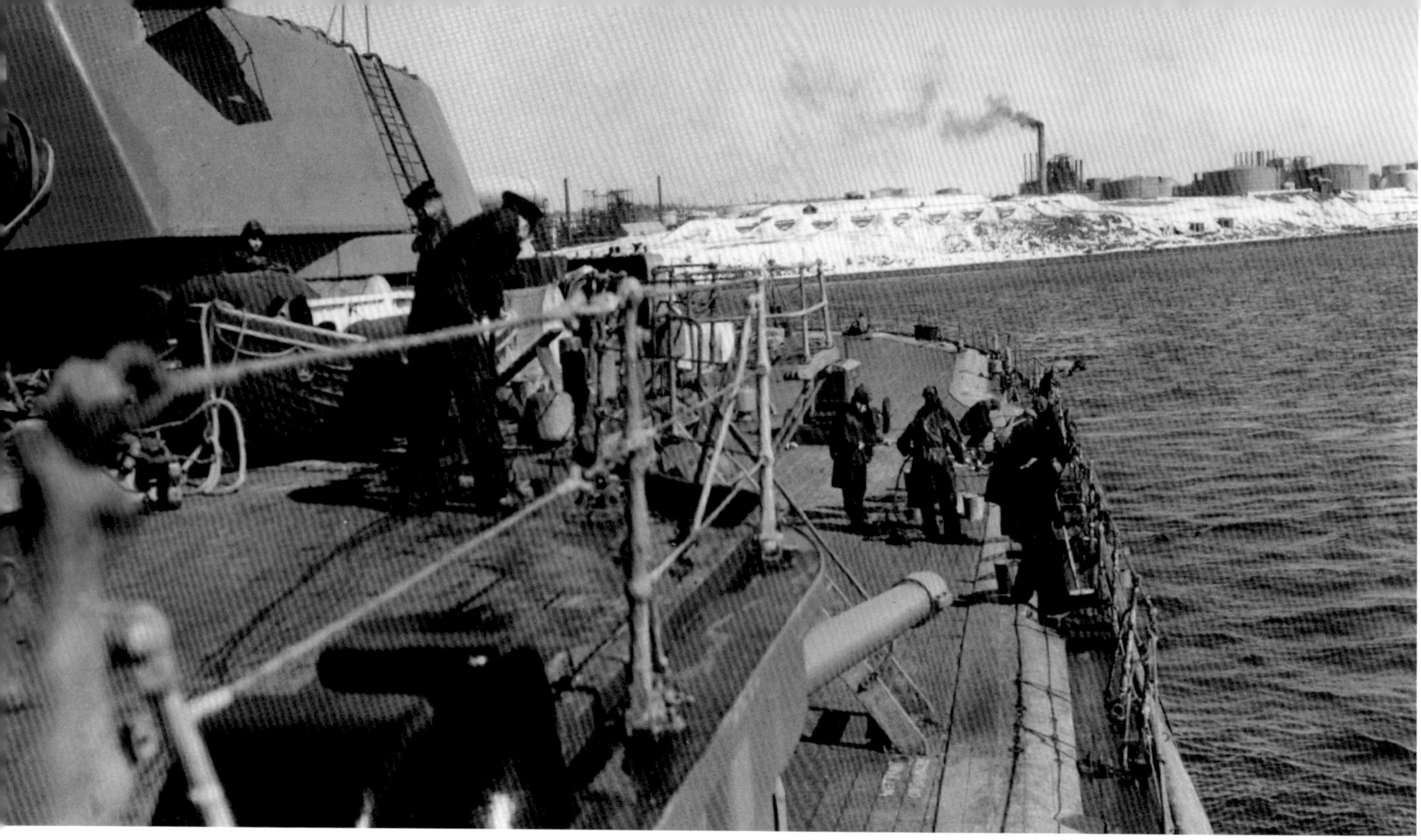

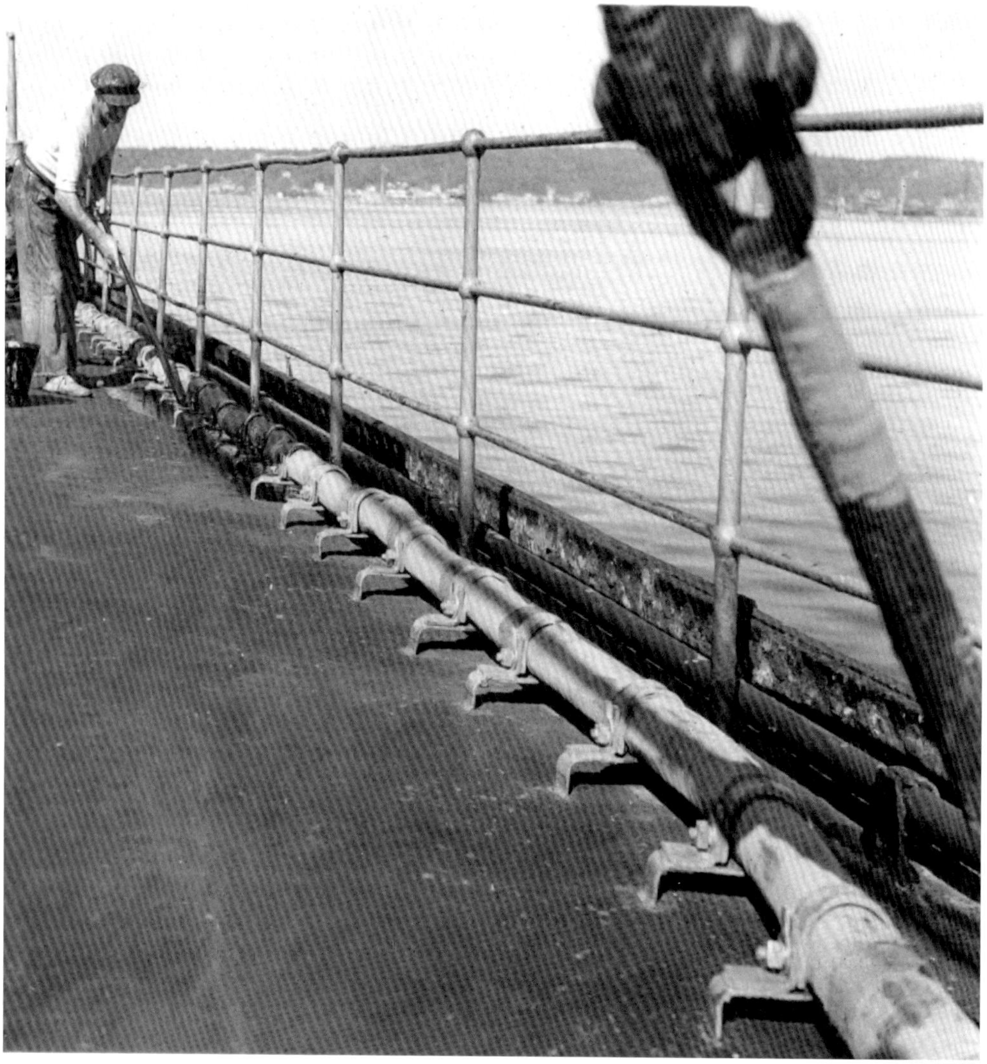

ABOVE: *Seen from the deck of the British battleship HMS* Ramillies *are the refining facilities of Imperial Oil at Eastern Passage. The company built a self-contained community, Imperoyal, for its employees. The refinery was totally dependent on oil transported along the Eastern Seaboard from South America and the southern United States. Most of the production was designated for Britain and, until America entered the war, its origins had to be "laundered" to comply with the laws of neutrality.*

LEFT: *Early in the war Germany developed the magnetic mine, which would explode from mere proximity to an iron or steel ship. British scientists quickly countered this threat by devising a method of demagnetizing, or "degaussing," a ship by encircling it with a massive electrical cable which, when energized from the ship's generators, neutralized the ship's magnetic field. This photograph shows the degaussing cable around the perimeter of the MV* Athel Crown. *The Nova Scotia Light & Power Company was responsible for outfitting ships with the degaussing apparatus, a task which, among many others, kept employees working around the clock throughout the war.*

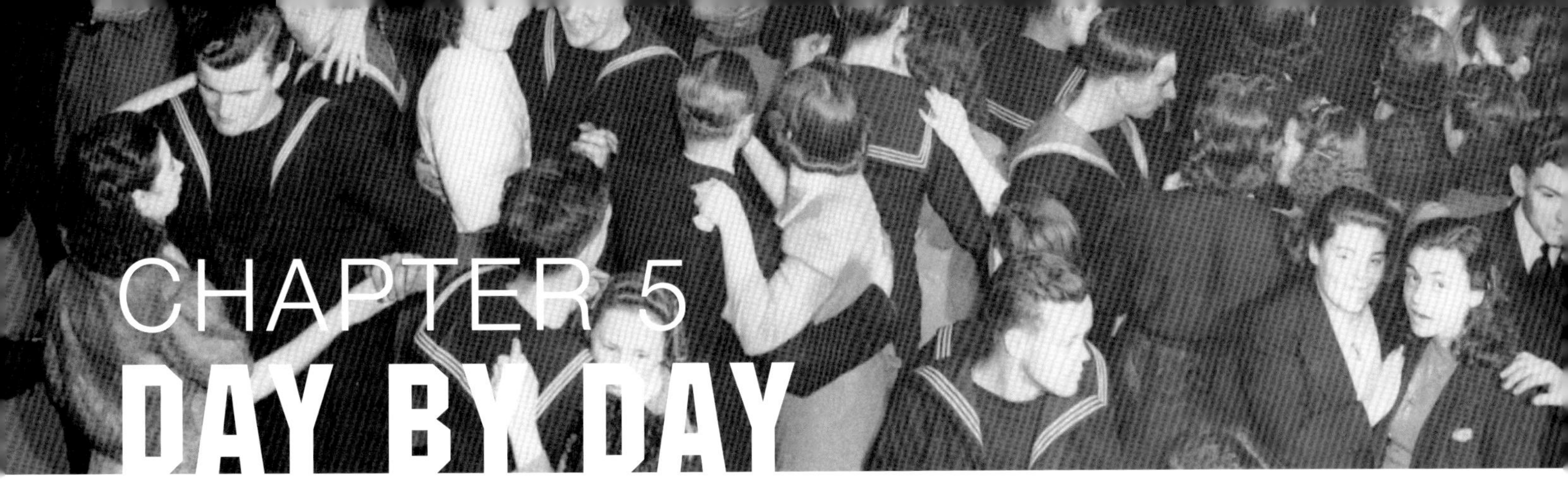

CHAPTER 5
DAY BY DAY

Life, as it always does, went on in the port of Halifax, in spite of increasing restrictions. These were not restrictions on people's freedoms, by and large. Censorship, imposed in the first months of the war, prided itself not on suppressing information but rendering it fuzzy enough that it would be useless to an enemy. Ship movements, being very sensitive, might be announced, but only once they were stale news. Political dissent, so long as it did not involve treason, was not an offense and there were many who made their disapproval of the national administration of Mackenzie King quite clear. Those who were youngsters during the war recall a freedom to go anywhere or do anything so long as you kept out of the way, a freedom that would be inconceivable a couple of generations later.

Since everyone was in the same boat, shortages, tiresome as they were, could be endured. Children, after the first disappointment of not being able to buy a chocolate bar on impulse, coped. School carried on, but while the course work and expectations remained the same, there was a definite shift to a wartime emphasis. Air raid drills, fundraising scrap drives, Air Raid Messengers for 12-year-old boys, cadets for high school boys, and volunteer work for the girls took up spare time in and out of classes. Every child studied aircraft identification and no German Messerschmitt or Japanese Zero could have penetrated undetected into the airspace of the "East Coast Port". Although women became increasingly welcome in the armed forces, it was not the case for school cadet corps, which remained a male preserve. For boys, it was made clear from age 16 on that military service was in their future when they left high school.

Adult life also went on more or less as usual, but it was circumscribed by travel restrictions, line-ups and shortages. Unlike children, adults had a wistful recollection of a time when there were more goods in the stores, preparation of the evening meal was not an exercise in make-do with Spam and last summer's root vegetables, and when Sunday meant a roast beef on the table and a drive in the country.

As with children, wartime activities took up much of the slack for adults: in particular Civil Defence. Scenes of civilian chaos as Europe collapsed ahead of the German juggernaut would not, if authorities had anything to say about it, be repeated in the city. Under the umbrella of the Air Raid Patrol, the community was divided up into districts headed by a warden. Every male householder was urged to join his neighbourhood A.R.P. headquartered in a nearby "hut." These units were charged with seeing that blackouts were observed and patrolling the streets during air raids to fight fires and assist civilians. Since there was wireless silence, communication between A.R.P. units and headquarters was carried out by boys on bicycles, called Messengers.

Paralleling the A.R.P. was a first aid network of Red Cross and St. John Ambulance workers, volunteer and professional. From time to time, in simulated air raids that encompassed the harbour communities, the whole organization was called into action with, to the enjoyment and entertainment of all, fighters and searchlights streaking across the sky, fake bombs exploding and the injured trekking to the first aid stations set up at designated intervals. It was all very exciting and the neighbourhood drills were as useful in enhancing civilian morale as they were in instilling confidence that the disasters their British contemporaries were dealing with on the newsreels could be handled.

In spite of shortages, there was still disposable income around and it was the policy of the Canadian government to soak up as much of it as possible to pay for the war. Through annual Victory Bond campaigns adults were persuaded to buy as many bonds as possible and it was made as easy as possible to do so. At the other end of the spectrum, in year-long campaigns, children were urged to buy, or persuade others to buy, 25-cent War Savings stamps. Shoppers were urged to use their spare change to buy them so as to ensure another Spitfire might take to the skies. Once their money was gone, householders were urged to comb their houses for scrap to feed the insatiable war machine. These campaigns were intensive and diverting, occupying much spare time and fostering citizen participation, often involving parades, public events, exhibitions of captured enemy aircraft and the like. Financially, it was a successful effort. As a nation, Canada was able to pay for its contribution to victory without resorting to foreign borrowing.

Spending money, left over after patriotic purposes were satisfied, went to movies and dancing, the main public recreations. To supplement these activities and provide entertainment for those for whom the fleshpots of civilization were inaccessible, the redoubtable Hugh Mills established the Halifax Concert Parties, whose hundreds of volunteers not only put on big revues but also went out alone or in pairs on a moment's notice to batteries, hangars, and ship wardrooms to lighten a sparse, stressful, and monotonous existence.

Public consumption of liquor was virtually forbidden, leading to serious problems in a city crowded with young men in the armed forces and the merchant marine. Immense efforts were made by committed civilian volunteers to provide support and entertainment in a community that had had little even before the war. Huts, canteens, and hostels juxtaposed with brothels and speakeasies on crowded and often chaotic downtown streets.

In the commitment of its citizens, young and old, in its crowded streets and its often riotous outdoor social life, downtown Halifax became a very different place from its shabby, genteel pre-war self. Although in treed suburbs around the Basin life went on without much change, there was a gradual realization in the city core that life was never going to be the same again.

ABOVE: *On the Home Front life went on, in many respects, as normal, even though there were constraints on "luxuries," the definition of which grew broader and broader after 1941. People still had fun, entertained themselves and others, the sun still shone, and in 1941 Maurice Bolbain had a birthday party in his backyard.*

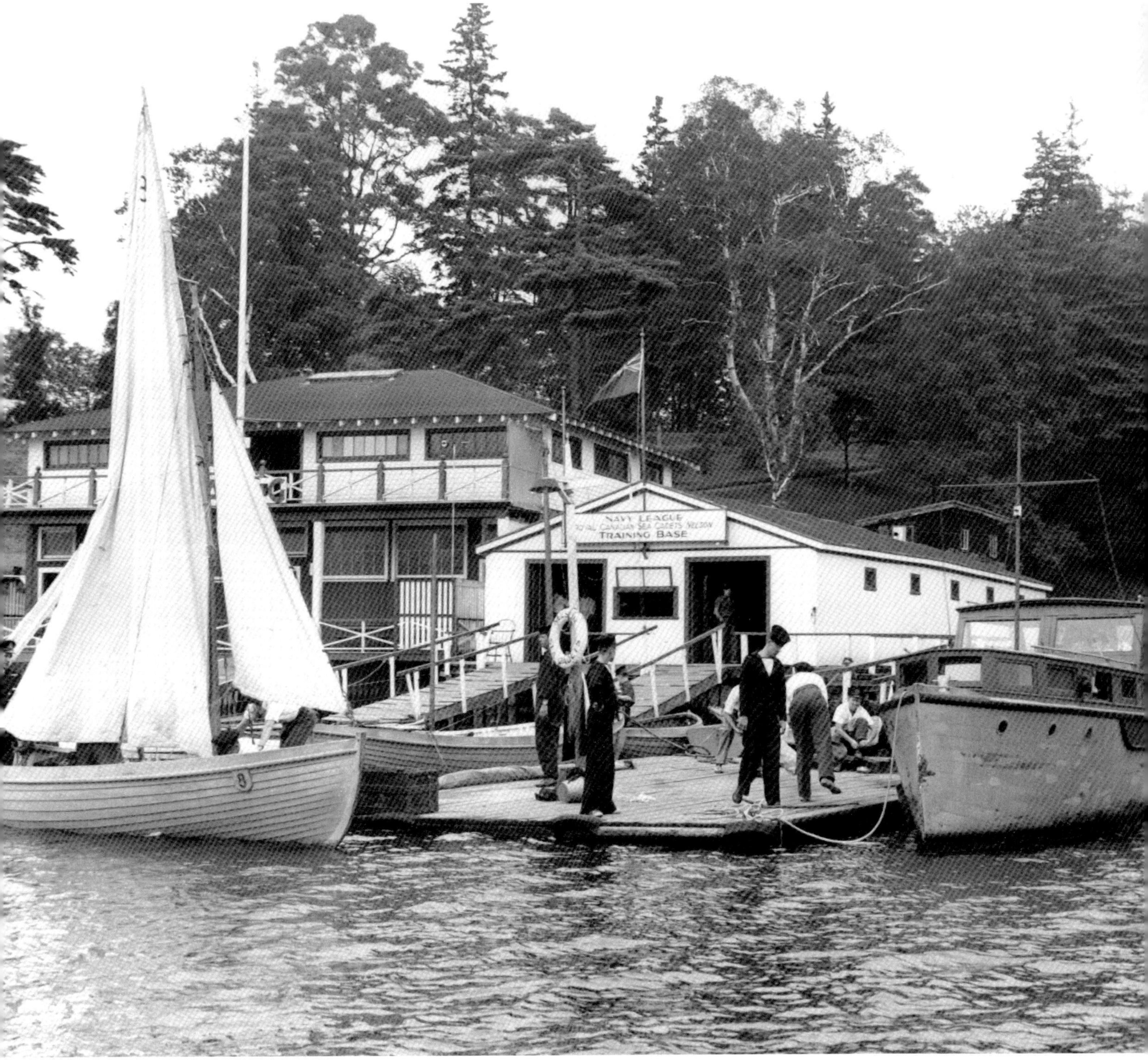
NAVY LEAGUE
ROYAL CANADIAN SEA CADETS NELSON
TRAINING BASE

ABOVE: *At the Waegwoltic Club on the Northwest Arm, people still enjoyed themselves during the summer months, but the club had also been co-opted to another role. As the men left, youth took up some of the slack and the Arm Patrol, which supervised the waters of Halifax's summer playground, was taken over by the Nelson Sea Cadets, seen here, who made their base at the club.*

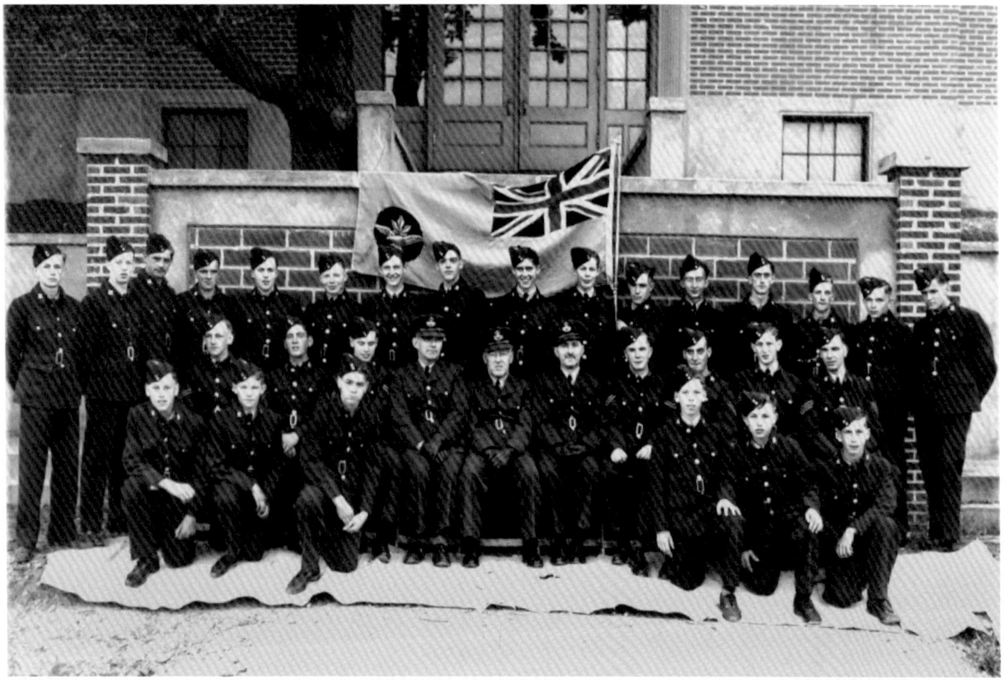

ABOVE: *Bedford R.C.A.F. cadets pose in front of their school. Cadets of all services were an integral part of the school curriculum. Large schools, such as Queen Elizabeth High School, had army, navy, and air force options; small schools might focus on just one of the services.*

RIGHT: *These cadets of the Nelson Sea Cadet Corps learned to tie bends and hitches as well as a variety of other skills useful for a military future, from rifle practice to signaling to parade ground drill.*

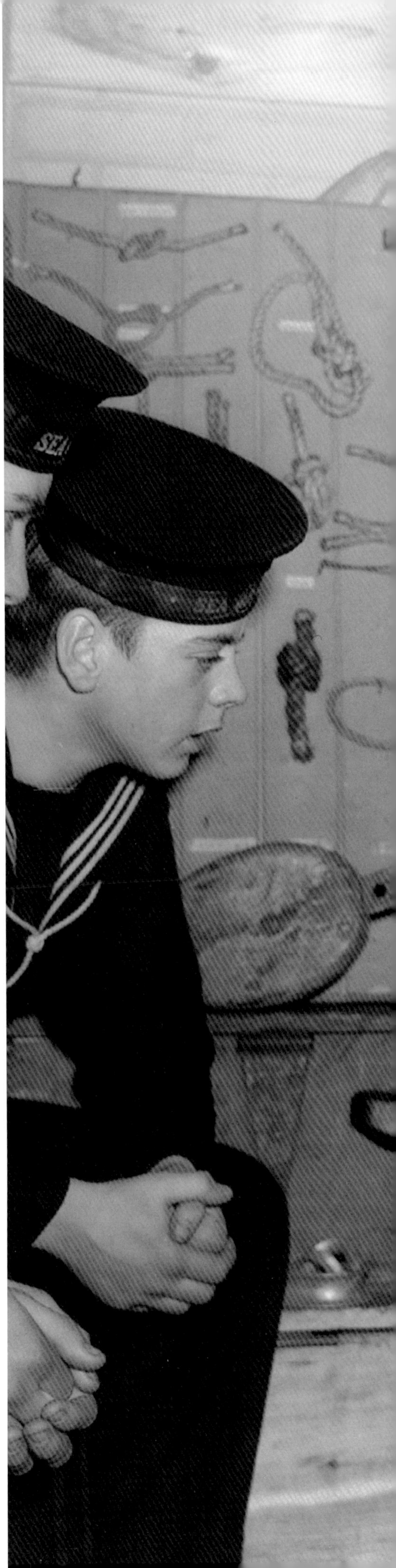

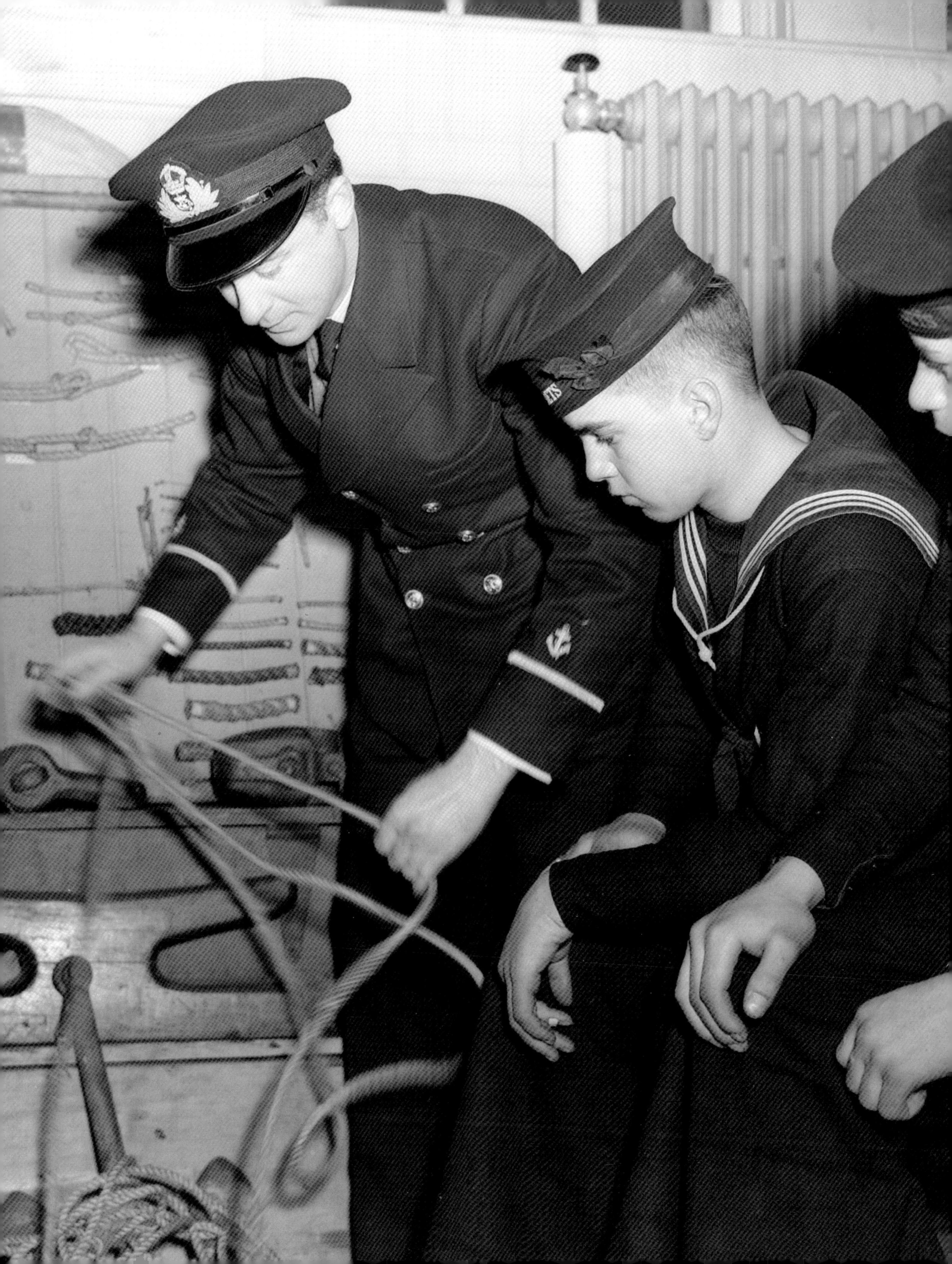

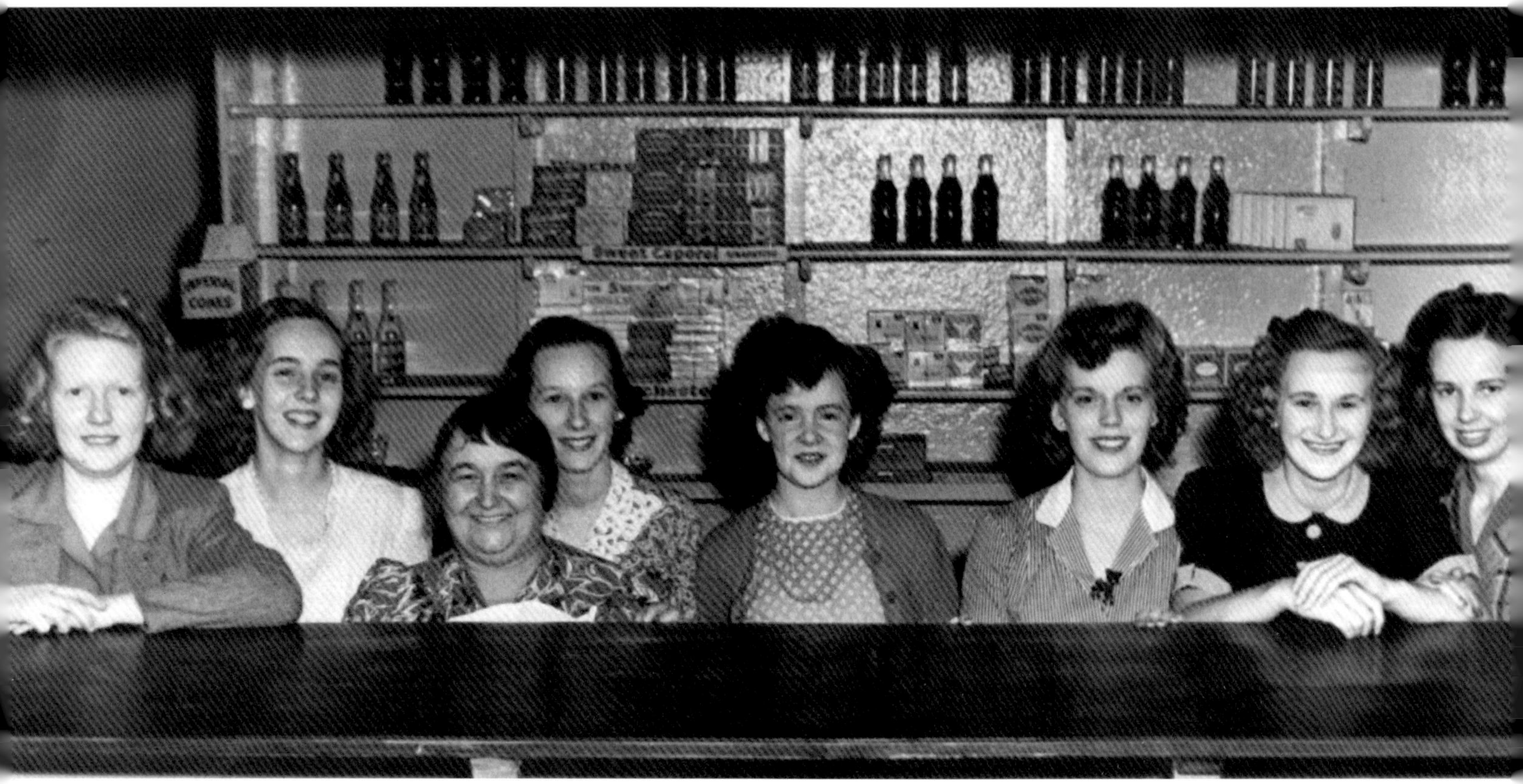

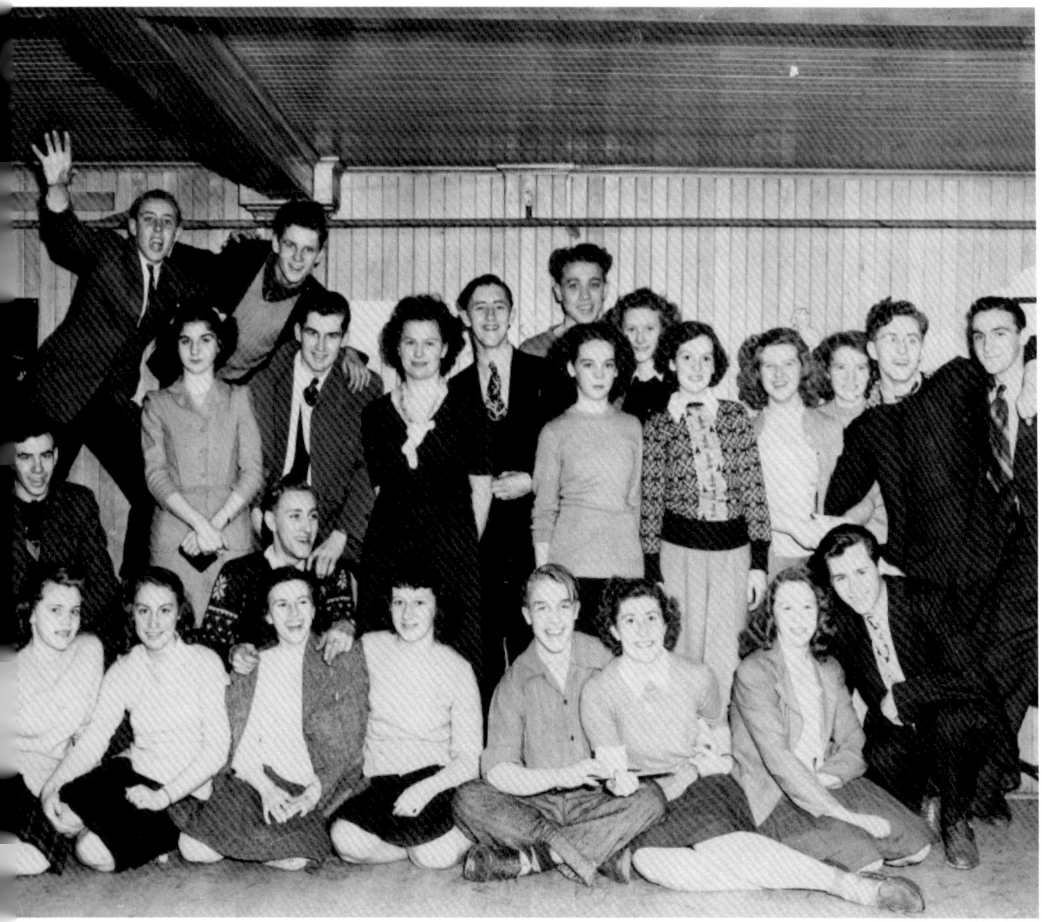

ABOVE: *While the boys marched, girls were encouraged to volunteer at one of the clubs, canteens or huts. While many remained uneasy, it is a measure of the effect of the social change wrought by the war that just a few years earlier no parent in their right mind would have allowed their daughters to do such a thing unaccompanied by an adult.*

LEFT: *Teenagers are bound and determined to have a good time in peace or war. This sparky group of Queen Elizabeth students who loved to dance got together, rented a hall on Isleville Street, and set up their own dance hall, Caper's Junction, as in capering about. In those innocent days no one seemed to think that this enterprise was out of line. Joyce Purchase, whose photo this is, recalls that everyone came from somewhere else and when the war was over they all scattered to the four winds. She never saw any of them again.*

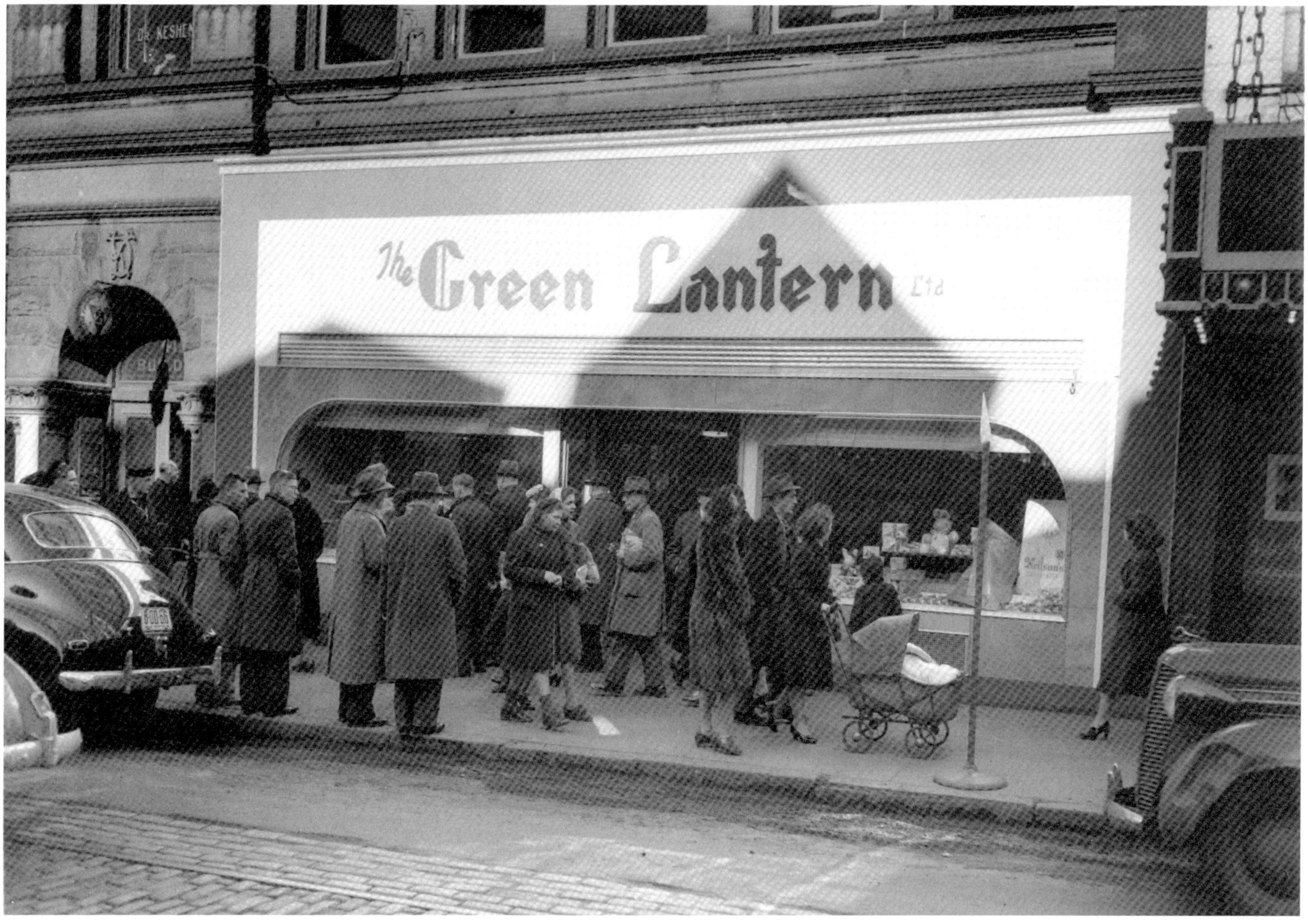
The Green Lantern Ltd

ABOVE: *Beside the Orpheus Theatre, one of the main movie houses in the city, the Green Lantern Restaurant, and indeed other restaurants such as Norman's at Hollis and Morris, never lacked for custom during the war, even though as rationing began to bite, it had few menu choices from time to time. Eating out and going to movies were among the few amusements widely available and there were often line-ups to do both. A leisurely restaurant meal became a fond memory when there were people standing at your shoulder waiting for you to finish. There was no such thing as an empty seat; if a place was empty, someone would take it. Small talk with complete strangers was a necessary skill.*

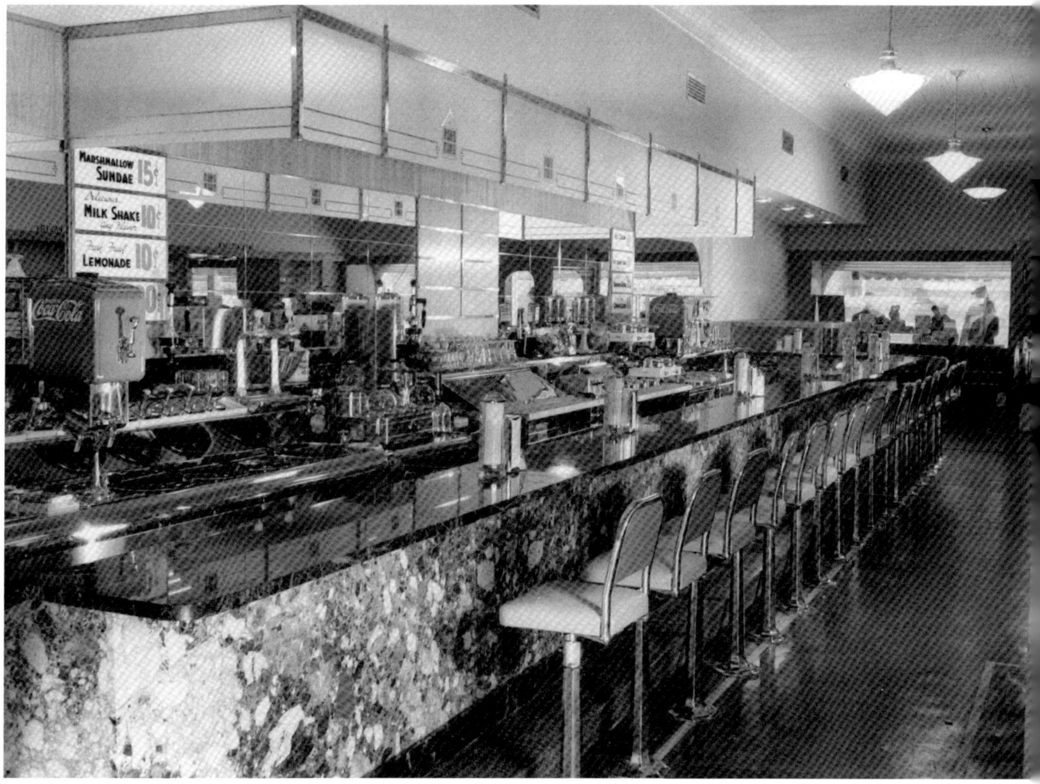
MARSHMALLOW SUNDAE 15¢
MILK SHAKE 10¢
LEMONADE 10¢
Coca-Cola

RIGHT: *Green Lantern Restaurant's soda fountain.*

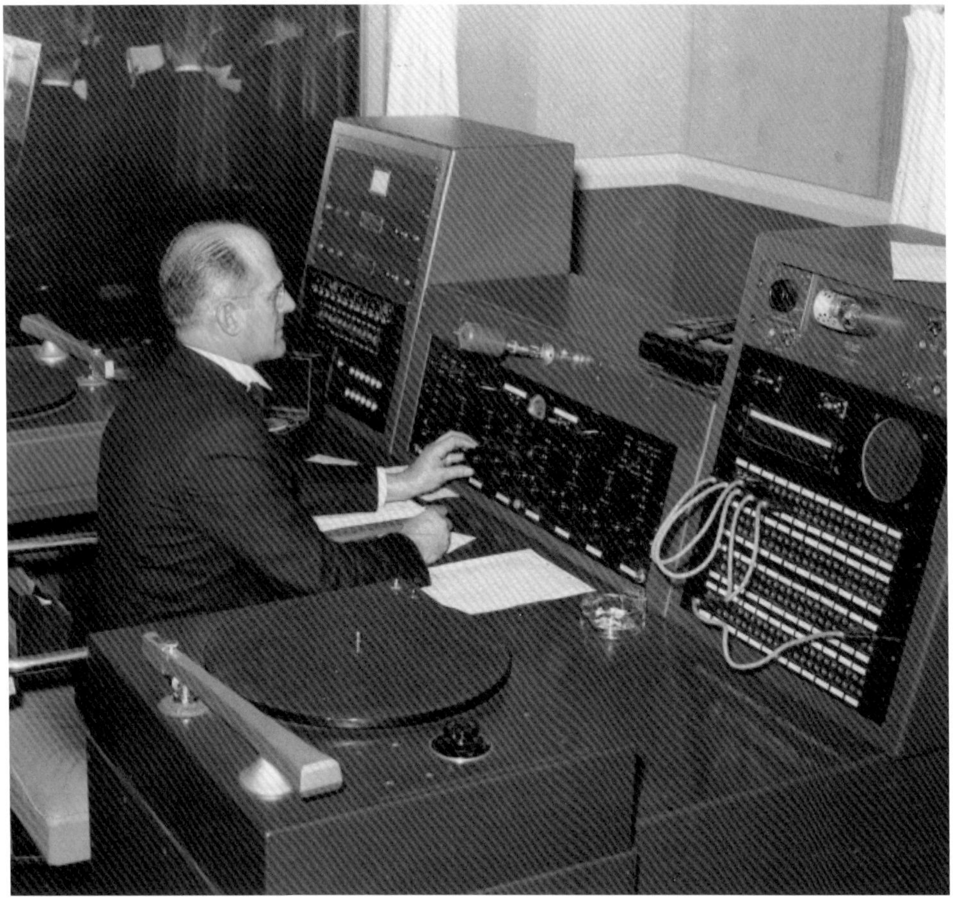

TOP: *Radio, still a new and exciting technology, came into its own during the war. From a government point of view, it was an ideal mechanism for getting information across (propaganda if you will), sometimes by earnest lectures, at other times through thrilling wartime serials such as "L For Lanky," an ongoing story of the crew of a Lancashire bomber in Europe. On the eve of the war, CHNS opened its new studio in a converted church on Morris Street.*

BOTTOM: *The Canadian Broadcasting Corporation, modeled on the BBC, ran a national network. Where it did not have its own radio stations, the CBC had agreements with local private stations to carry programmes. CHNS, like other private radio stations, carried popular American comedy and music programmes; but in-house productions were also important. Seen here in the CHNS studio, in progress, is the Farmer's* Dairy Quiz Kids *broadcast.*

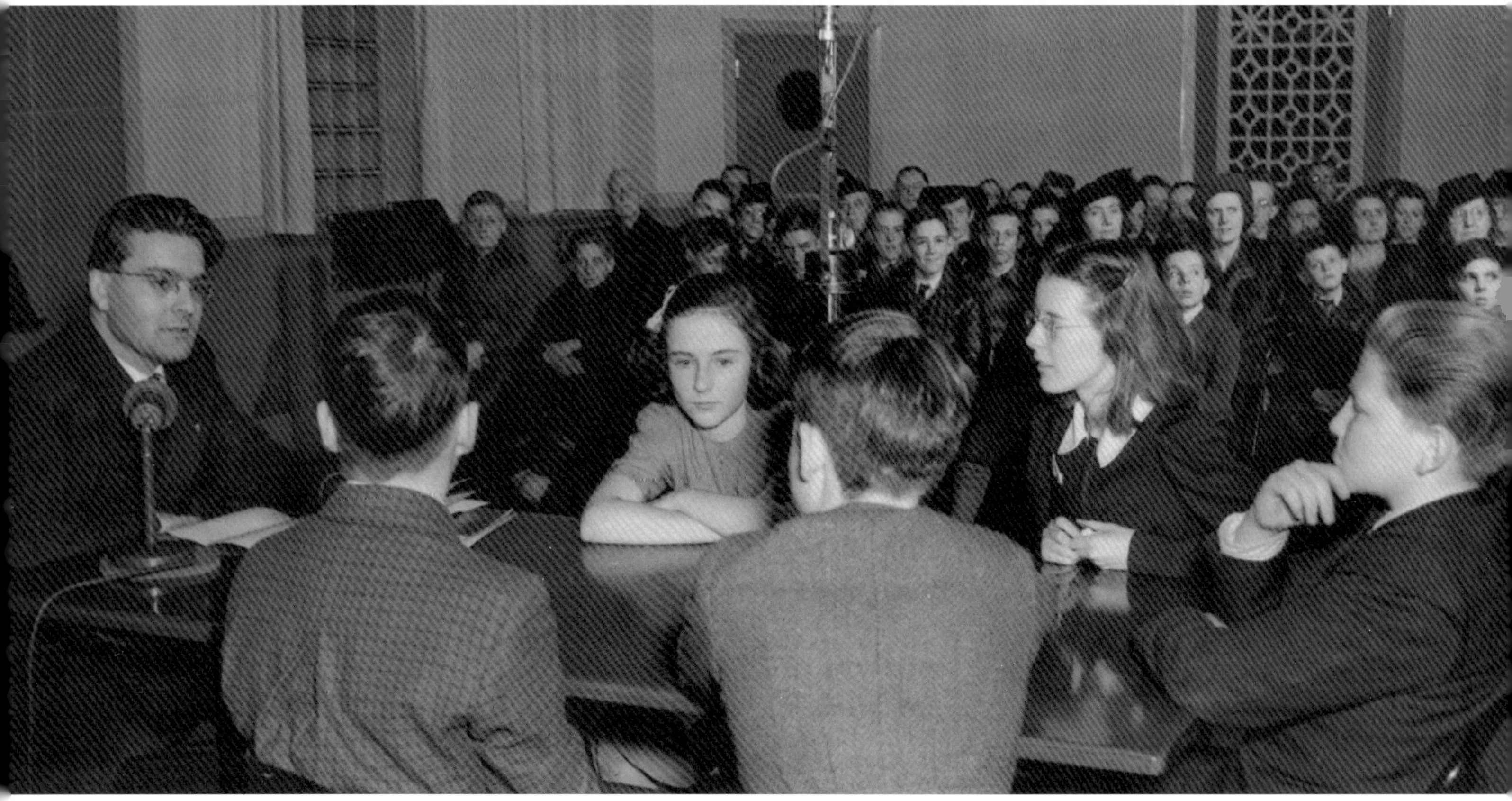

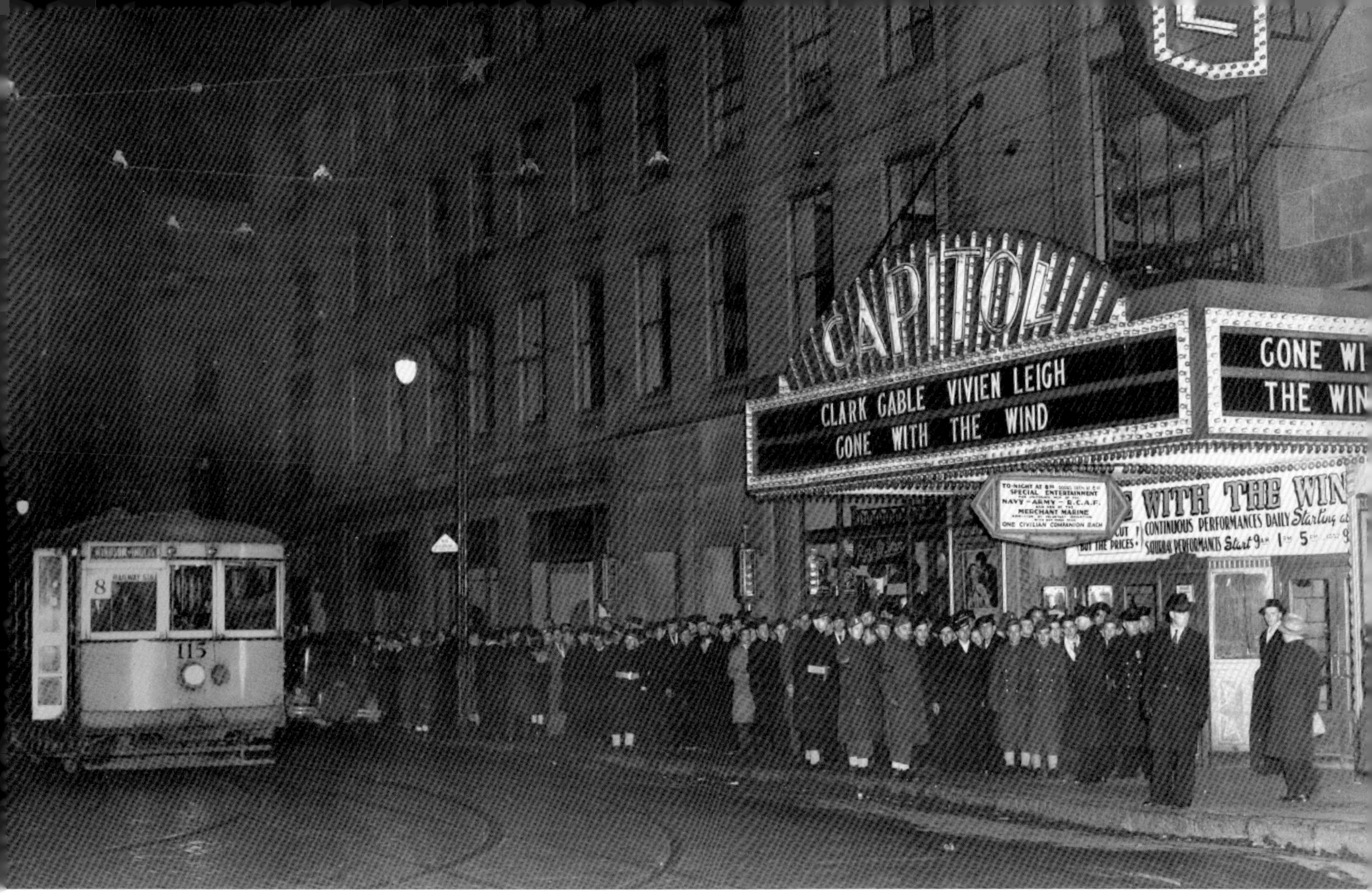
CAPITOL
CLARK GABLE VIVIEN LEIGH
GONE WITH THE WIND
CONTINUOUS PERFORMANCES DAILY

ABOVE: *This line-up at the Capitol Theatre was the norm. All of Halifax's theatres were busy. Although they complained bitterly about the wartime entertainment tax imposed on their tickets, they never wanted for business, given that there was not much else to do. Patrons went to the theatre at any time, not just when the feature began, irrespective of what film was on or whether they thought they might like it. The Capitol, a movie palace the equal to any elsewhere, was a first-run house, showing all the new releases first.*

RIGHT: *Another movie line-up at the Orpheus Theatre, just down the street from the Capitol. The Orpheus was also a first-run house.*

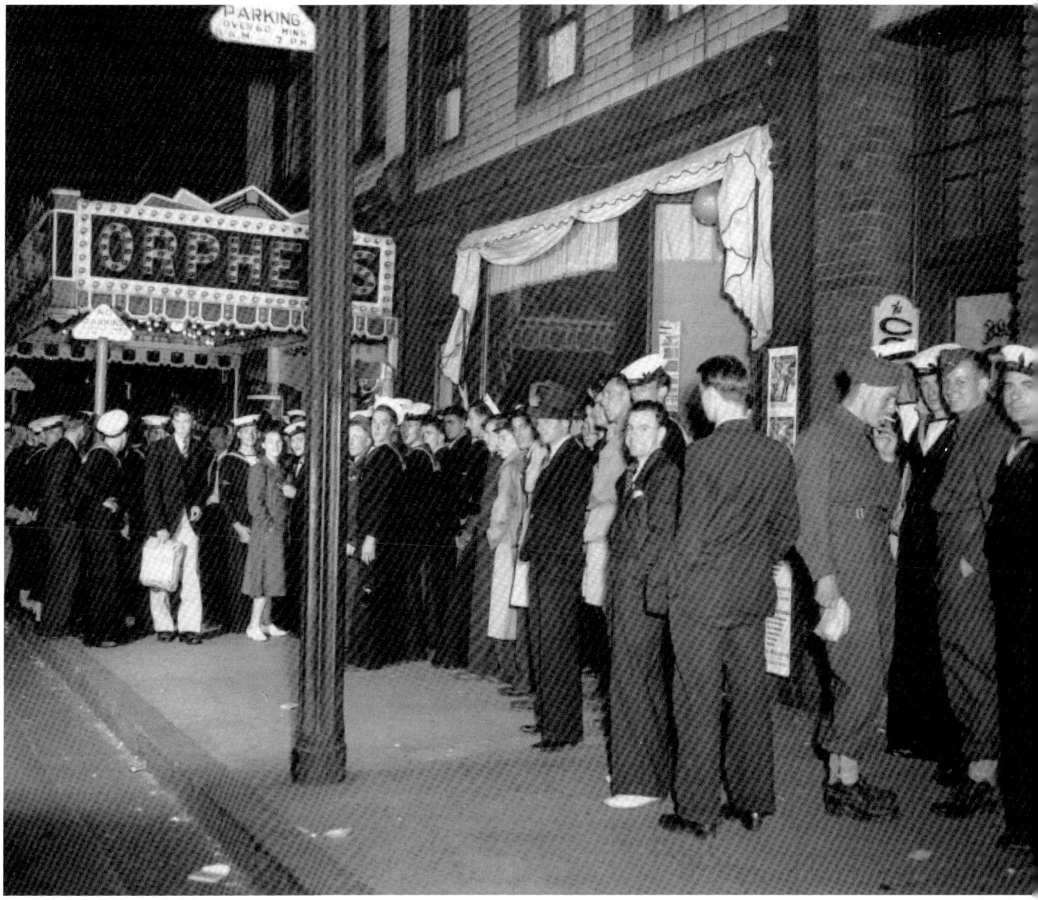
PARKING

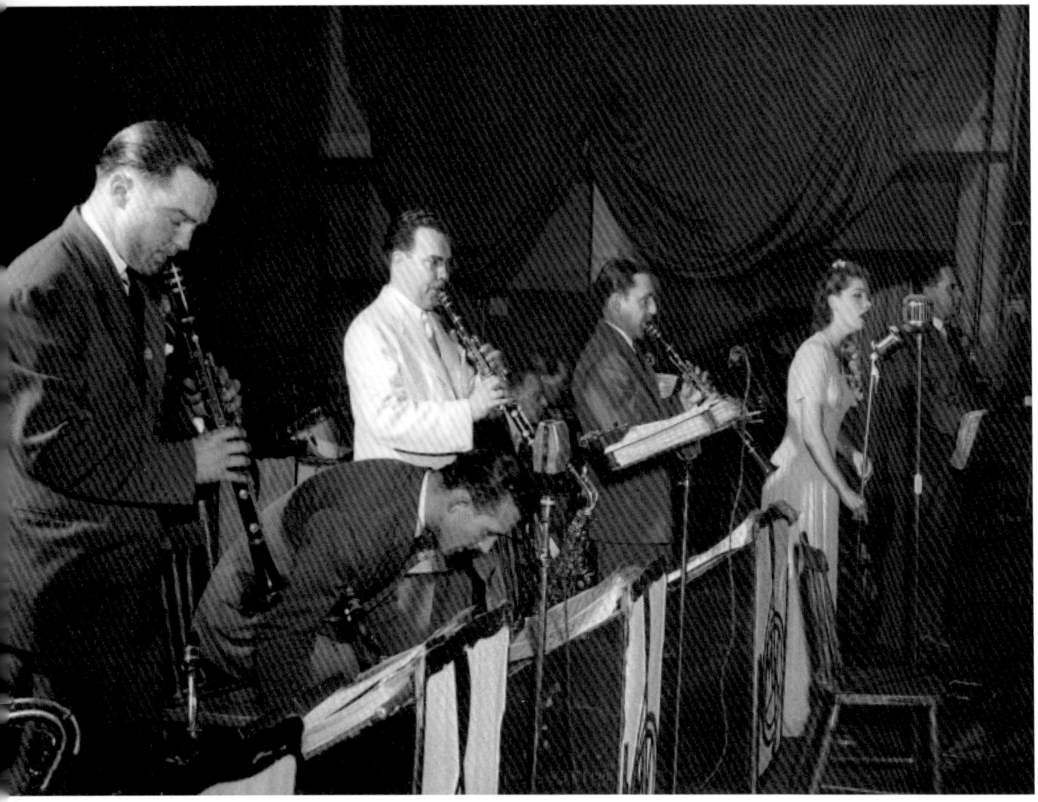

ABOVE: *It was the "Big Band" era and in a city hungry for entertainment, bands were a huge draw. Canadian Mart Kenney is seen here performing at the Dalhousie University gym, a favourite venue along with the Halifax Forum. Hundreds went to hear the music and to dance.*

RIGHT: *Most of all, however, people loved to dance. Private dance halls sprang up where none had existed before. Social organizations could be sure of a crowd if they sponsored one. Live music was preferred, of course, and amateur bands of varying quality emerged, thrived and died according to what ship or regiment was in town and for how long. Service personnel and transients comprised the bulk of the musicians. They were also the bulk of the dancing partners, a boon for the Halifax girls who also loved to dance.*

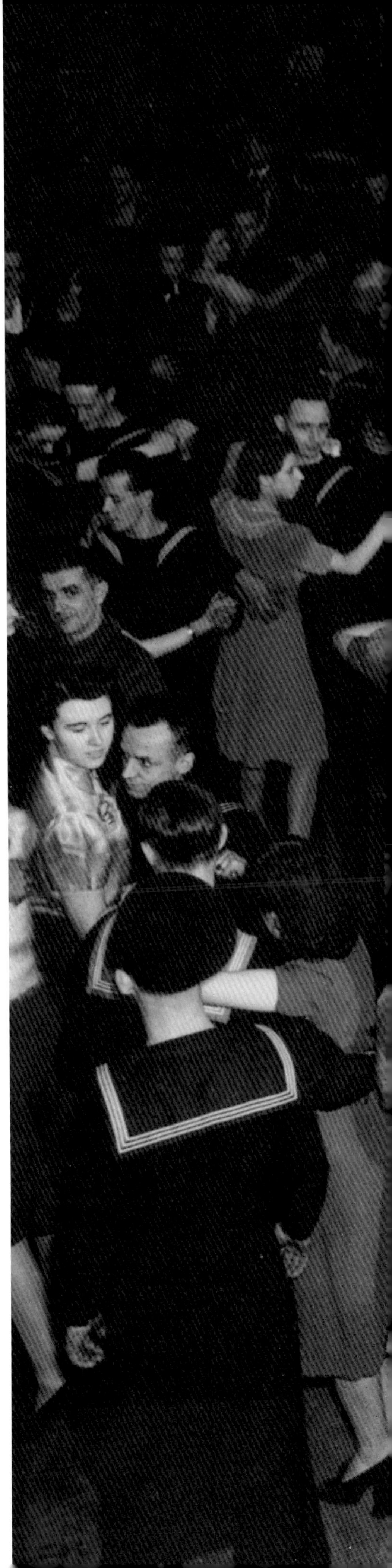

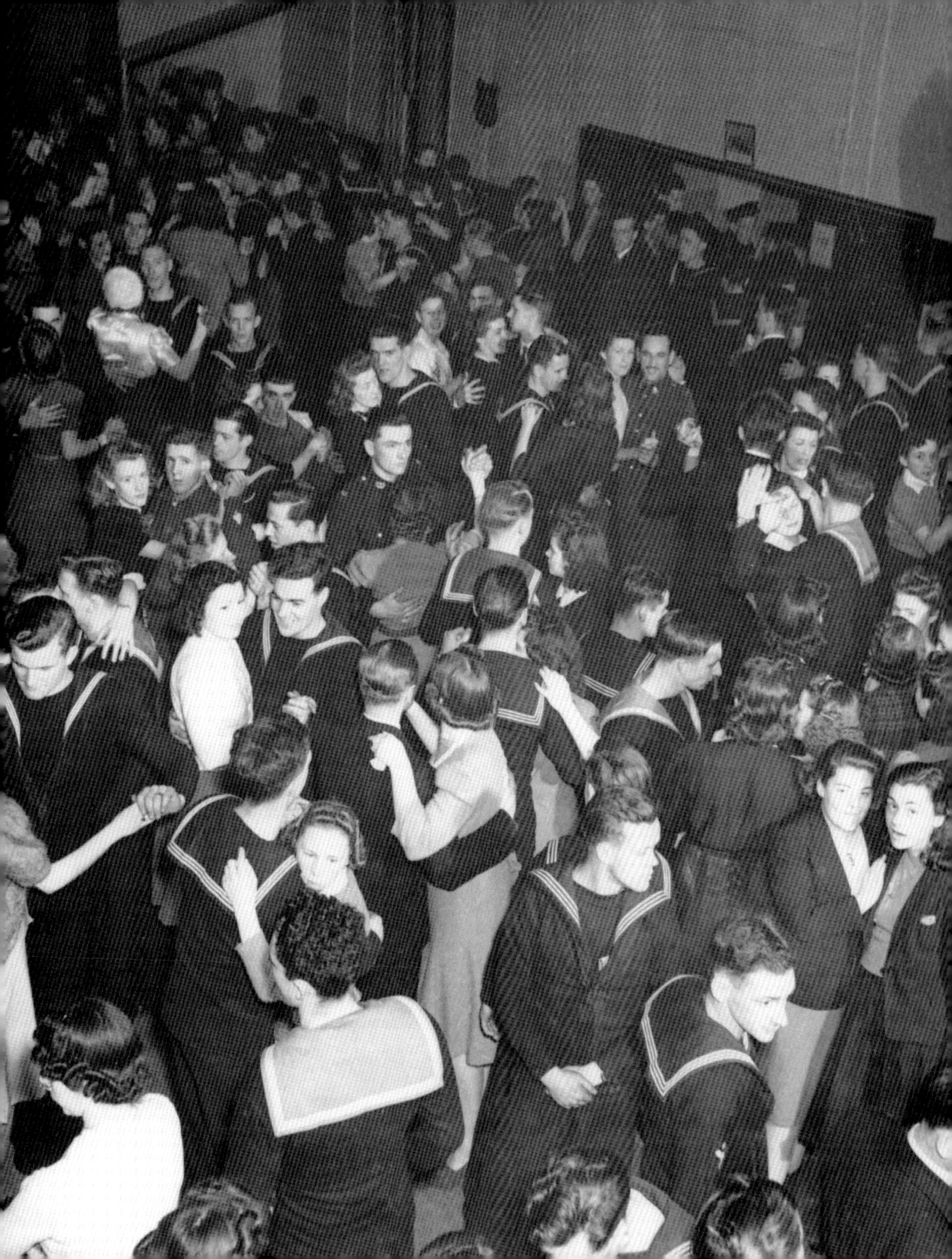

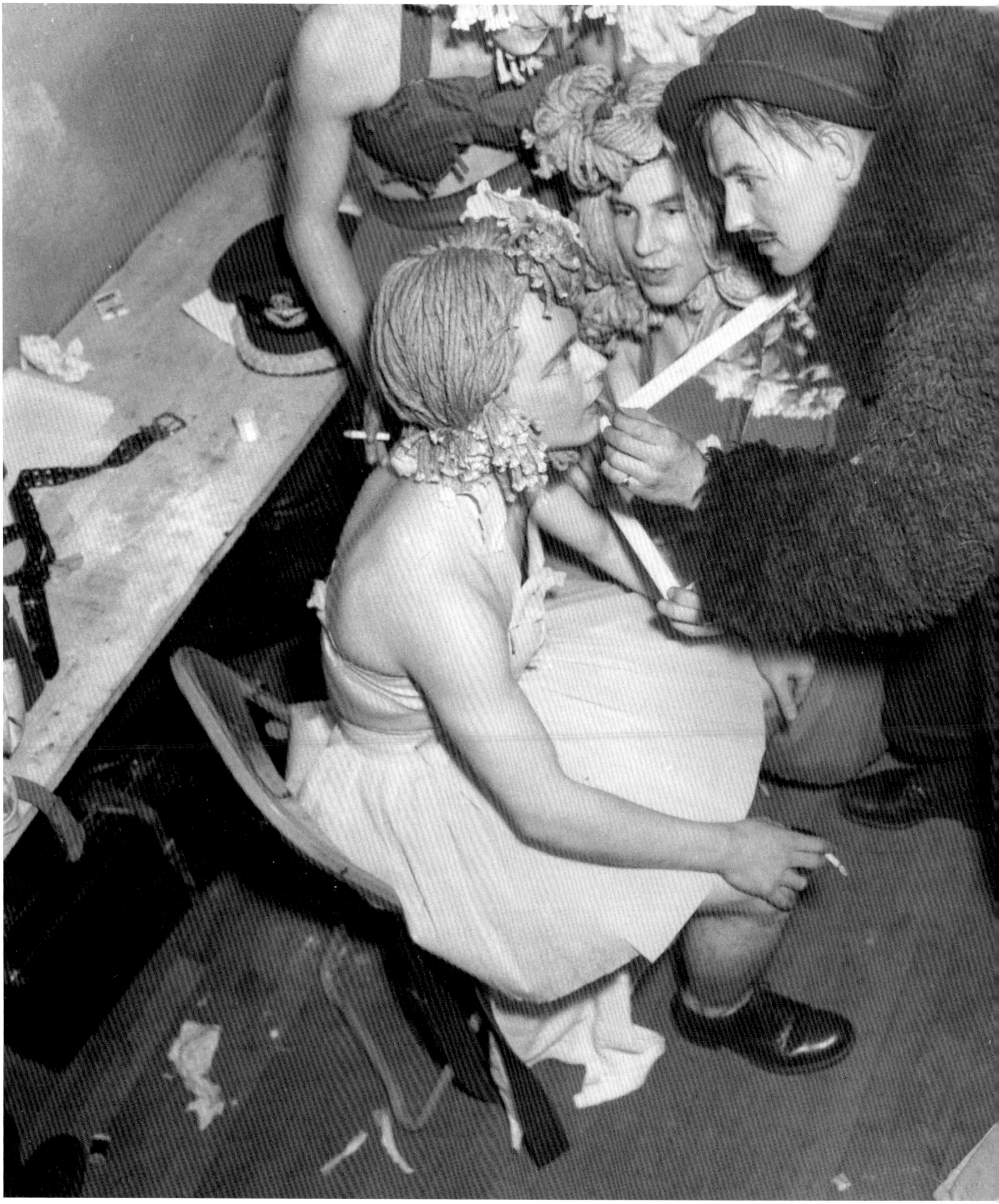

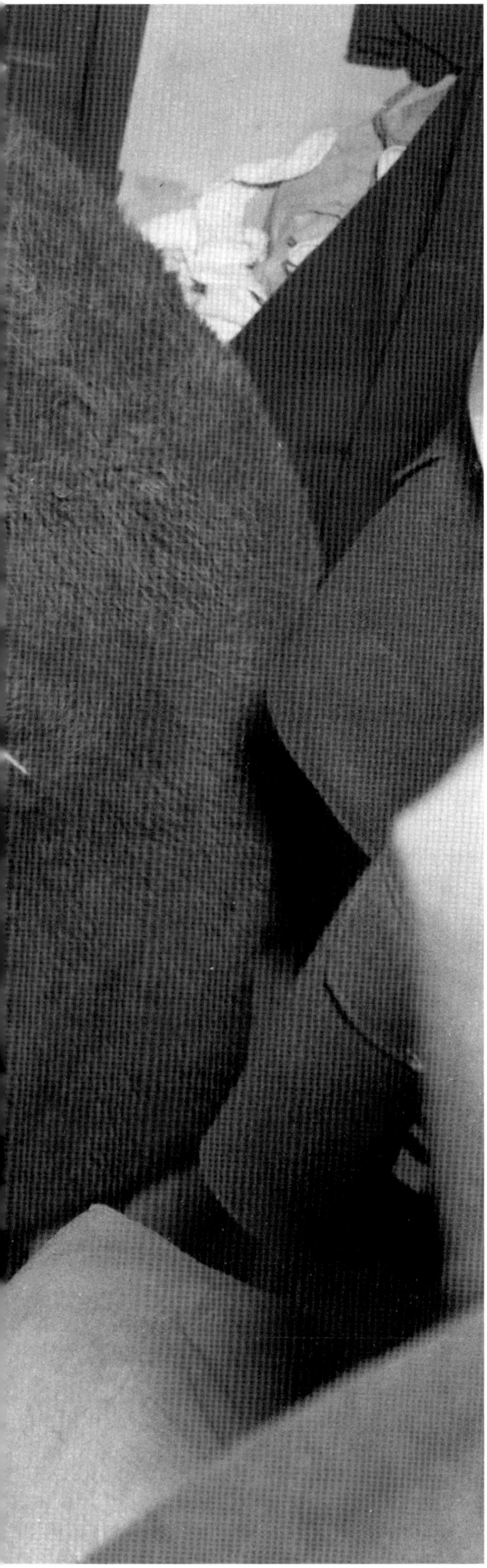

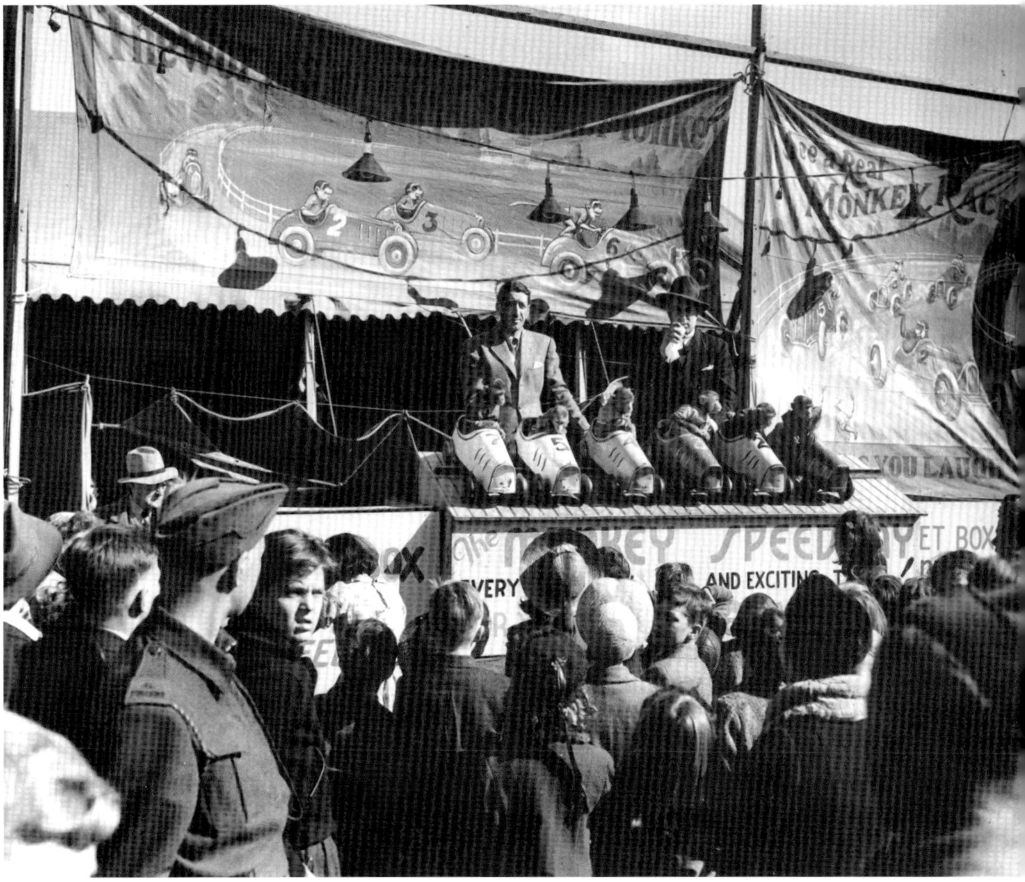

LEFT: *R.C.A.F. personnel seen here putting on the play "Straw Bags," which featured, to the amusement of all and the scandal of none, men in women's roles. Amateur performances such as these were common and great morale boosters for both performers and audiences.*

ABOVE: *In the summer of 1941, there was the always popular standby from peacetime, the Bill Lynch Shows, with its side shows and midway. Their arrival on the Commons was, tradition had it, a sure forecast of rainy weather. Some things never change.*

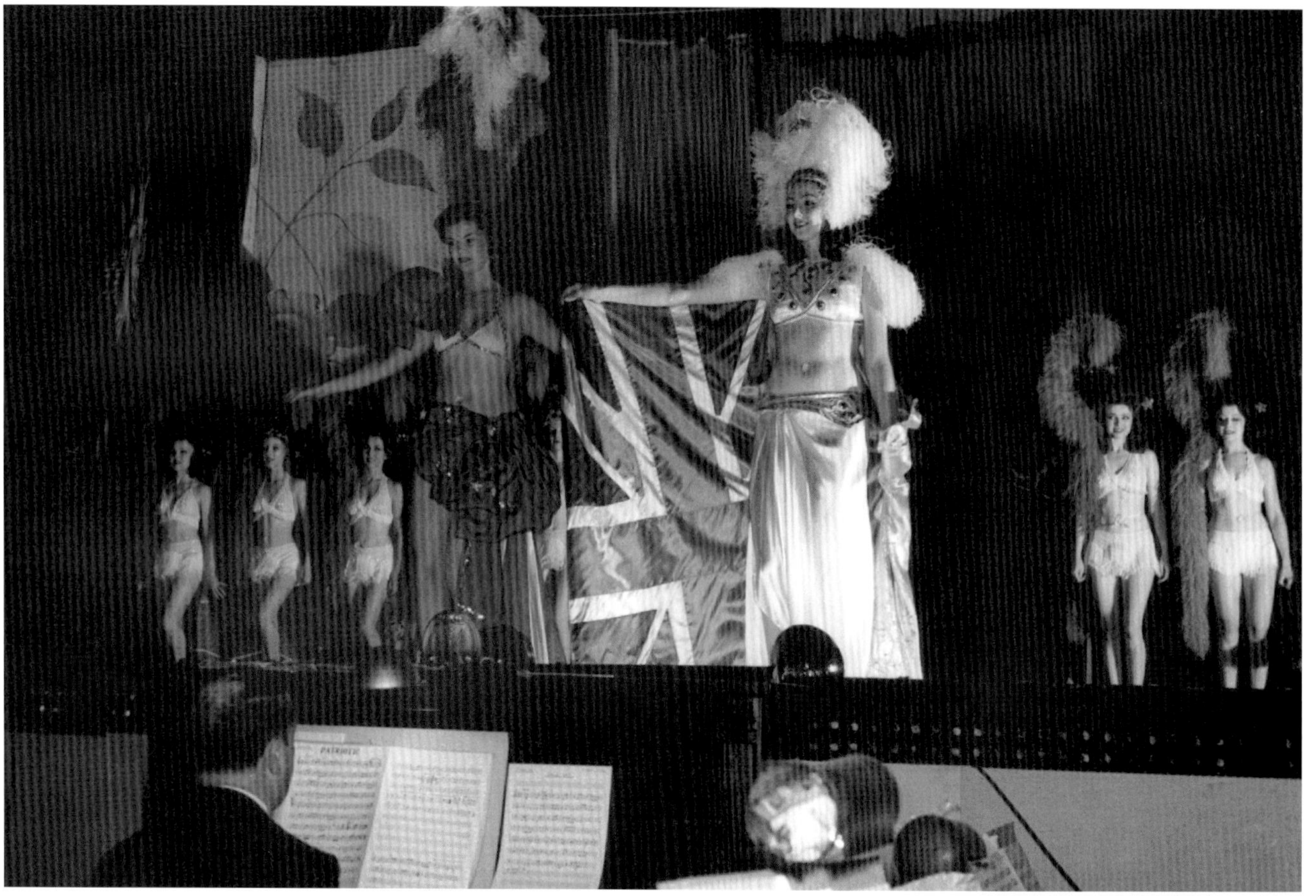

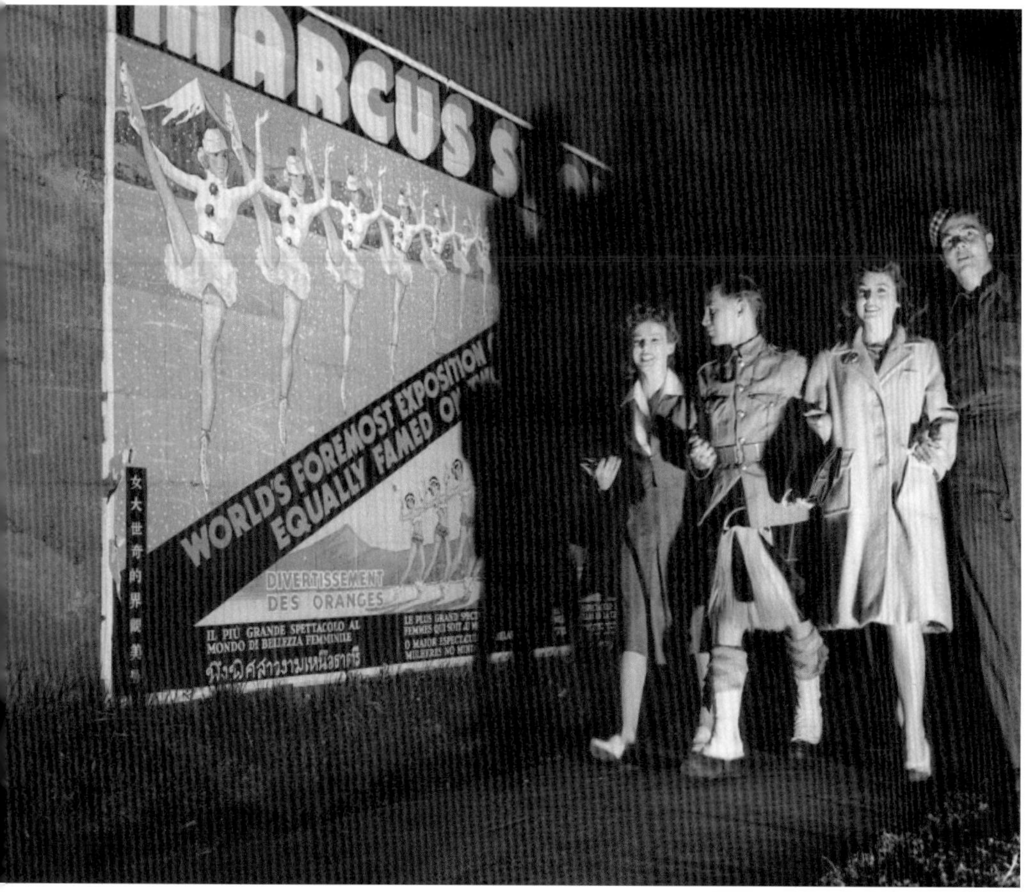
MARCUS S
WORLD'S FOREMOST EXPOSITION
EQUALLY FAMED
DIVERTISSEMENT
DES ORANGES
IL PIU GRANDE SPETTACOLO AL
MONDO DI BELLEZZA FEMMINILE

ABOVE: *Another entertainment import was the* Marcus Shows, *heavy on pretty girls in scanty costumes, lots of dancing, and good comedians.*

LEFT: *Fortunate indeed was the soldier who persuaded one of the* Marcus Show *girls to go on a date.*

RIGHT: *Everybody loves a parade and they certainly were a frequent feature of life on the Home Front. Parades were a particular aspect of the Canadian government's determination to pay for the war without resorting to international borrowing. This goal meant persuading Canadians to lend money to the government in addition to accepting heavy taxation. In this effort the government was especially successful. Canada's contribution to World War II was entirely financed within the country. Eight successful Victory Loan campaigns were a part of this effort. Parades, such as this one on Barrington Street, were an important means of involving the public in the campaigns and promoting the purchase of bonds.*

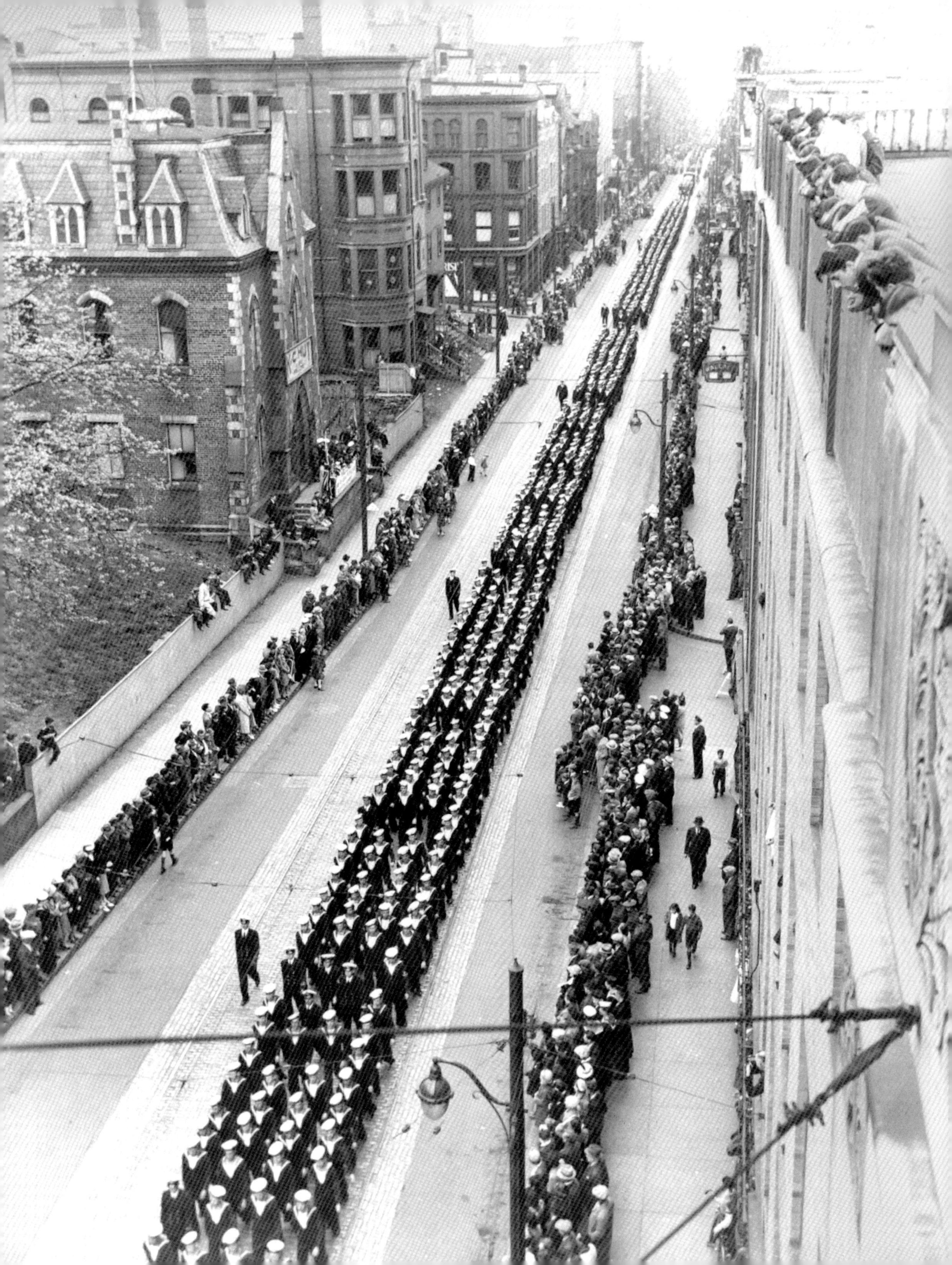

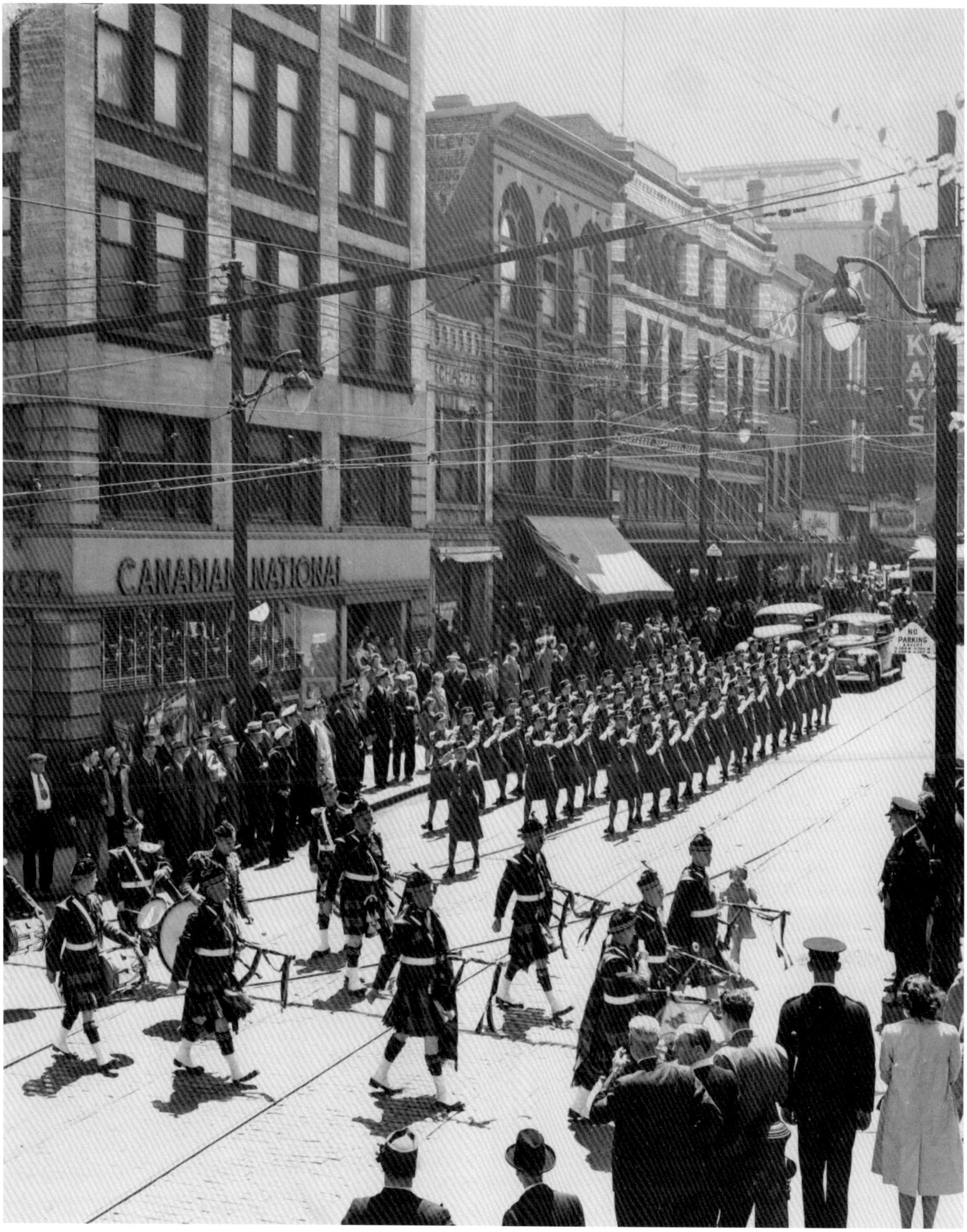
CANADIAN NATIONAL
KAYS
NO PARKING

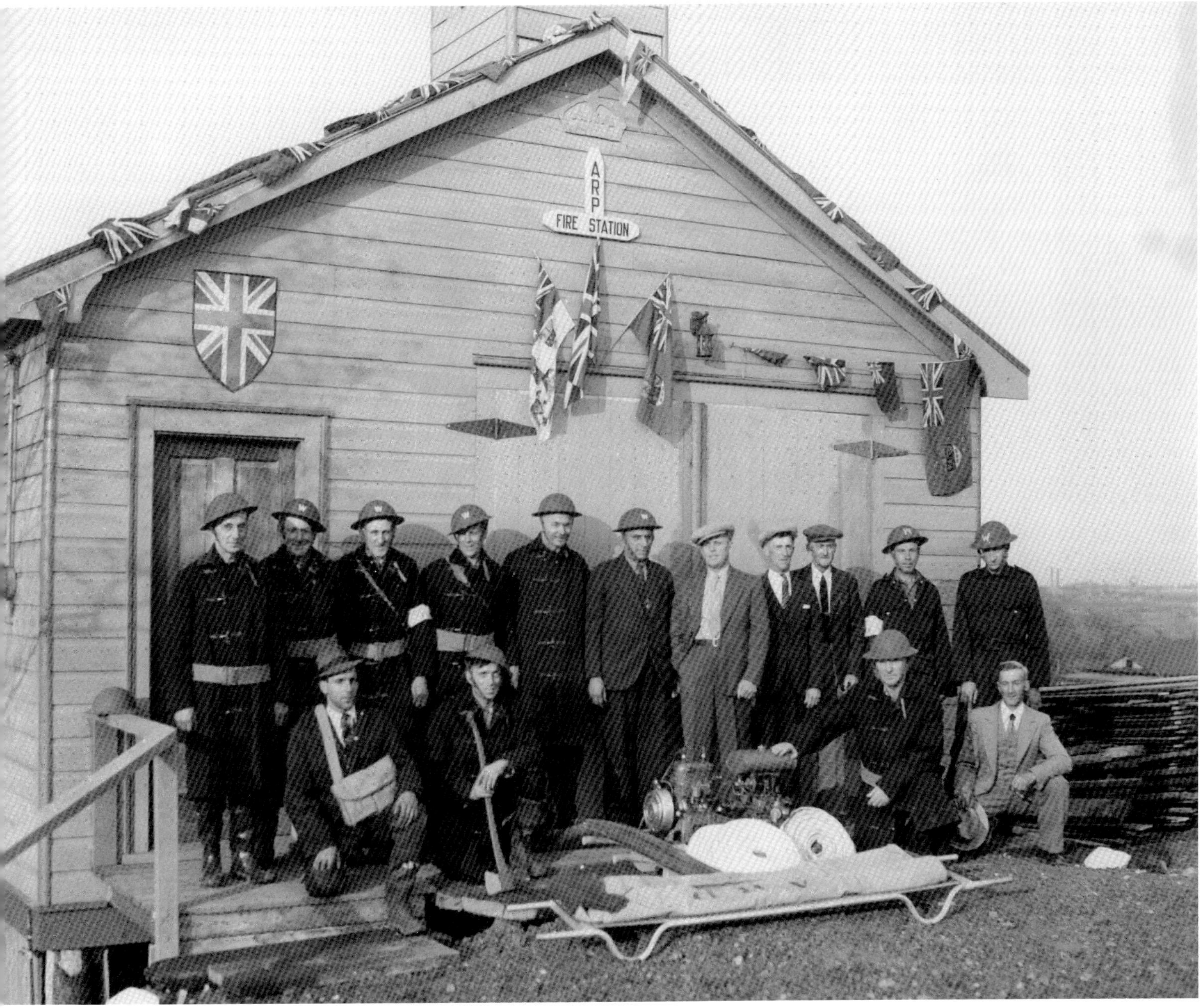
A
R
P
FIRE STATION

LEFT: *Parades also served the secondary purpose of regularizing the radical concept of women in the military, as in this photograph of the R.C.A.F. Women's Division, seen wheeling into the Grand Parade at Barrington and George Streets.*

ABOVE: *For the more sedate members of the Home Front, it has been mentioned earlier that Civil Defence, with its focus on neighbourhood organization, was as important for its social function as its actual purpose of combating the effects of an air raid. These Fire Wardens, the Fairview A.R.P. Firefighters and their Hall, dressed to the nines on a sunny day in November 1944, demonstrate a real pride in the contribution they are making to the war effort.*

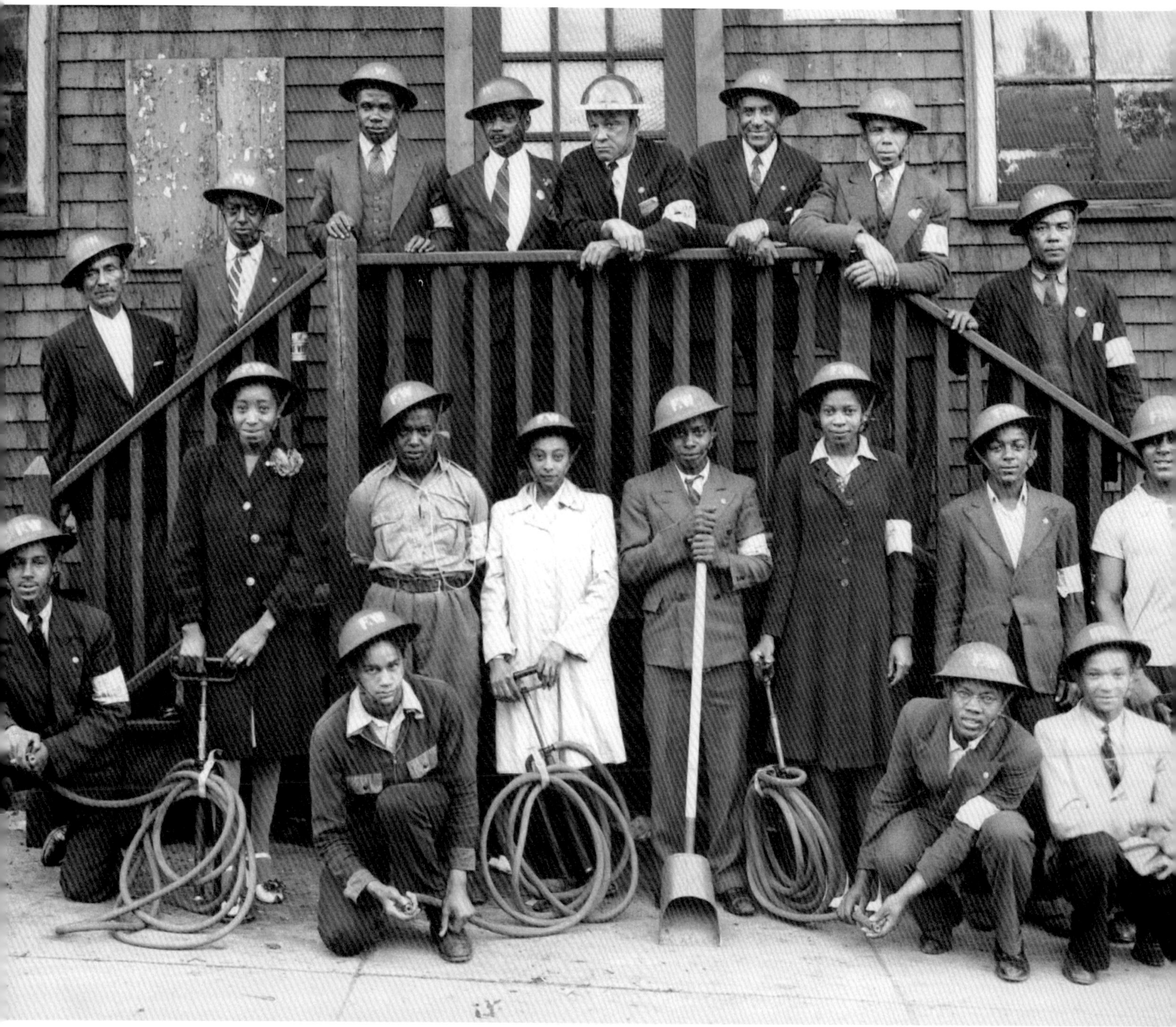

ABOVE: *Black citizens also played important roles in their communities, as is demonstrated by No. 7 Platoon A.R.P., sec. E2, Fire Watchers and Wardens, located in the blocks between Gerrish and Cunard Streets.*

LEFT: *Who, after all, could resist the appeal of these Dartmouth-based "Miss Canada Girls," Elinor Teasdale and her friends Joyce and Ruth, dressed in neat uniforms and selling War Savings Stamps, while the boys were off drilling in cadets.*

BOTTOM: *When the Japanese overran the rubber plantations of Malaya and the Dutch East Indies, overnight rubber became so scarce that it disappeared from formerly essential items such as elastic bands in underwear. No old tire, not even the inner tube retired to the beach, was safe. These youths at Dartmouth High School are bringing their spoils to a collection point.*

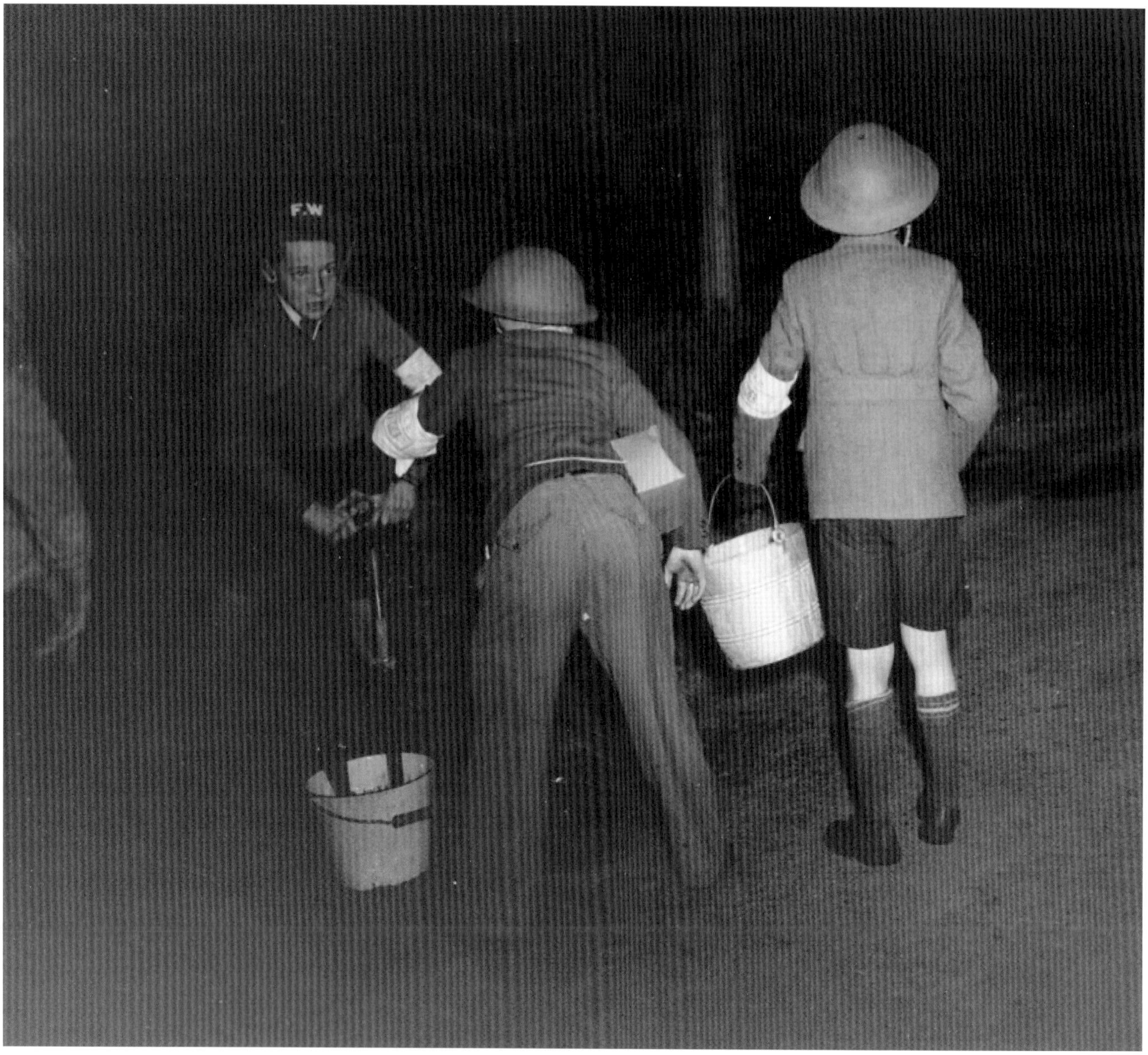
F.W

ABOVE: *Those not even old enough to be Messengers could be Junior Fire Watchers, probably long after their bedtime.*

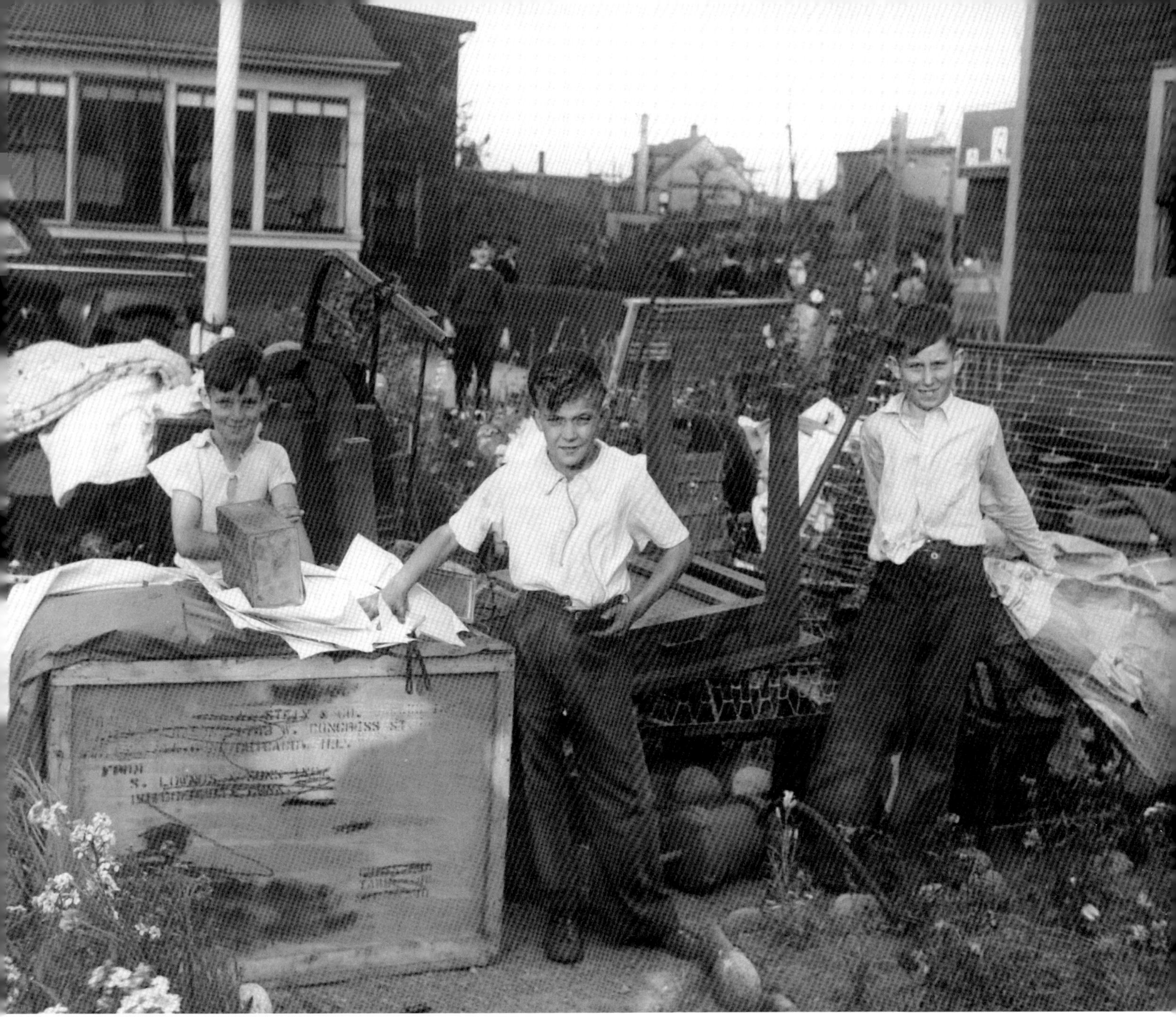

ABOVE: *Money was not the only thing collected. Serious shortages of raw materials at the same time as demand from the war industries building planes, tanks, ships and ordnance increased, made it vital to scour the nation's attics and scrap yards. Children, either individually or collectively through school campaigns, were energetic and relentless in ferreting out unused pots and pans, collecting tin foil from gum and cigarette packages, and saving huge lumpy balls of string and mason jars of bacon fat and soap ends.*

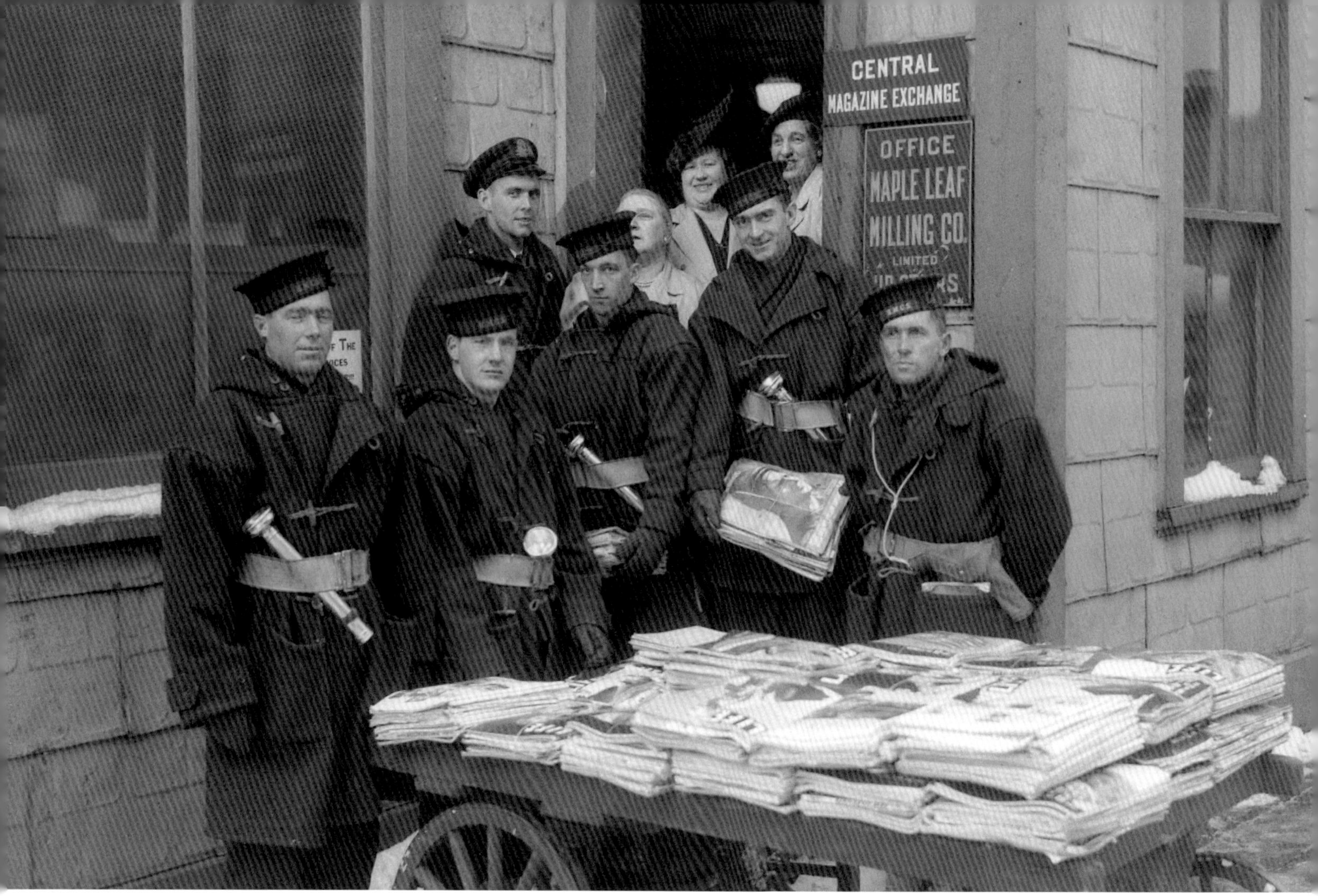
CENTRAL
MAGAZINE EXCHANGE
OFFICE
MAPLE LEAF
MILLING CO.
LIMITED

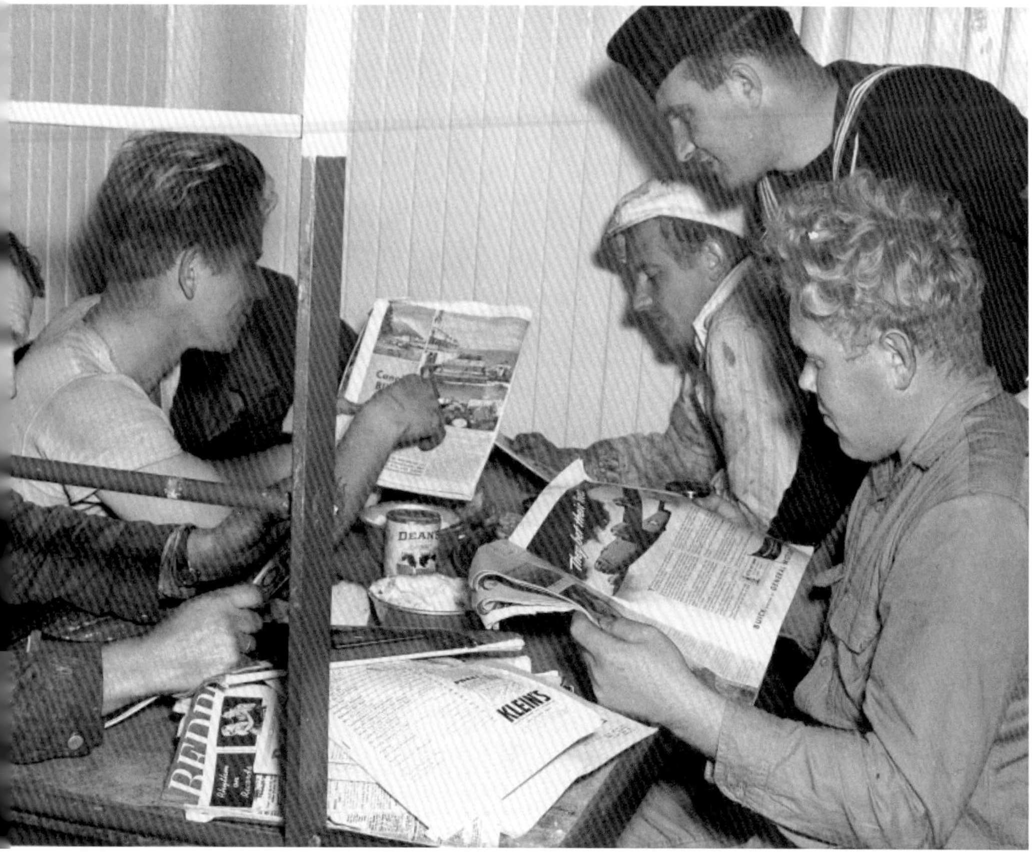
KLEINS

ABOVE: *A group of Halifax women organized the Magazine Exchange, which took on continental proportions. Collected by service clubs from all over North America, used books and magazines were shipped free to Halifax by the Canadian National Railways, sorted in bundles, and sent out to isolated garrisons and to merchant and naval ships.*

LEFT: *The Magazine Exchange was immensely appreciated by the recipients and helped ease the boredom and tension of long idle hours on duty and off watch in cramped fo'c'sles or barracks.*

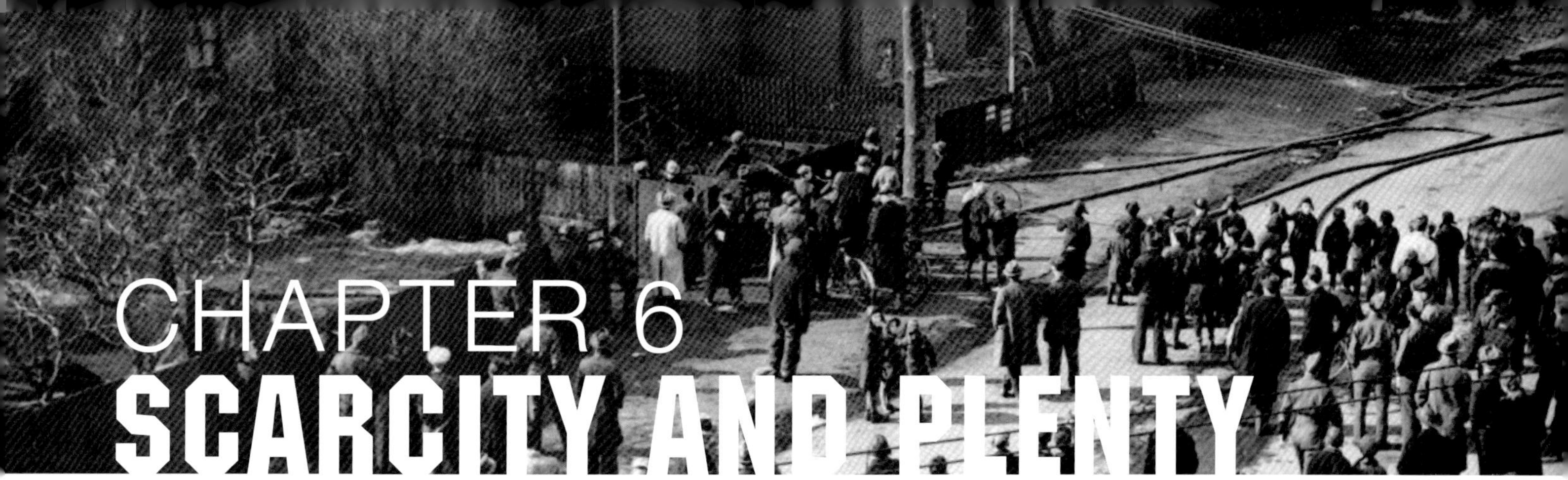

CHAPTER 6
SCARCITY AND PLENTY

Halifax and Dartmouth in 1939 contained about 67,800 and 10,000 souls respectively. Official figures for 1944 show an increase to about 107,000 and 17,200, and anecdotal accounts add more. Whatever the figures, housing was a serious problem and authorities were slow to respond. The need was desperate and as a result official efforts to control abuses were honoured more in the breach than the observance, so that in some areas housing stock, never good to begin with, deteriorated. Once-tidy neighbourhoods started to fray around the edges. The Navy in particular was reluctant to build barracks to house shore-based or shore-leave personnel, fearing it would be surplus after the war, and so gave thousands a small allowance and sent them to fend for themselves in the free market. The Army and the Air Force in particular handled their responsibilities better; but it was no help that many civilian and service personnel brought family to live against all warnings that there was no room for them.

In one limited area of housing for shipyard workers, appropriate steps were taken as part of a national programme to house war workers. Beginning in 1941, the Canadian government set up Wartime Housing Limited, which produced four standard designs for prefabricated houses and 1,546 were built in the city. Never intended to be permanent, nevertheless they were well-built, their neighbourhoods well-designed, and the need continued after the war. Eventually sold to veterans and occupants, most of them survive today, perhaps the most enduring homefront memorial to World War II.

The population explosion meant that there were crowds everywhere — hotels were crowded, trams were crowded, sidewalks were crowded, restaurants were crowded, and taxis were scarce as hen's teeth.

The restrictions that the citizenry had to live with were those that arose from the gradual disappearance of consumer goods as the economy shifted to a war footing. Slow at first, this shift accelerated in 1942 as German successes in the Battle of the Atlantic and Japanese successes in southeast Asia reached a peak. In the former case, every cargo that a U-boat torpedo sent to the bottom had to be replaced by the Canadian economy, whether it was food for Britain or war matériel for the invasion of Europe. In the latter case, the loss of the rubber and spice plantations and oil fields were just a few of the commodities produced in Malaya and the Dutch East Indies which seriously affected sources of supply.

In spite of promises to the contrary, food rationing began with sugar in July 1942 and rapidly progressed to encompass every food group. Rationing was accomplished by a level of government control and regulation which had no parallel in peacetime. Not only food, but also cars, appliances, clothing, shoes, consumer goods of all types virtually disappeared or fell under tight rationing controls. Private automobiles spent most of the war in their garages or up on blocks as gasoline and rubber were diverted to the military. Housewives scoured grocery stores, often stripped to supply the needs of departing convoys, for anything more than the basics. "Make a friend of your butcher" was good advice followed by every wise housewife.

From time to time, some U-boat captain lurking off the harbour mouth provided a temporary relief available only to the citizens of the "East Coast Port" and their neighbours. Torpedoed tankers or freighters that drifted ashore offered a source of unrationed goods to all those as determined to salvage as the R.C.M.P. was determined that they would not.

The public services of a small coastal community, in need of capital investment to begin with, staggered under the double load of too many people to service but not enough people to maintain and repair, and no spare parts to maintain with. A partial exception was the Dartmouth Ferry Commission's cross-harbour ferry operation. It went to 24-hour-a-day operation and somehow finagled the construction in 1942 of a new ferry, the *Governor Cornwallis*. With four ferries, the operation functioned well until a December 1944 fire destroyed the *Governor Cornwallis*. For the rest of the war it was a struggle to keep up.

The gas and electrical services of Nova Scotia Light & Power coped well and never faltered, but the company's street railway service in Halifax suffered severely. Trackage and equipment were utterly worn out by war's end. Equally overwhelmed was that city's municipally operated water supply system. It was so decrepit that it became impossible to fight a major fire and water a ship at the same time. Under heavy pressure from the Canadian government and fire insurance companies, it was taken over by the provincial Public Utility Commission and farmed out to a private engineering firm for overhaul and operation.

There was no question that by 1945, in spite of constant appeals for patriotism, the citizens of the East Coast Port were getting sick of the war, of shortages, of making-do, of shabbiness, of crowds and line-ups. The resentments were made worse by the autumn of 1944, if not before, by the knowledge that Germany was on the ropes. The war was effectively over, but still the restrictions, regulations, shortages, and crowding went on and on and on. A level of frustration was slowly building beneath the surface that would, when conditions were right, bubble to the surface in a way that would have been inconceivable in pre-war years.

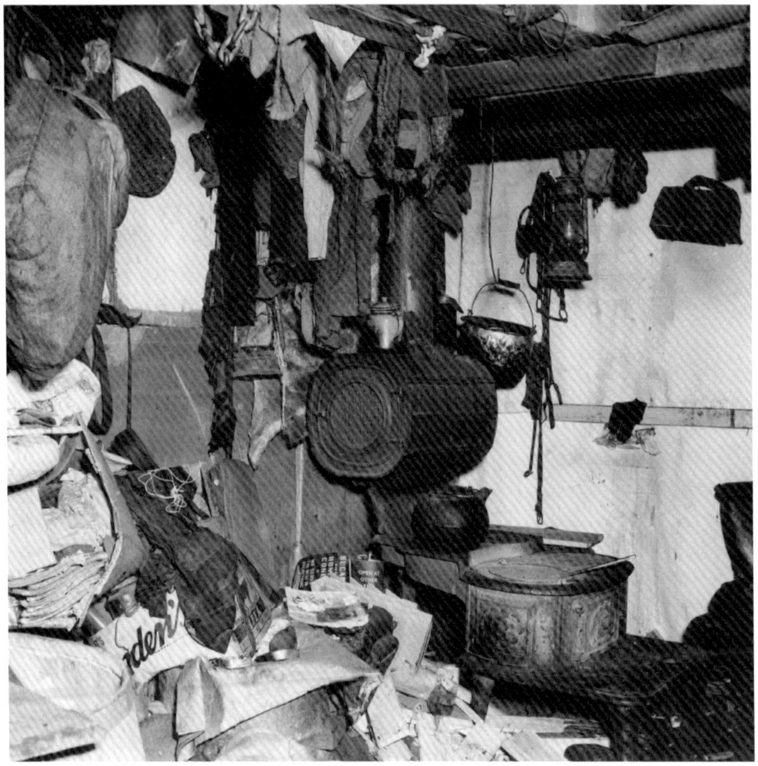

LEFT: *Some housing, such as this place ordered demolished by the Board of Health, was "third world," and shocked transient visitors. Such conditions were remembered long after the war by many who never came east again and defined the city for them for the rest of their lives.*

BELOW: *Greenbank was a southend neighbourhood where fine homes on the heights above the railway cut overlooked the shabbier ones below. The almost overnight population explosion exerted immense pressure on the existing, barely adequate housing stock. With the best will in the world, it would have been almost impossible to meet demand, but wartime scarcity and restrictions made a bad situation worse in certain areas of Halifax.*

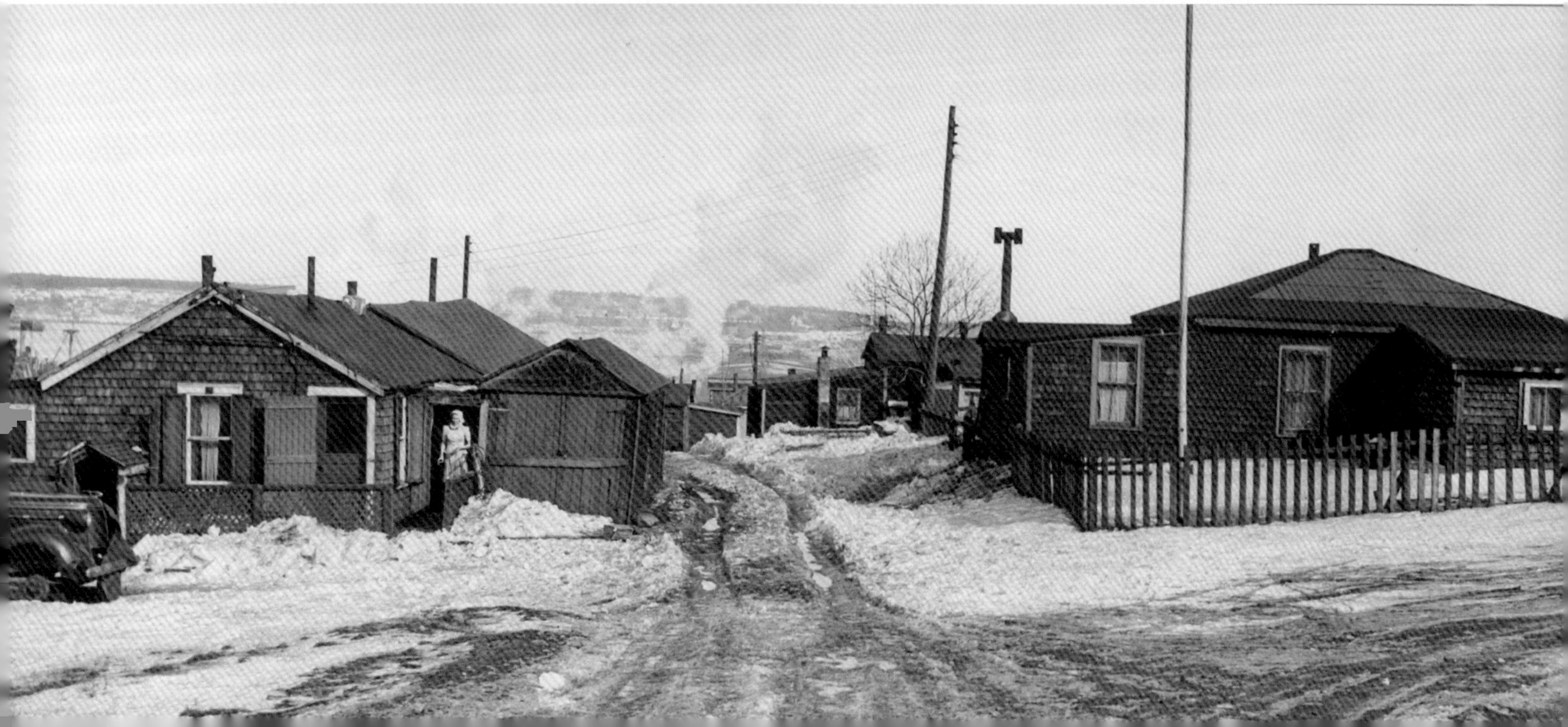

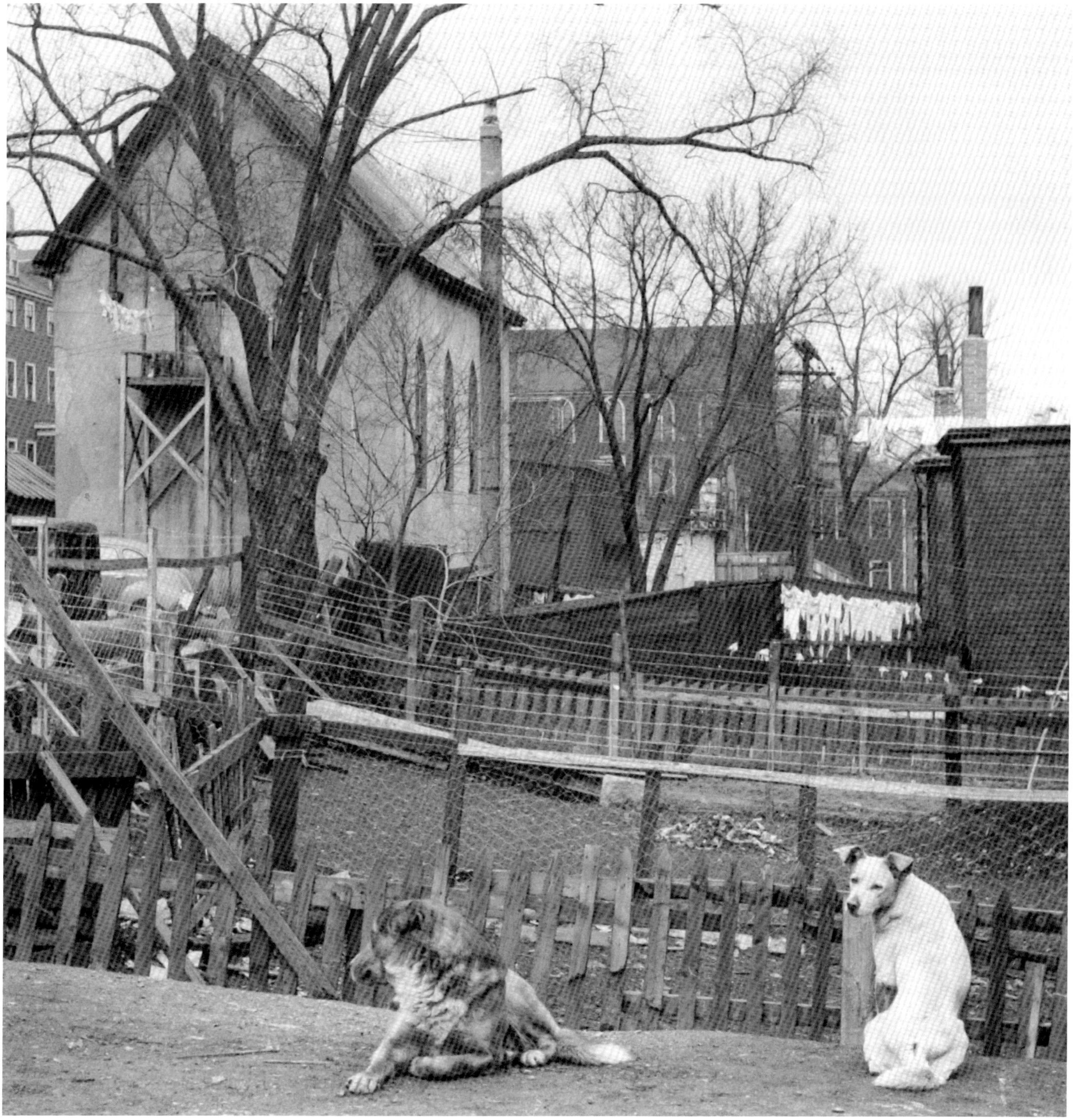

ABOVE: *Some parts of peninsular Halifax were neat and tidy and among the nicest in the country, but others were not, suffering from the pressure of overcrowding and neglect. Here a former church near Cornwallis and Brunswick Streets is used as housing.*

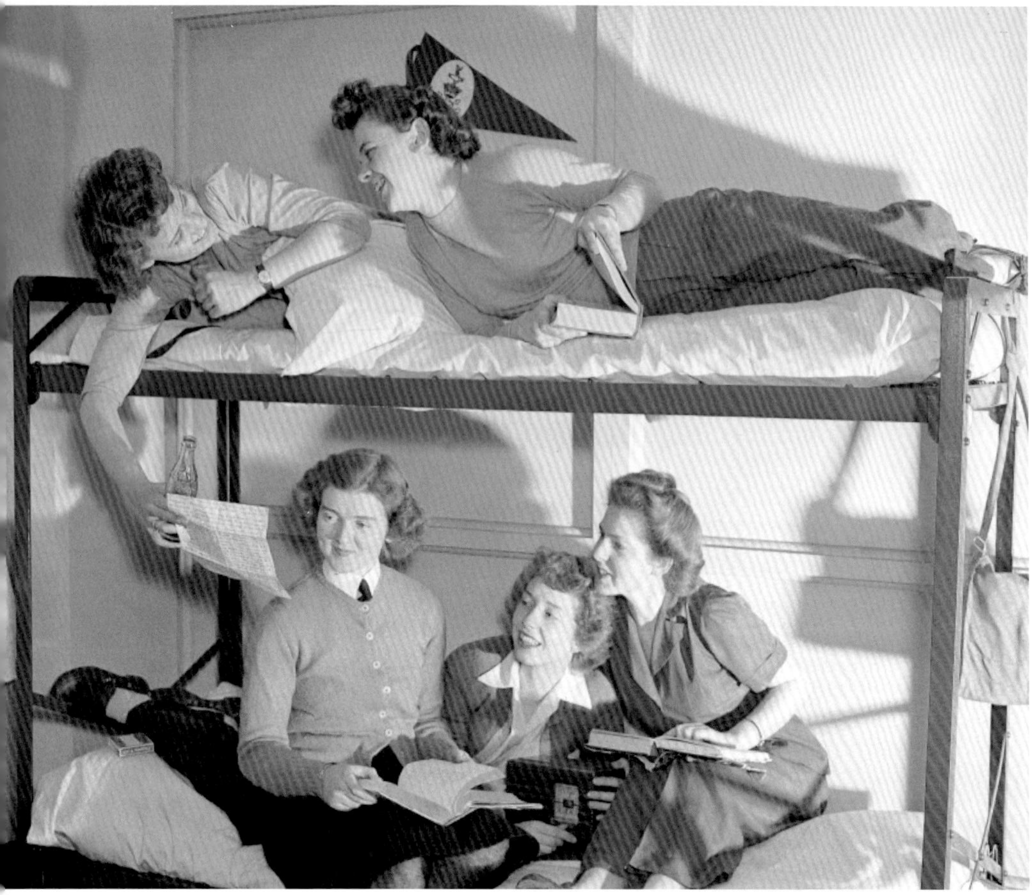

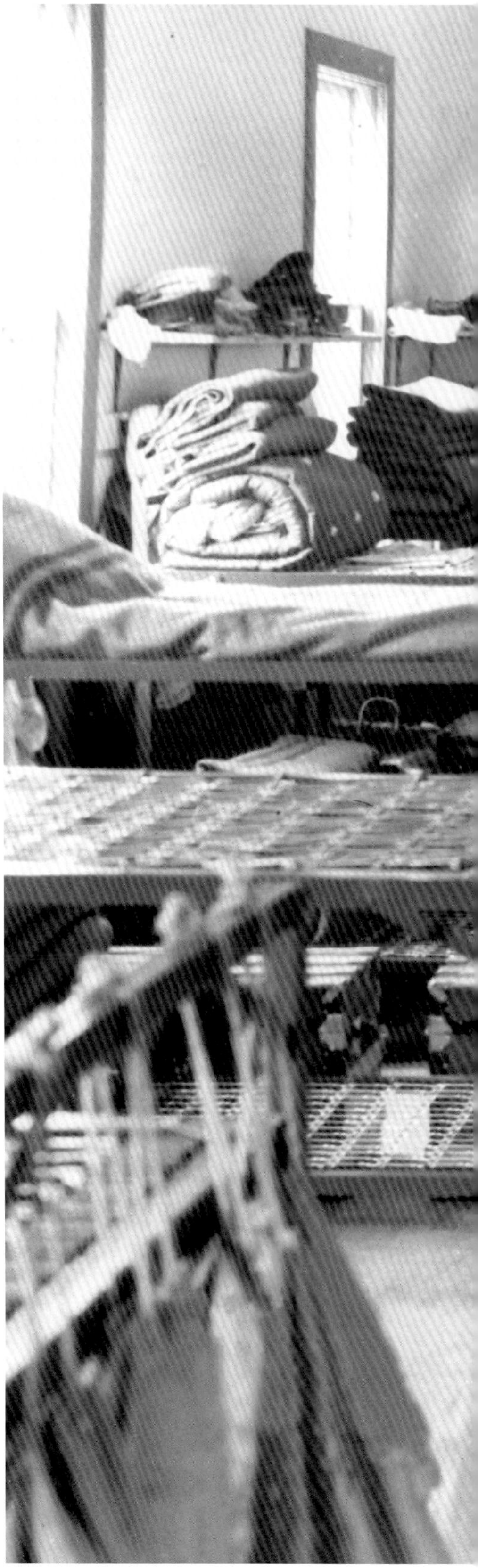

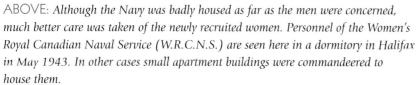

ABOVE: *Although the Navy was badly housed as far as the men were concerned, much better care was taken of the newly recruited women. Personnel of the Women's Royal Canadian Naval Service (W.R.C.N.S.) are seen here in a dormitory in Halifax in May 1943. In other cases small apartment buildings were commandeered to house them.*

RIGHT: *There was not much privacy for R.C.A.F. recruits in the newly built RCAF Dartmouth, whose Block F Barracks is seen here in a November 1939 photo.*

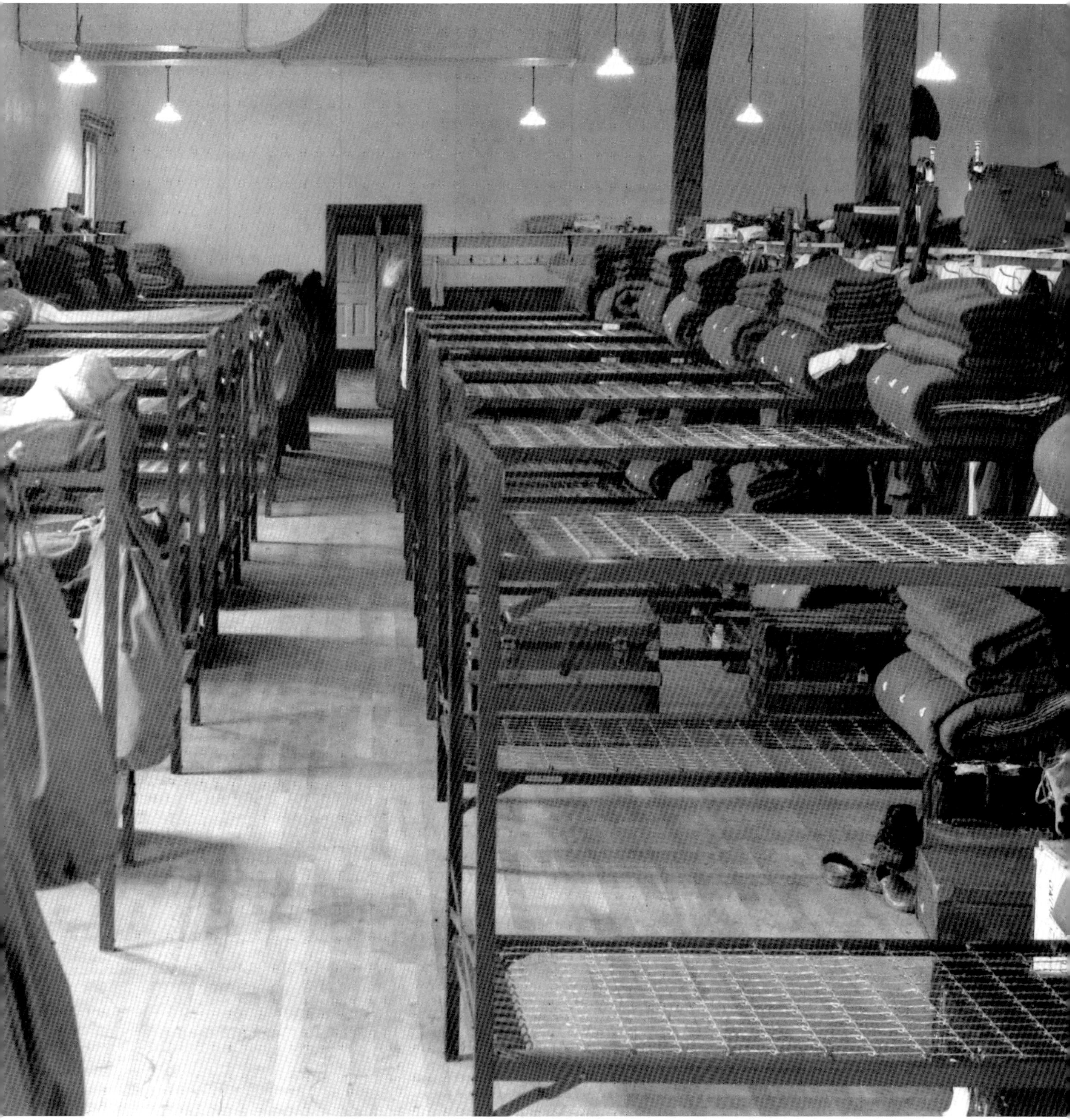

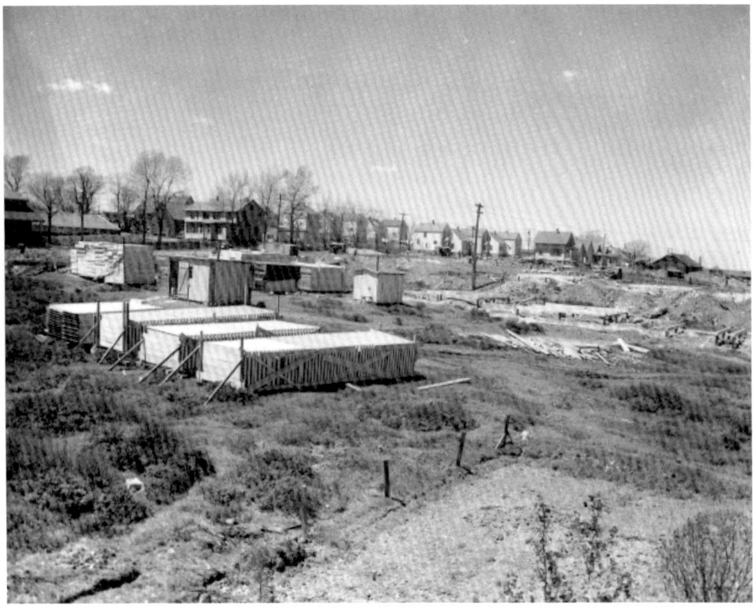

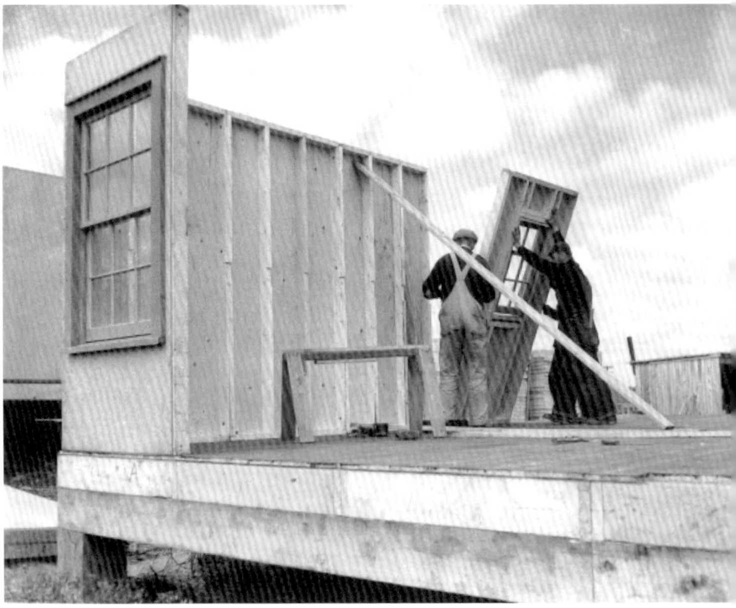

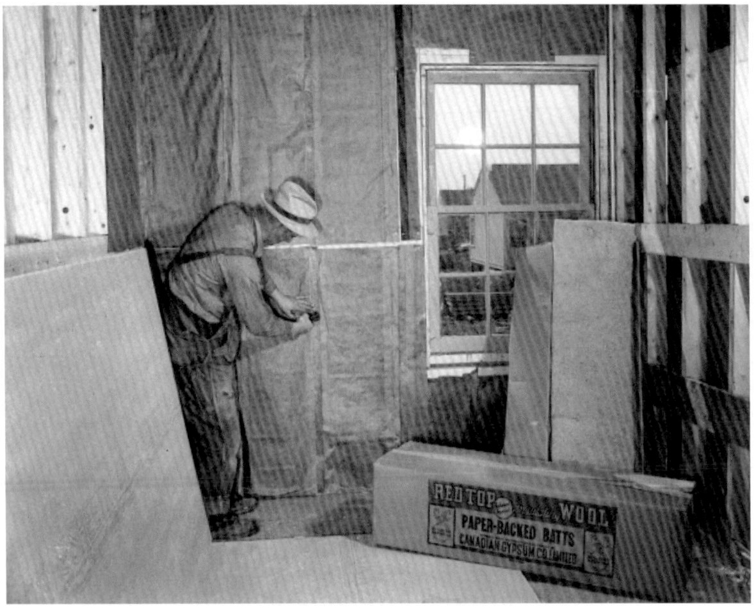
RED TOP WOOL
PAPER-BACKED BATTS
CANADIAN GYPSUM CO. LIMITED

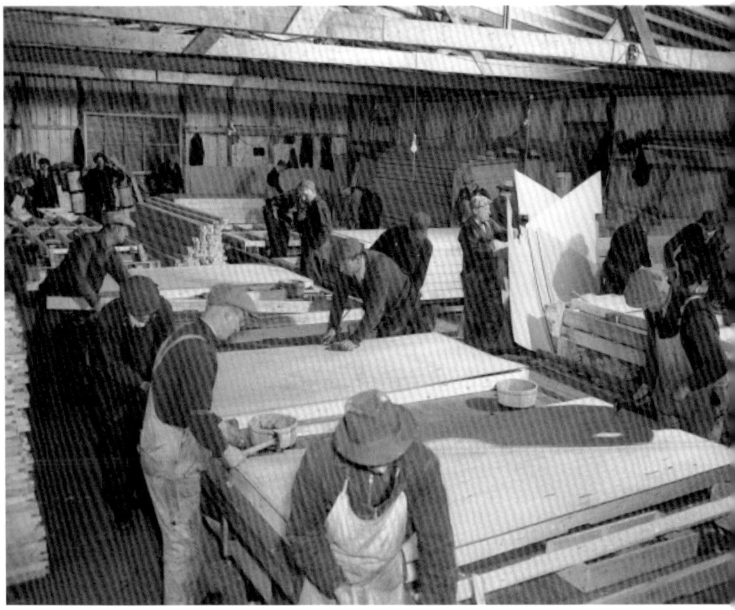

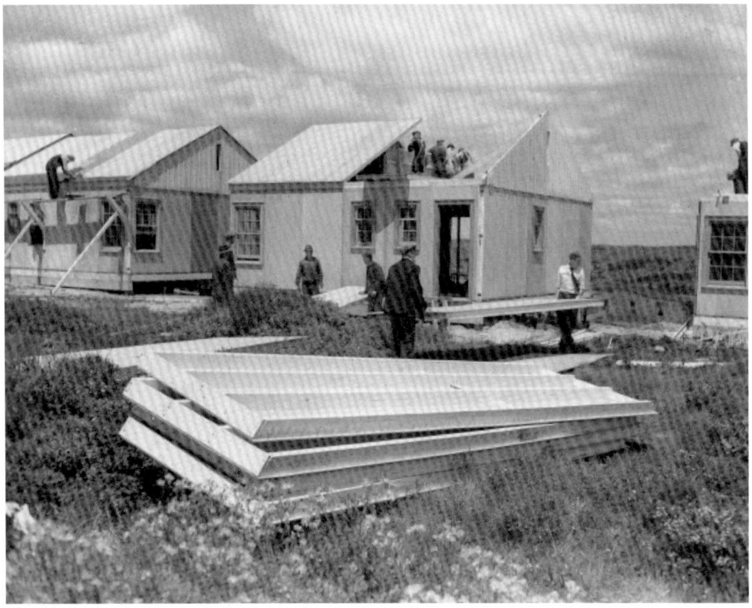

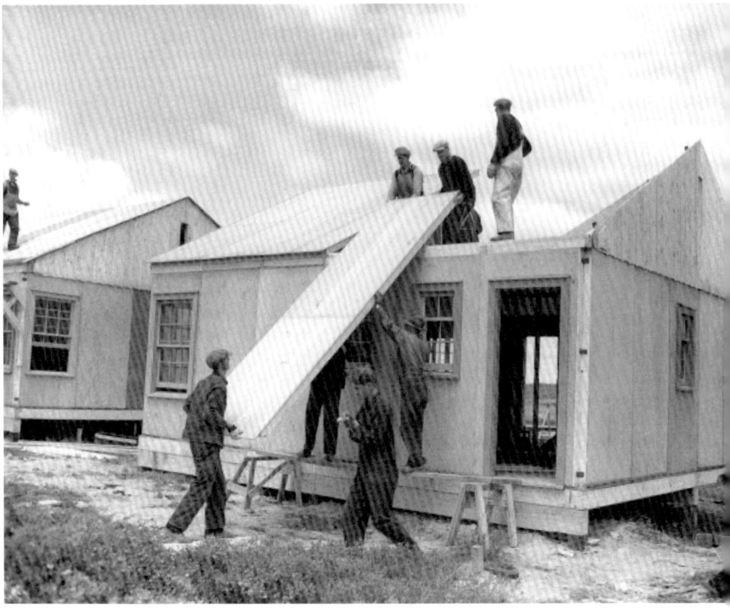

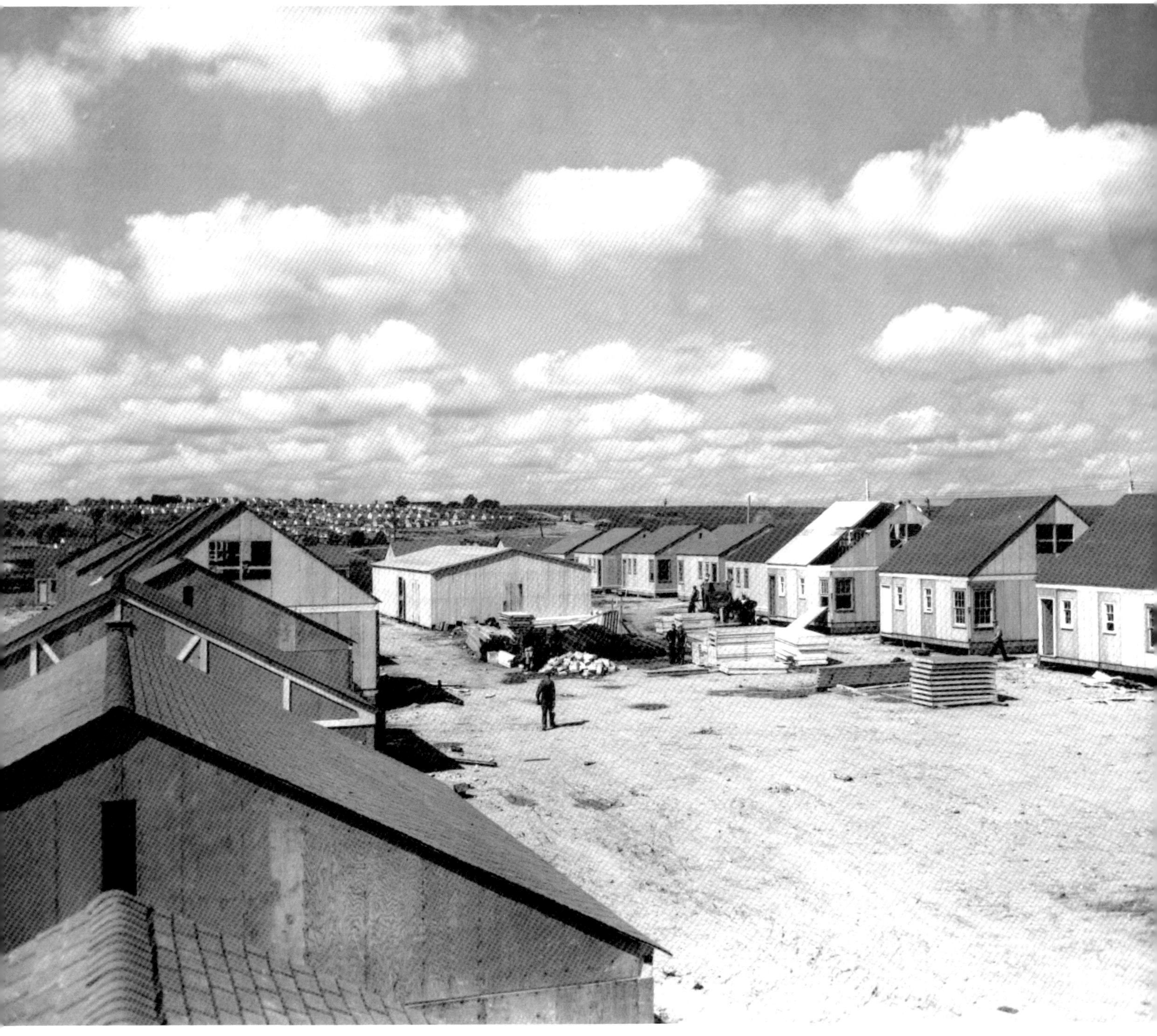

ABOVE AND LEFT: *Although government accepted little responsibility for most service personnel, authorities realized that they would not get the war workers they needed, especially for the shipyards, if there was no place for them to live. Here and elsewhere, beginning in 1941, Central Mortgage and Housing produced standard designs for this wartime housing, providing modest but comfortable homes for workers.*

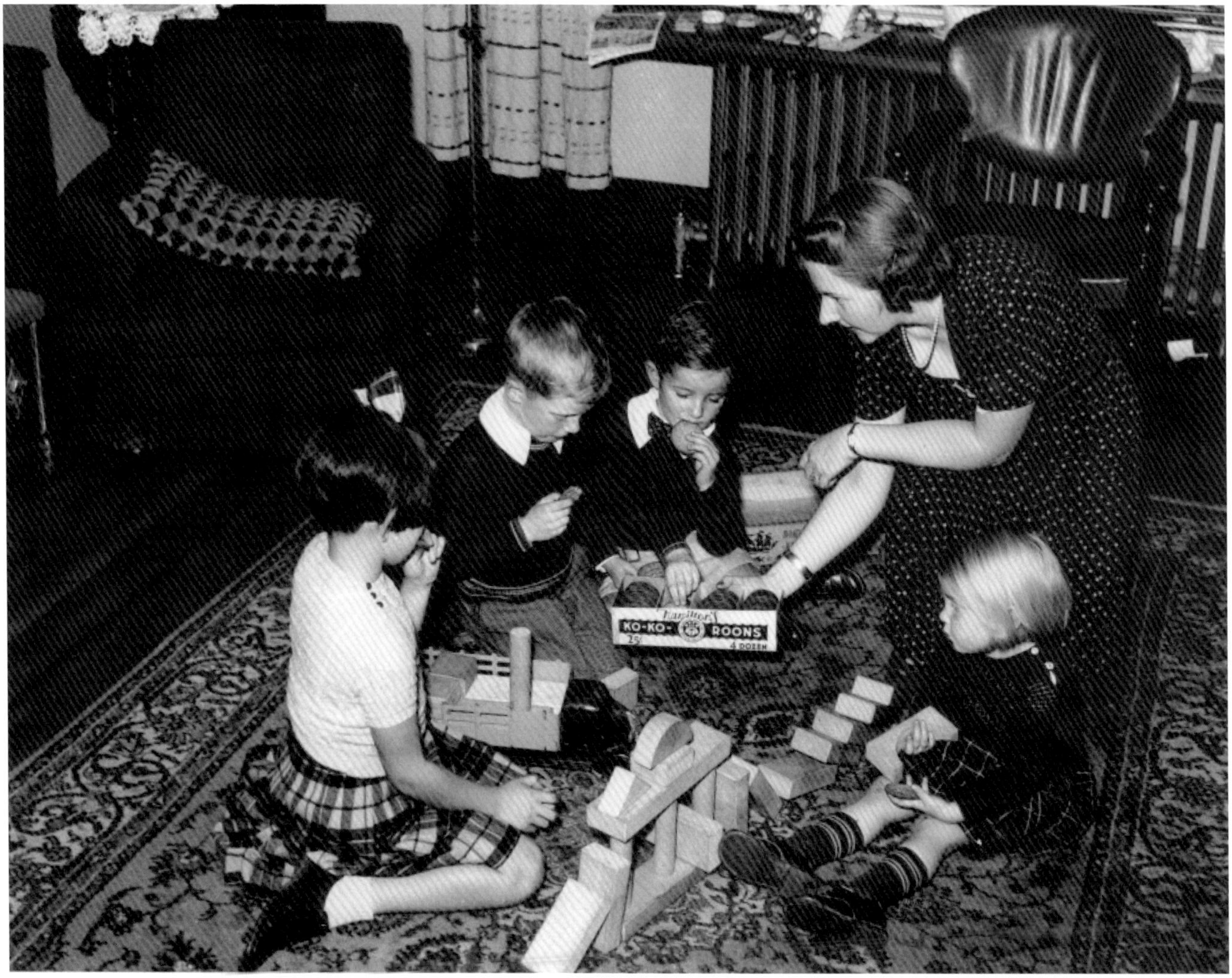
KO-KO-
ROONS
4 DOZEN

ABOVE: *This 1941 advertising photograph shows children eating Hamilton's "Ko-Ko-Roon" cookies in the Mart Livingstone home. They likely had to live off this delicious memory for some time.*

RIGHT: *As a consumer event, Christmas slipped in importance during the war, although it was always a family festival. In the Simpson's Toyland of December 1941, there were still goodies on the shelves. By the next year and for the duration of the war, toys and treats got scarcer and scarcer.*

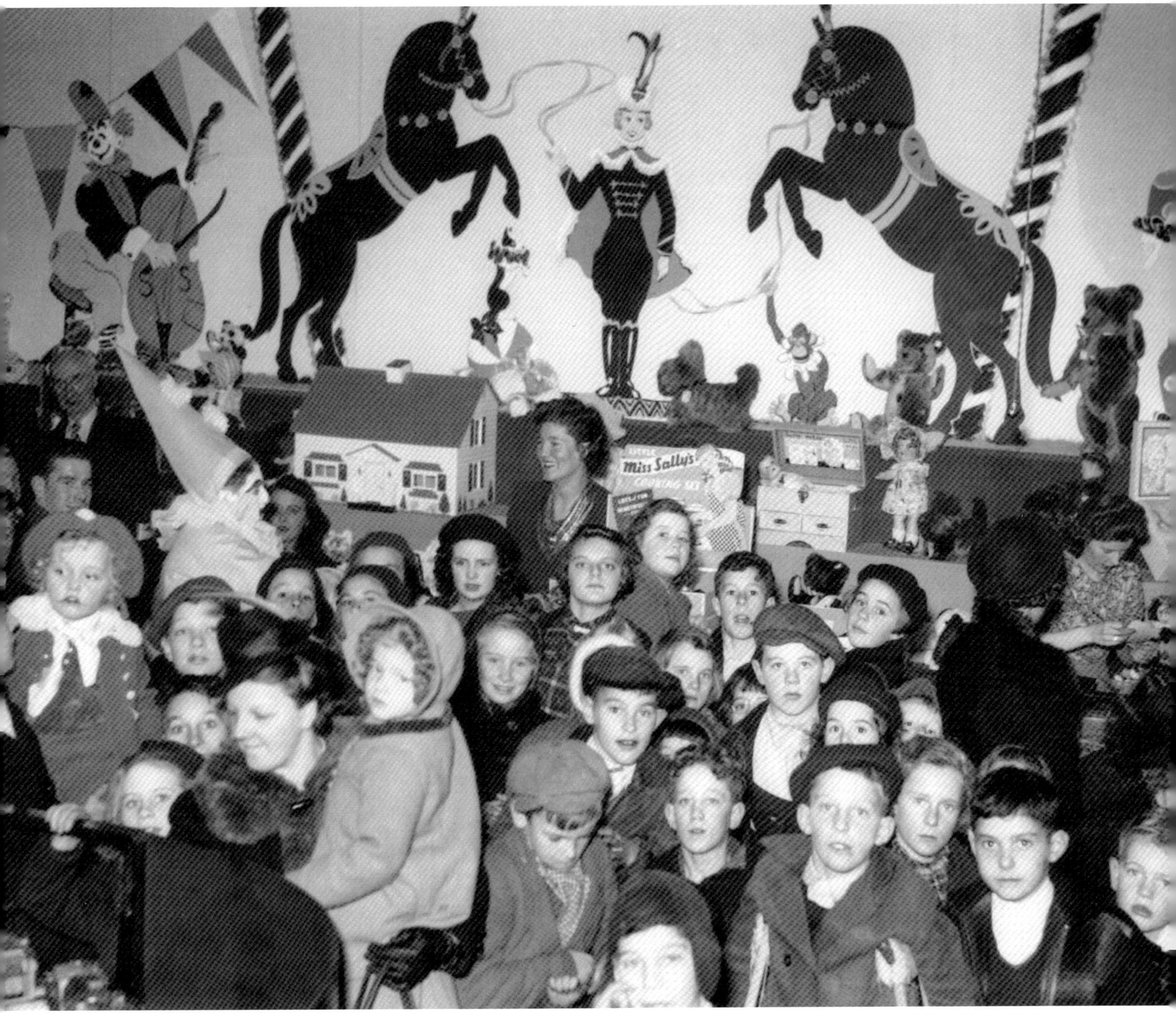
Miss Sally's

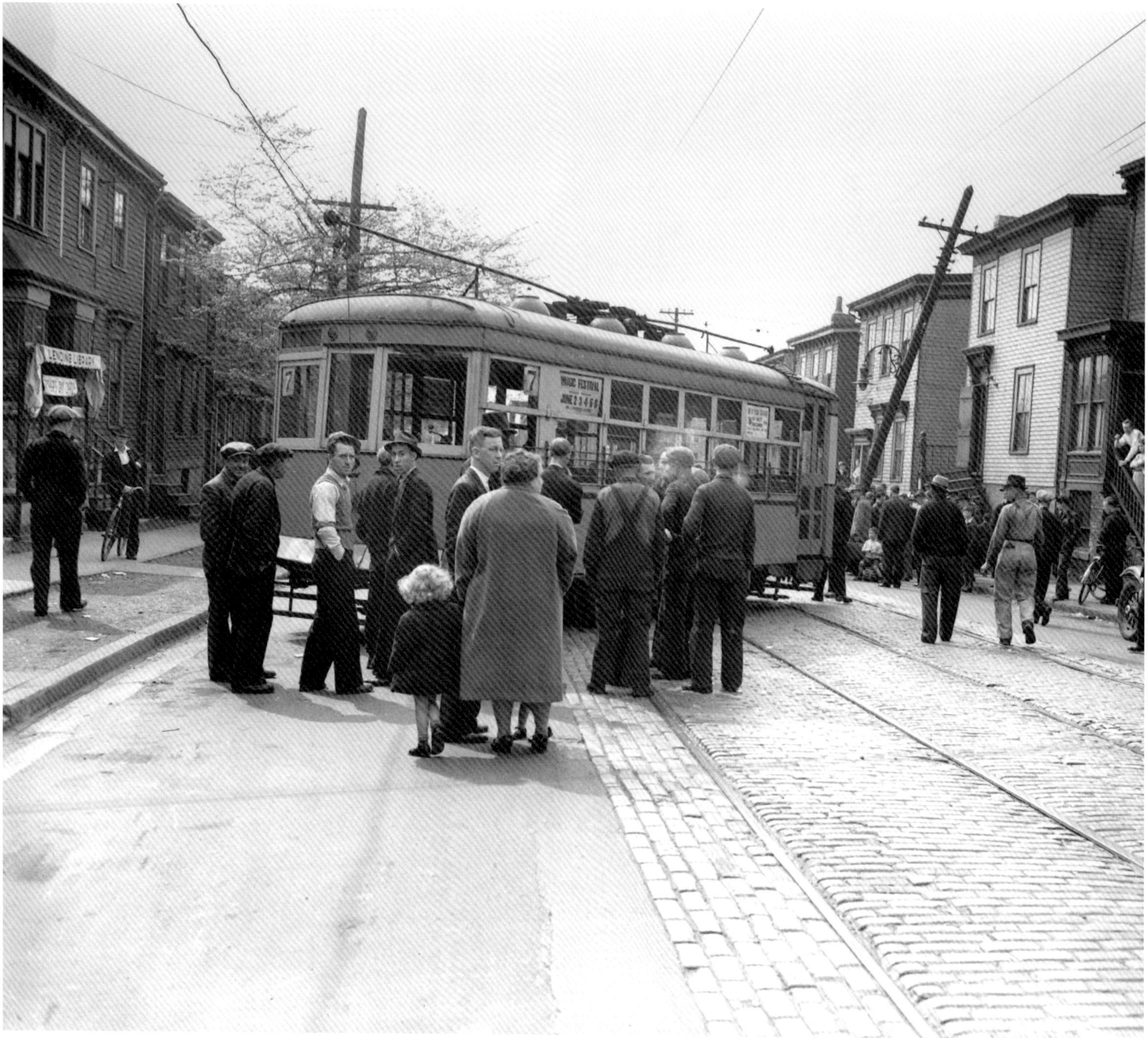
LENDING LIBRARY
7

ABOVE: *The private motor car became an endangered species on the streets during the war, but military traffic ramped up and more than took its place. The streets were full of noisy trucks and mobile ordnance, night and day. In peacetime or wartime, when an irresistible force meets an immoveable object, the results were the same, only with different players, as seen in this tram car and bren gun carrier collision on Agricola Street.*

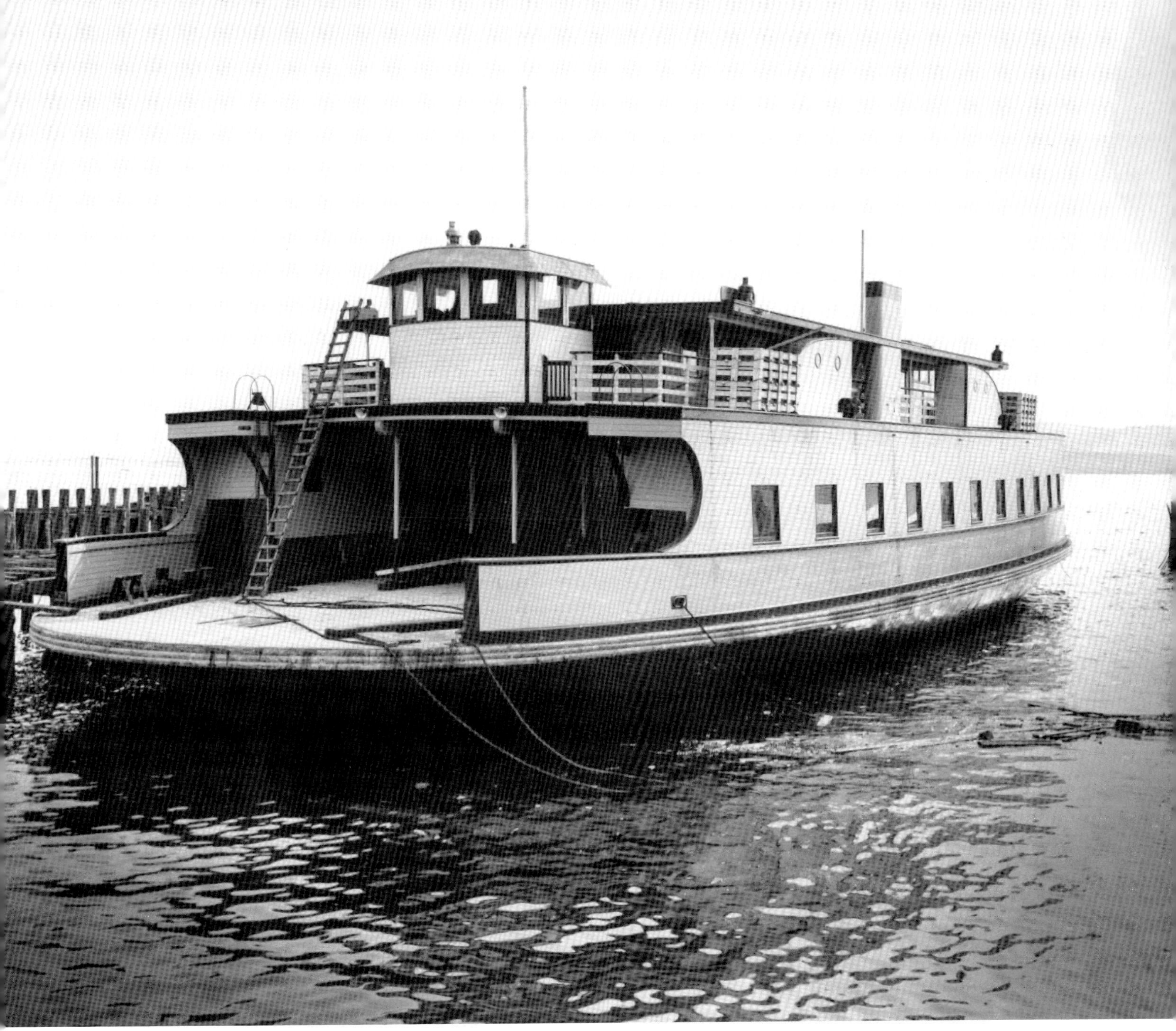

ABOVE: *A critical part of the public transportation infrastructure was the cross-harbour ferry system run by the town of Dartmouth through the Dartmouth Ferry Commission. Dartmouth's ferry terminal with the brand new addition to the fleet,* Governor Cornwallis, *is seen here. The establishment of RCAF Dartmouth, followed by the construction of Elkins Barracks in 1941, a large Army facility nearby, brought the ferry system up to a 24-hour operation on New Year's Eve 1942. Previously, missing the last ferry meant spending the night in Halifax for anyone without the means of driving around Bedford Basin.*

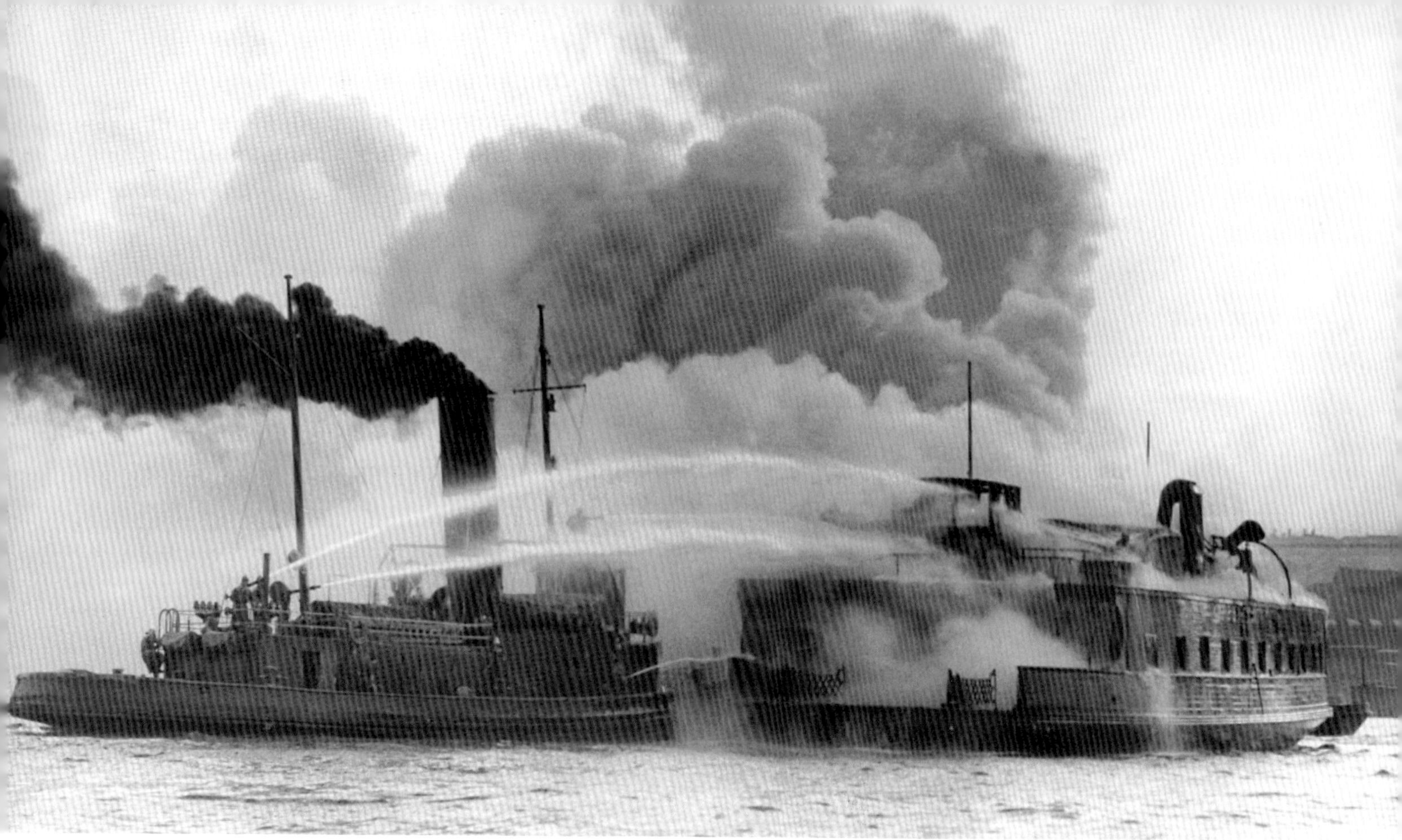

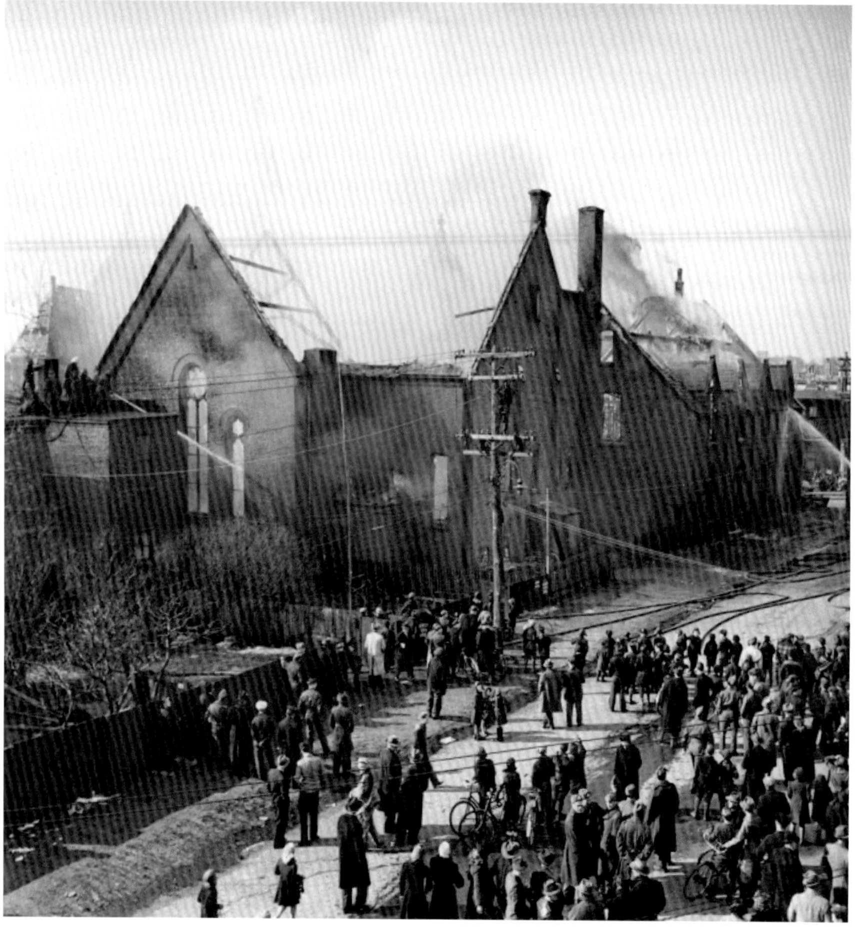

ABOVE: *The addition of the* Governor Cornwallis *was a boon to the Ferry Commission because with four boats the system could handle the traffic. Thus, it was a disaster when on leaving the Halifax terminal on 22 December 1944, the engine room crew noticed that ceiling insulation had caught fire. To avoid a mid-harbour panic the crew fought the flames in silent desperation, landing safely in Dartmouth and disembarking the cars and passengers just in time. For the ferry it was too late. Overwhelmed by flames it was towed out into the harbour to burn to the waterline and then beached on George's Island. For the rest of the war the ferry service struggled to cope.*

LEFT: *Fires were a serious issue for peninsular Halifax during the war because its water system, a creature of the City Council, was highly politicized, ramshackle, unsanitary, broke, and barely functioning. The additional pressures of the war were the straw that broke the camel's back. Watering ships in a convoy was a tedious process which lowered pressure in all the mains. It is said that the First Baptist Church at Spring Garden and Queen, seen here the morning after, burnt to the ground on 21 March 1942 because the* Queen Mary *was taking on water and there was no pressure in the hoses.*

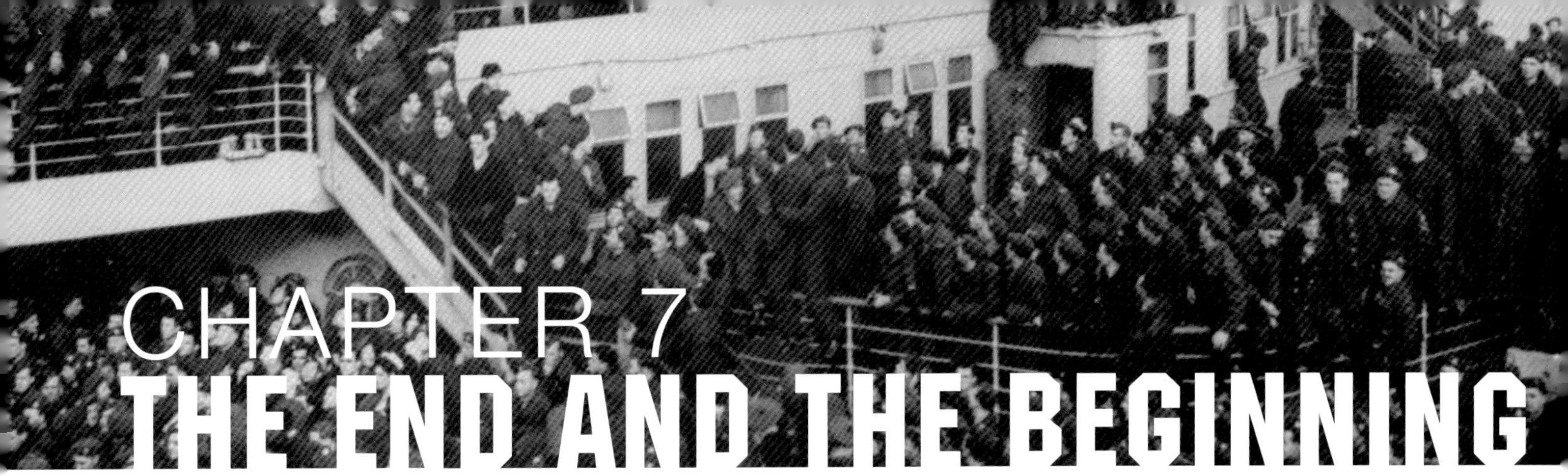

CHAPTER 7 THE END AND THE BEGINNING

When at last the end came on 7 May 1945, after weeks of hand-to-hand fighting in the ruined streets of Berlin, it was really no surprise. What was a surprise, at least to those who planned a sober, thoughtful and alcohol-free celebration in the provincial capital, was that a large proportion of the military and civilian population wanted nothing of the sort and set out to celebrate V-E Day, 8 May, without the restraints that they had lived with for the past six years. When the dust settled after the "celebrations," the downtown was in a shambles, the city's liquor stores were cleaned out, Nova Scotia Light & Power was short two trams, three were dead from the excesses of riot, the career of Admiral Leonard Murray, in spite of his making the Royal Canadian Navy a byword for competence and respect, was in ruins. Sadly, even though ample evidence showed that the Navy had plenty of help from the general population, naval personnel were blamed by civilians for the wanton destruction in what became known as the Halifax V-E Day Riots.

It is said that it is an ill wind that blows no good. A hot dry wind was blowing at suppertime on 18 July when a stray spark landed in an ammunition-laden lighter at a Bedford Magazine jetty. The resulting explosion scattered flaming brands over the Magazine's tinder-dry hillsides, setting them immediately ablaze. Although the facilities were state-of-the-art, they had been overwhelmed by massive quantities of ordnance deposited by ships returning from the Battle of the Atlantic. Stacked everywhere, it began to explode and each new explosion in its turn spread the blaze even wider. Because it did not happen, citizens of the port of Halifax never knew how close they came to the kind of disaster that had been visited on the bomb-ravaged cities of Europe. In among the piles of shells, torpedoes, and depth charges was a cache of a new, secret, and highly volatile explosive, RDX. That the flames never reached it was owed to the battle waged on flaming, exploding hillsides by naval personnel, backed up by municipal and A.R.P. firemen. If, for the past two or three years wardens had wondered what all the drills were for, the Civil Defence organization wondered no more. It sprang into action with smooth efficiency so that the civilian evacuation of the north ends of Dartmouth and Halifax on a warm summer night is remembered by most as an exciting diversion, almost a celebration, at war's end. Although there were many bangs, the worst did not happen and on the evening of the 19th the "All Clear" was sounded. The evident heroism of those who had faced death on a flaming hillside did not go unnoticed, and insofar as the Magazine Explosion restored a working relationship between civilians and the Navy in the port of Halifax, it was a good thing.

Now that the war was over, it was time to get on with life. The big liners which had taken the troops away were now bringing them back by the thousands and the Seawall hummed with activity. They also brought back thousands of War Brides, most of them British, because the troops had not spent all of their time fighting Germans.

They all came to a new world of hope and expectations, a future with new social support systems and the promise of education for service personnel who just a few years before would never have dreamed of such a thing. Chastened by its wartime experience, and perhaps more ashamed of its wartime shortcomings than it needed to be, Halifax determined to build itself anew. It wanted finally to erase the sense of shabbiness that was in the minds of many who had passed through during the past six years, who had overwhelmed the kindness and sacrifice of countless volunteers, who had tried to civilize their stay. To a waiting public, on 16 November 1945, after three years' work, the Civic Planning Commission introduced a Master Plan that would link Halifax and Dartmouth with a bridge and bring the war-weary communities into a new post-war world of cars, refrigerators, vacuum cleaners, a baby boom, and suburbs.

There was a determination among civic authorities and citizens alike that the East Coast Port would not resemble the city that had existed in September 1939, but present a modern image to a world now poised to reap the benefits of victory and a new peace.

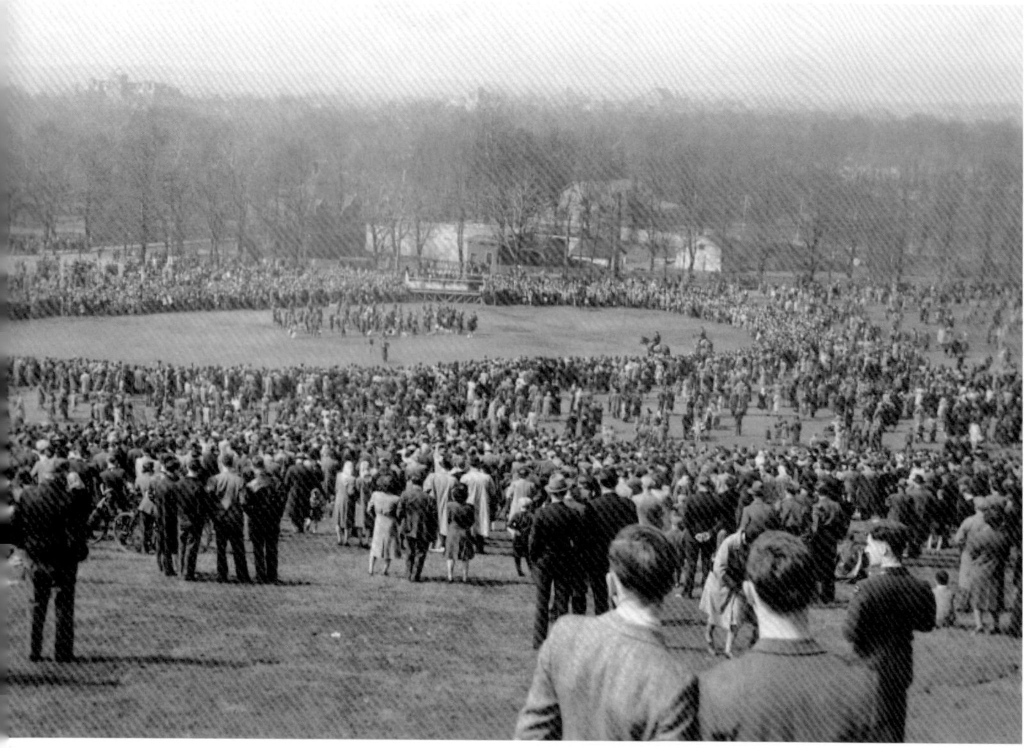

LEFT: *On 7 May 1945, General Alfred Jodl signed a surrender document at Rheims, France. It was a long time coming because by the autumn of 1944 it was obvious to everyone but the Germans that Germany had been defeated. Word of the surrender leaked out on 7 May, well before the official announcement, and the streets of Halifax filled up rapidly on the warm spring day. Since peace was no surprise, planning for the event was already in place. 8 May was proclaimed V-E Day and celebrations on the theme of thanksgiving were announced for that morning. As this photograph of "A Peaceful Celebration V-E Day at the Garrison Grounds" shows, official gatherings took place and were largely attended.*

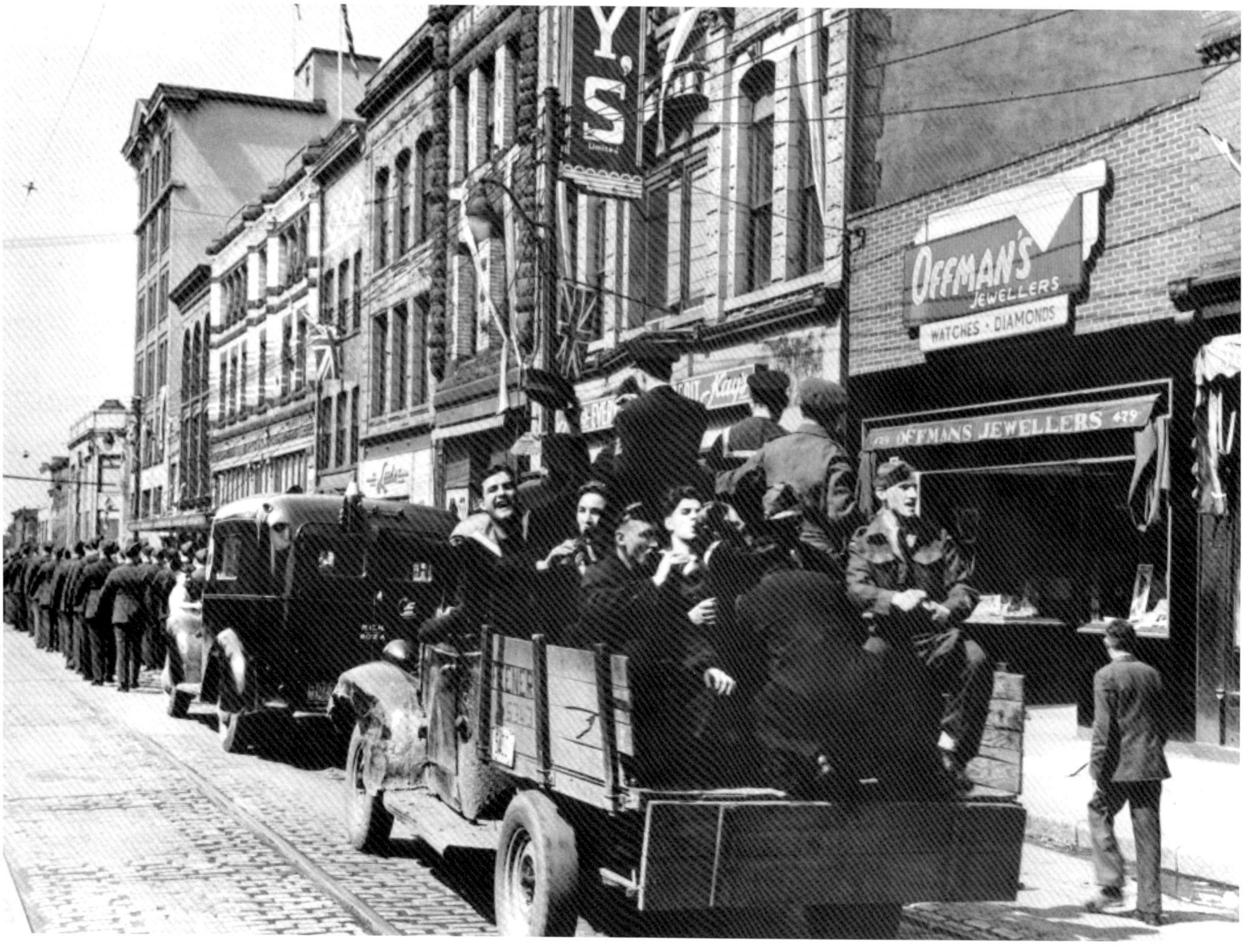
OFFMAN'S
JEWELLERS
WATCHES · DIAMONDS
479 OFFMANS JEWELLERS 479

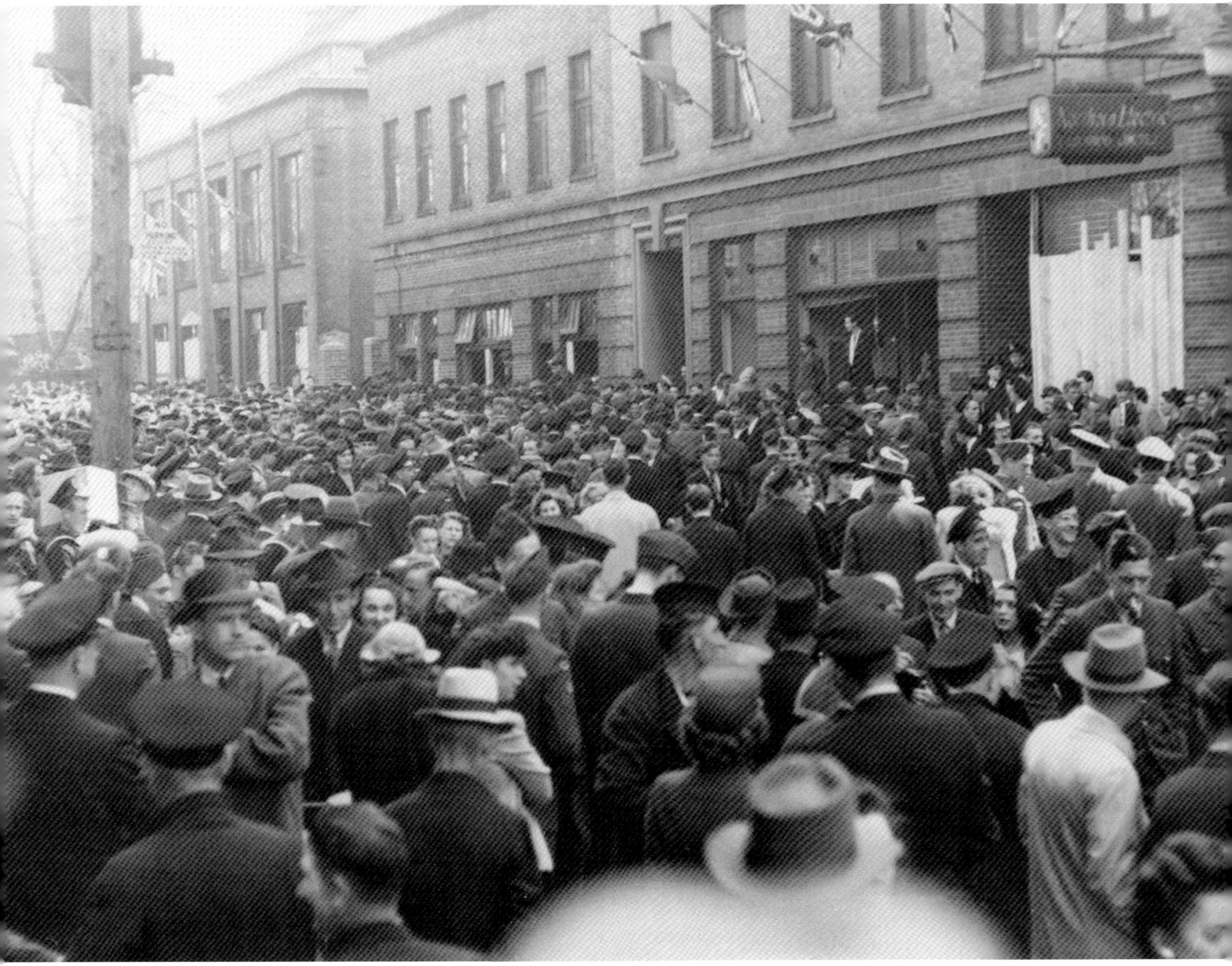

BOTTOM LEFT: *Celebration was not, however, going to be that simple. The warm and pleasant evening of 7 May saw some raucous behaviour in spite of fireworks on the harbour and a street dance on South Park. The high-minded decision to close liquor stores, so that celebrations would not be sullied by the consumption of alcohol, prompted theatre and many restaurant owners to follow suit. This action, combined with years of real or imagined grievances, rankled civilian and military personnel. The streets were full of naval ratings who, unlike their air force and army colleagues, were not required to return to base. In the warm evening crowds surged through the downtown, accompanied by the sounds of breaking glass, the smell of a burning tram car and a burning police car. It was hoped that with the Thanksgiving Service the next morning that things would calm down, but it was not to be. This photograph may represent the beginning of events on 8 May. As the troops paraded out of the Thanksgiving Ceremony at the Garrison Grounds the marching units began to disintegrate, lured away by the siren song of colleagues offering them liquor looted the night before from the closed stores.*

ABOVE: *One noteworthy aspect of this crowd, to more casually dressed later generations, is how nicely turned out everyone was. Moreover, though the crush of people on Barrington Street represents a riot in progress, everyone seems to be enjoying themselves, as indeed they probably were as long as they were not a merchant or police constable.*

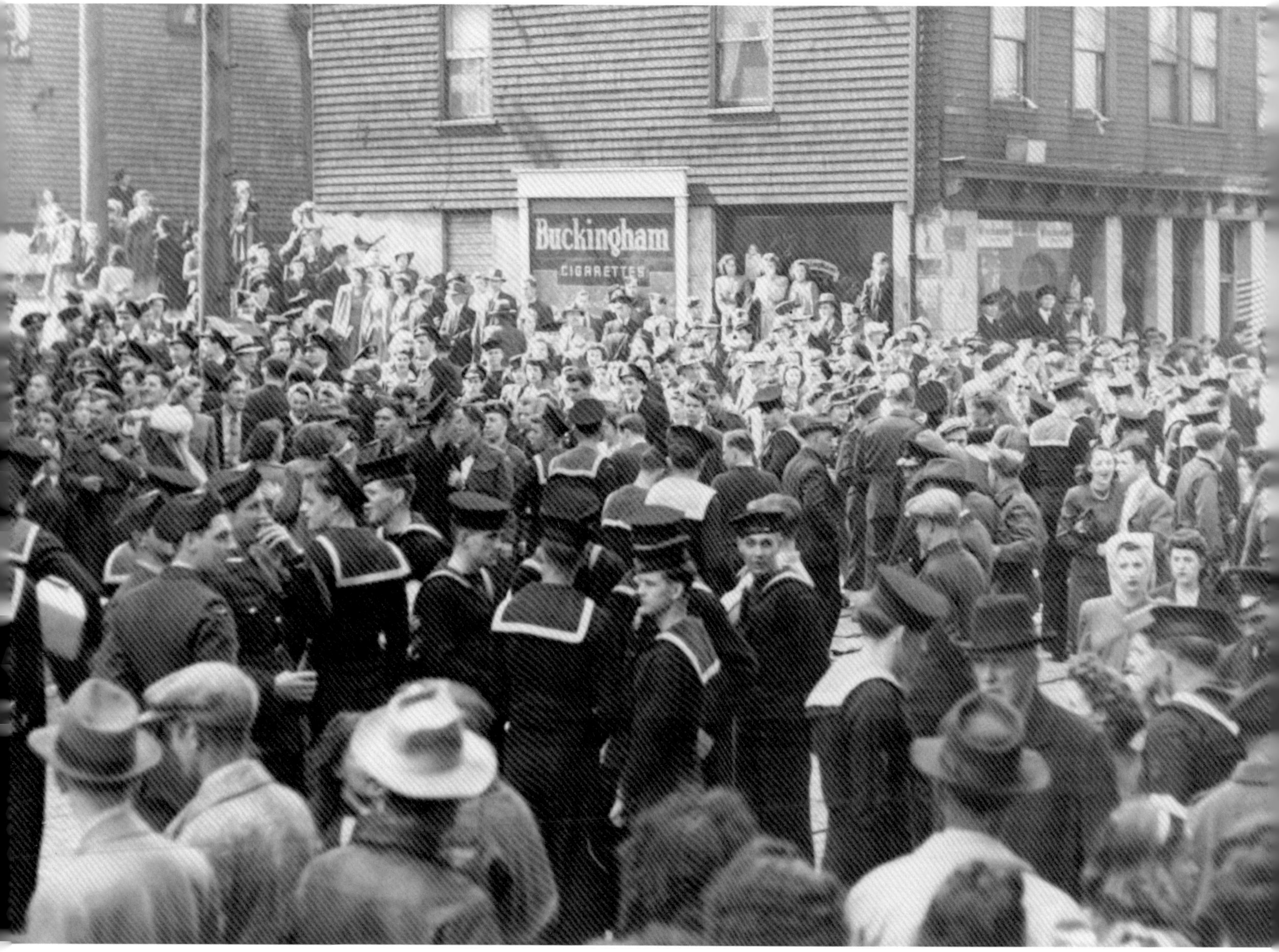
Buckingham
CIGARETTES

ABOVE: *Somewhere a thin line was crossed and a mob mentality ignited. What the mob wanted was booze, always a touchy issue for the military in Nova Scotia, and now a focus for long-suppressed resentment. With police forces still shaken from the events of the night before and, down Salter Street from Barrington the warehouse of Keith's Brewery looming like a pot of gold at the end of the rainbow, the crowds once again got out of hand.*

RIGHT: *Early on the police, of which there were 540 in Halifax, including military, R.C.M.P., and city, essentially gave up. Instructions had been issued as part of the planning leading up to V-E Day that the Halifax police were not to take a hard line in the event of any difficulties, so they did not. The Police Chief of Dartmouth had no such instructions. He stopped the ferries and issued night sticks to his men. It could be argued that his actions were the reason why no serious problems developed there.*

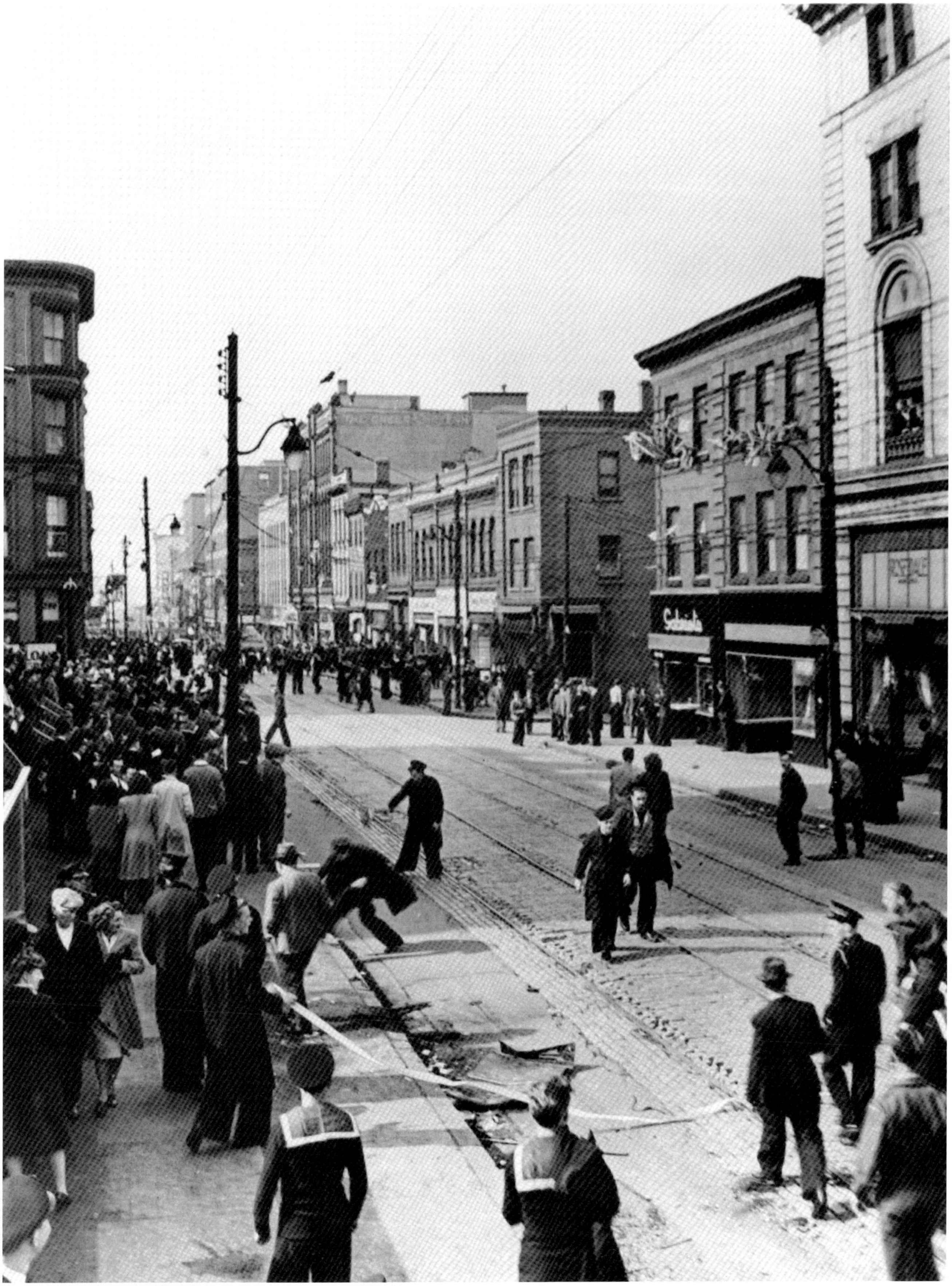

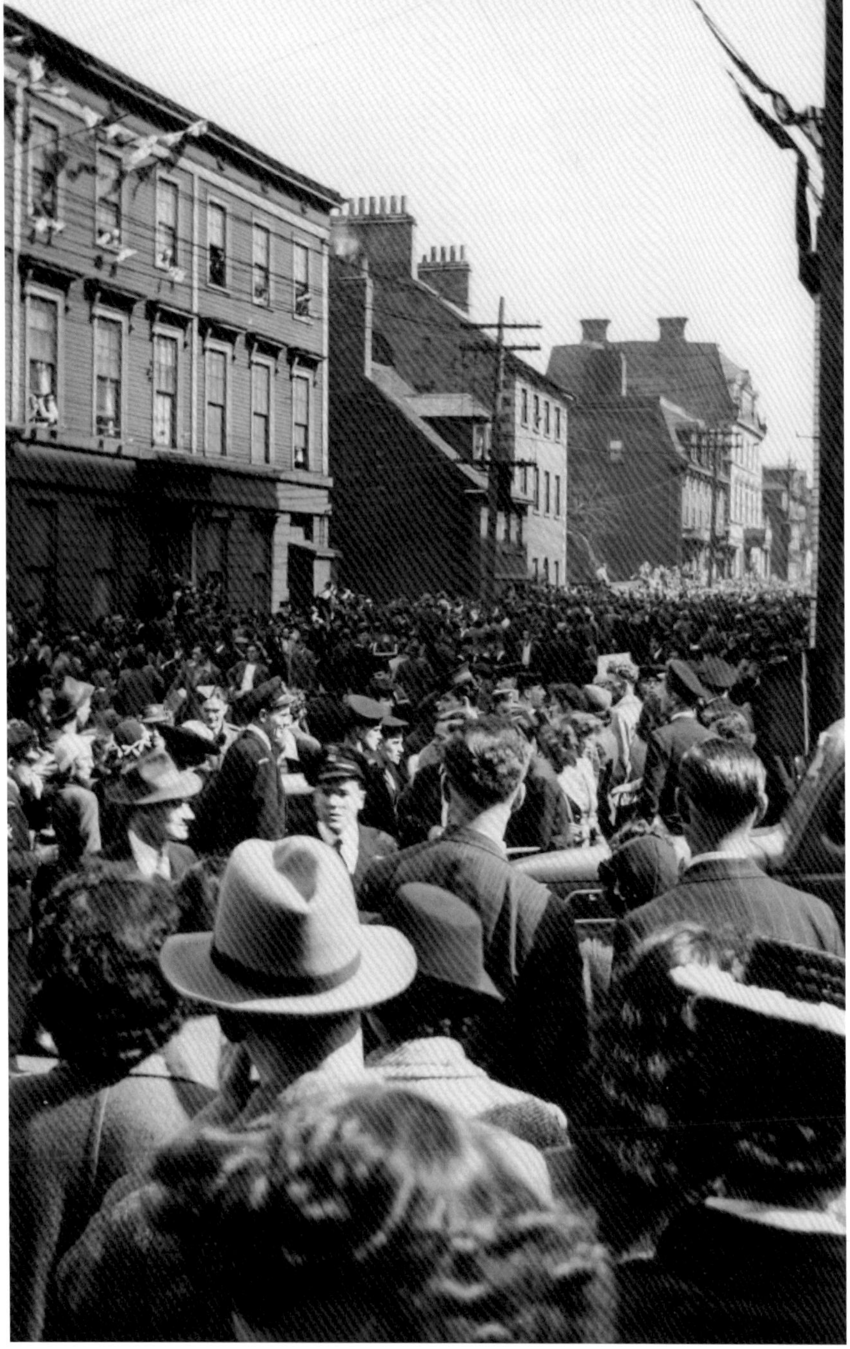

ABOVE: *This shot, in the vicinity of the Hollis Street liquor store, is typical of much of what went on, with masses of onlookers out to watch the fun as the store was emptied of its contents. When the looters drifted off to enjoy their booty (once they had their fill, smashing bottles against the curbs was as much fun as drinking it), so did the sightseers, leaving the empty street a litter of debris and broken glass. Boarded-up windows would be a feature of downtown for weeks until shipments of window glass could be brought in from the United States.*

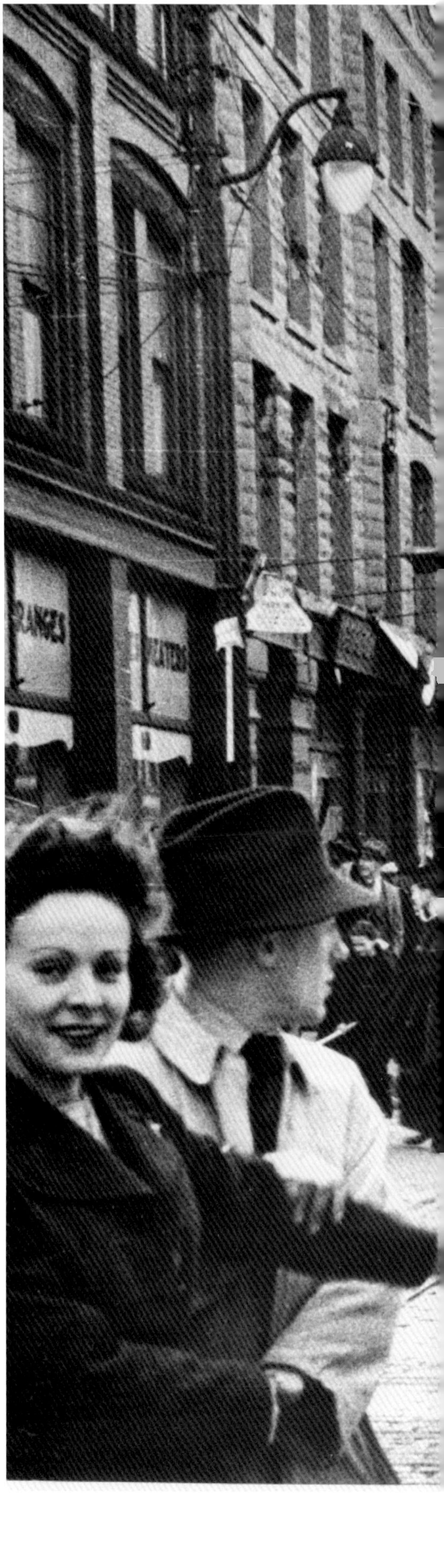

RIGHT: *It is hard not to see in the V-E Day riots an element of celebration and, even by later standards, innocence among the mayhem. At last the war was over, the pressure of endless exhortations to sacrifice, to save and scrimp, to say farewell perhaps forever to sons and husbands, was coming to an end. The sober reflection of official celebration was all very well, but it was not enough of an outlet for the overwhelming sense of relief and release from living in a pressure cooker for six years.*

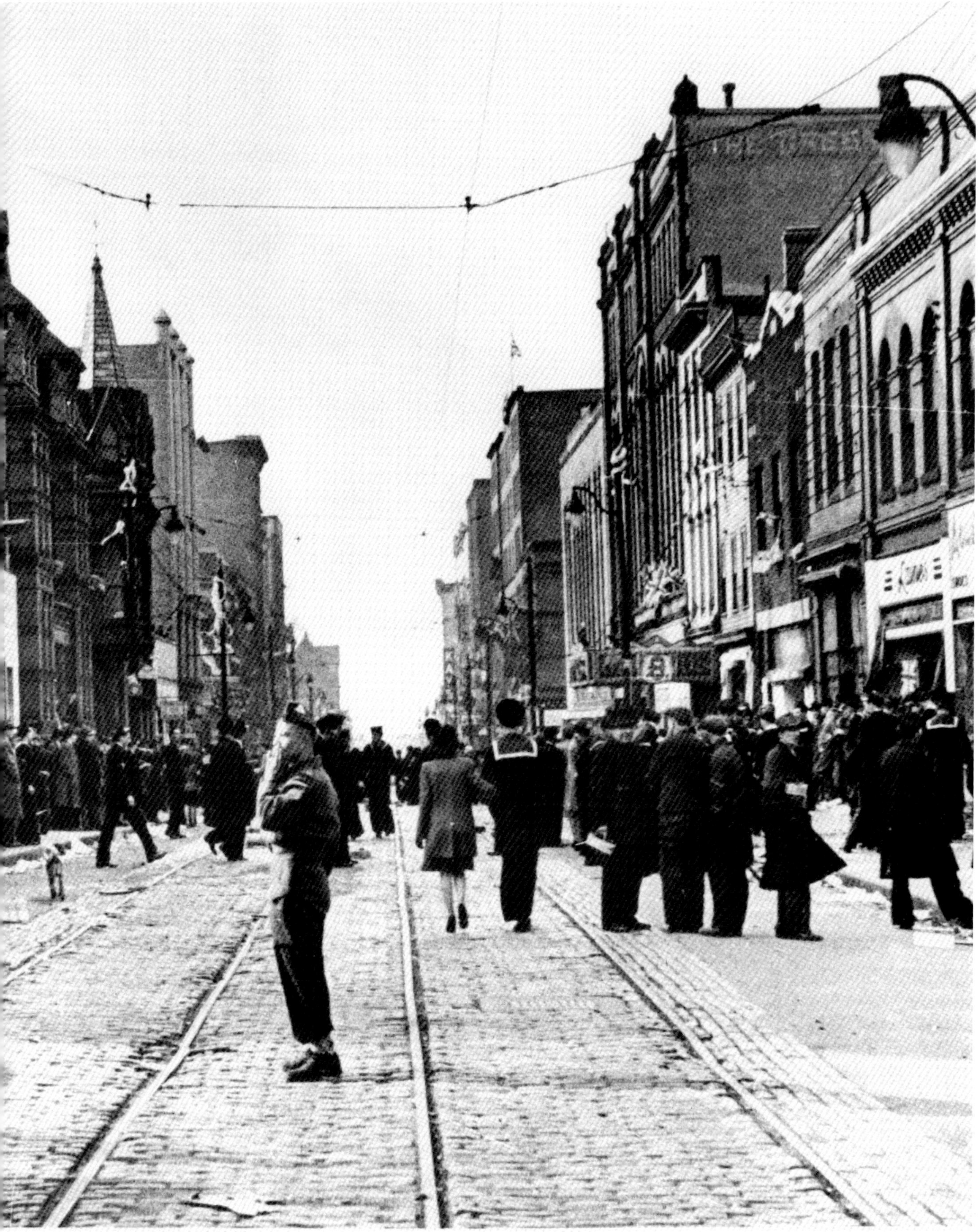

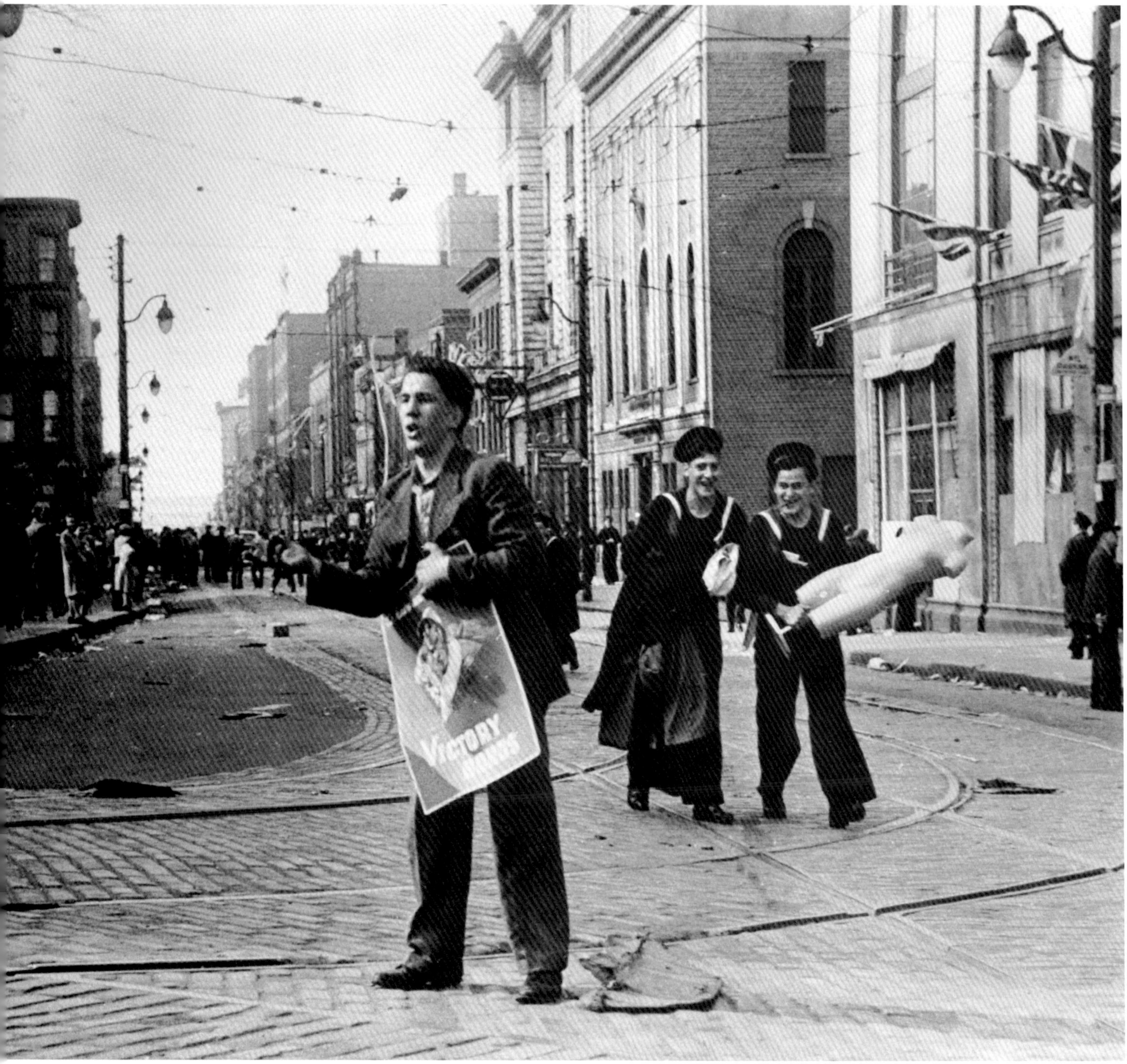
VICTORY

ABOVE: *At the corner of Barrington Street and Spring Garden Road. The Navy was criticized for allowing its men to run wild. It was true that of the hundreds of naval officers in the city, few if any were seen on the streets during the riots attempting to restore discipline; but this inaction may have been a wise course. In part, their absence was intended to avoid confrontations which would have escalated the mere letting-off of steam to another level, involving more serious actions of disobeying orders that could lead to charges of mutiny. Admiral Leonard Murray, who became the government's scapegoat for the affair, in his defence was still preoccupied with the very real fact that fanatical Nazi submarine captains continued to wreak vengeance upon allied shipping.*

RIGHT: *Barrington Street hung over on the drizzly morning after the night before. Halifax hit the news for its riotous reaction to the German surrender, but it was not alone. Riots and liquor store raids erupted in Sydney, New Waterford, Dominion, Kentville, and Yarmouth.*

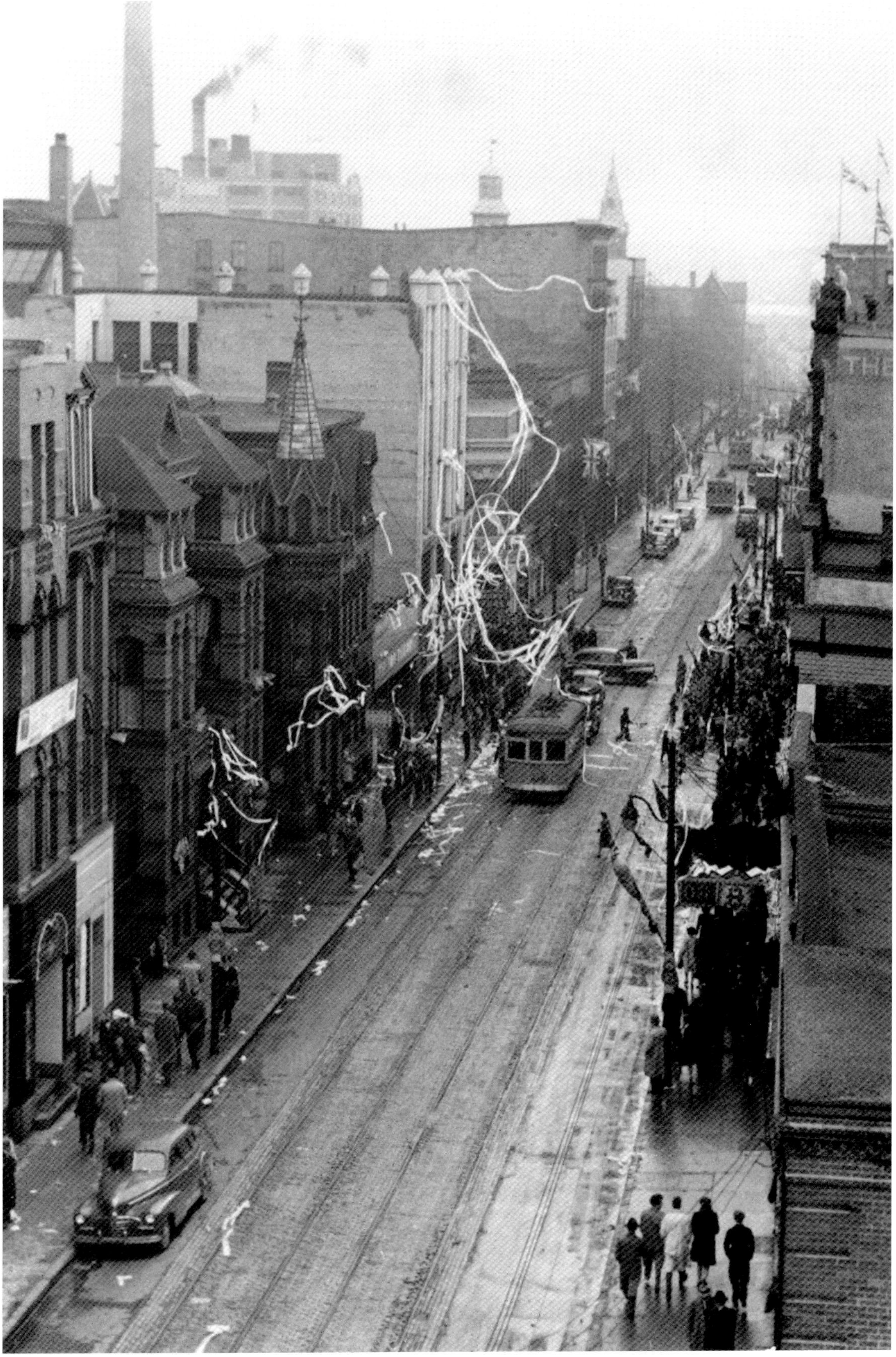
THE

RIGHT: *As sailors and civilians marked the official end of the war with varying degrees of intensity, there was still war work to be done. Here Fairmiles at the entrance of Halifax Harbour escort a U-boat that has surrendered.*

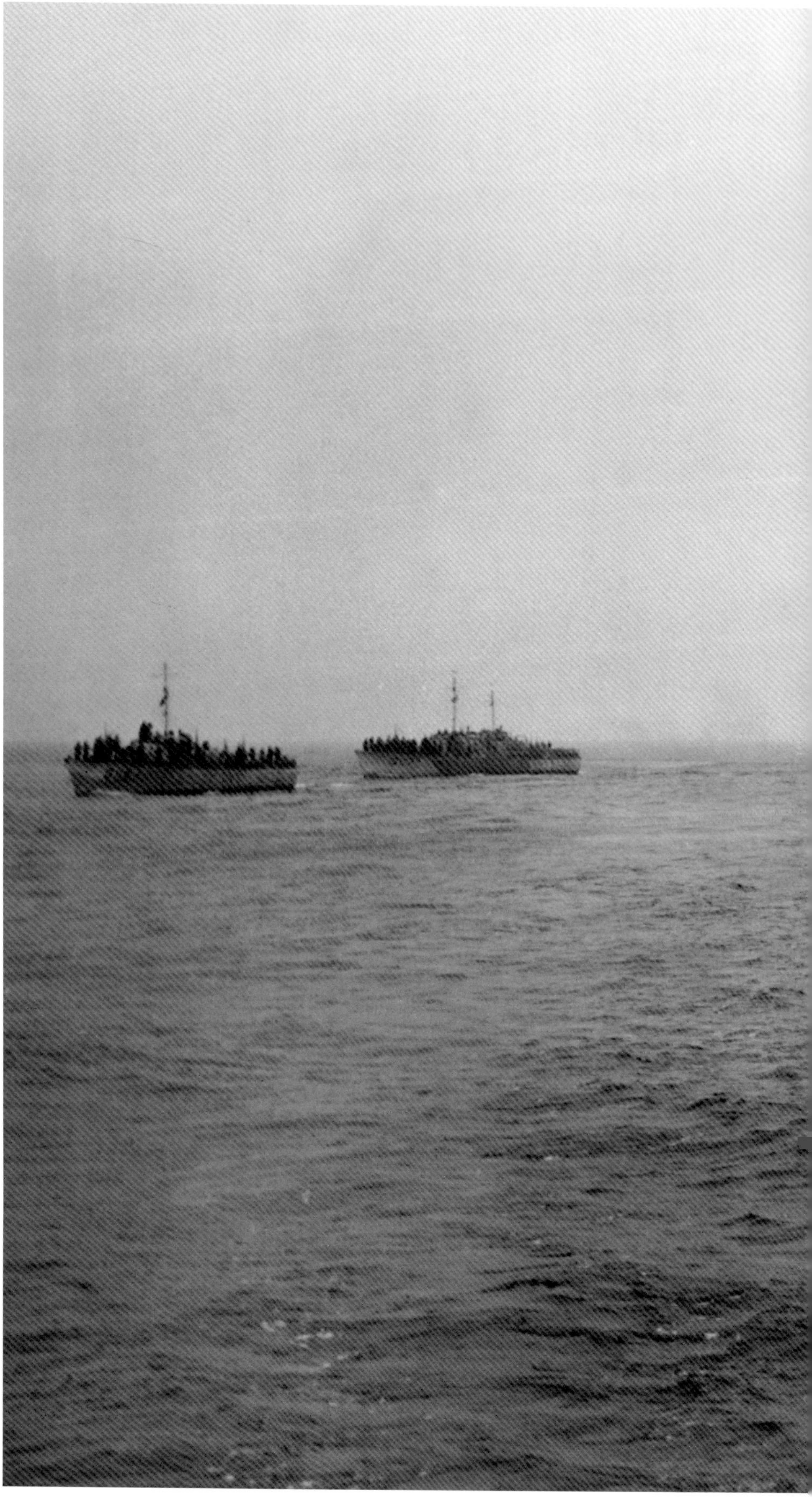

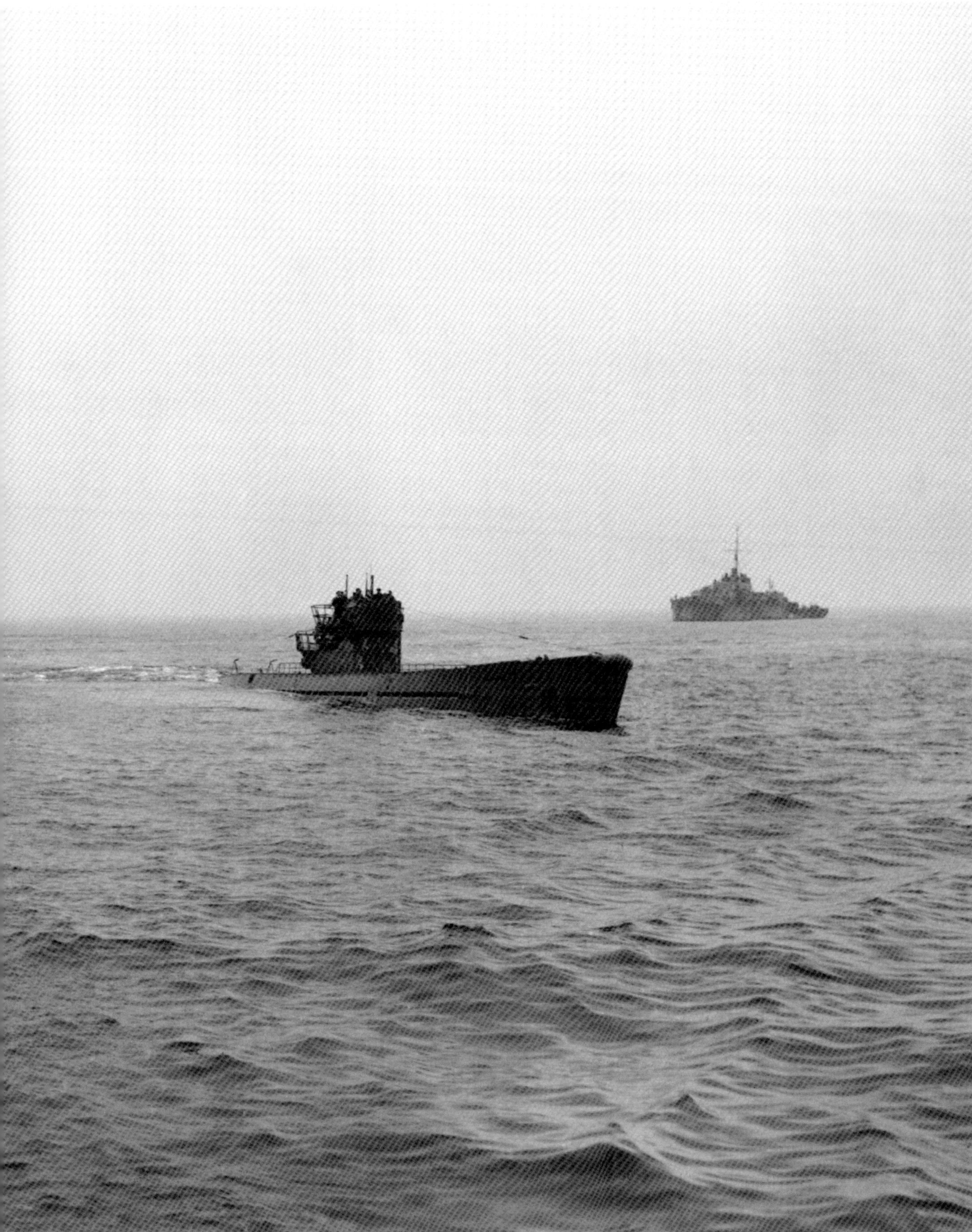

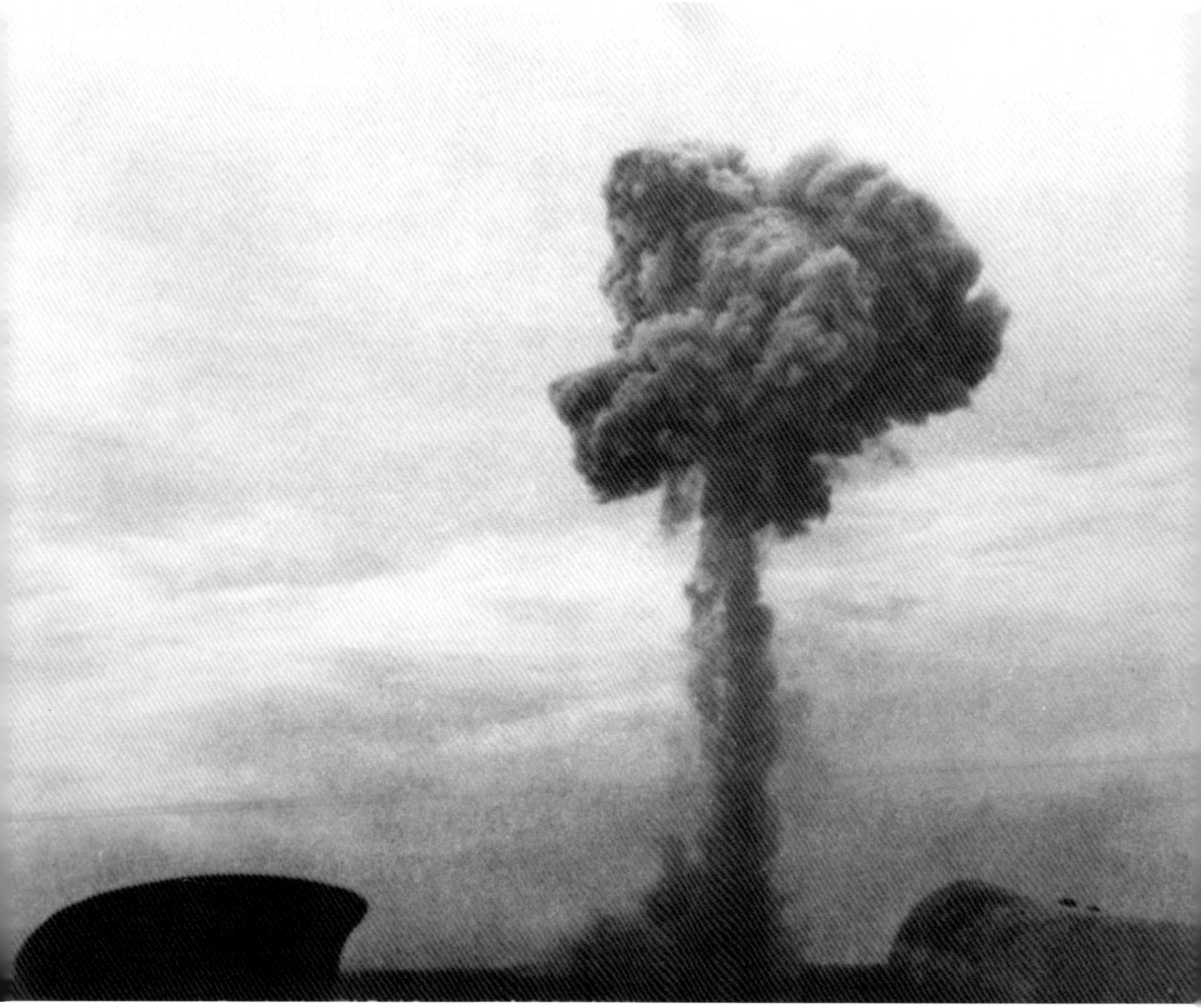

ABOVE: *At suppertime on 18 July, after days of hot sunny summer weather, the unthinkable happened. For weeks HMC ships returning from the North Atlantic and coming into harbour made the wharf of the Bedford Magazine their first call, depositing ammunition and depth charges before decommissioning. Although the storage facilities were modern and up-to-date, magazine staff were swamped by the rapid influx and explosives were piled everywhere. It was an accident waiting to happen and it did. Perhaps it was the flick of a forbidden cigarette butt, perhaps it was something else, but the fire and subsequent explosions continued for hours. Only the heroic efforts of Civil Defence units and armed forces personnel prevented a repeat of the disaster of 1917.*

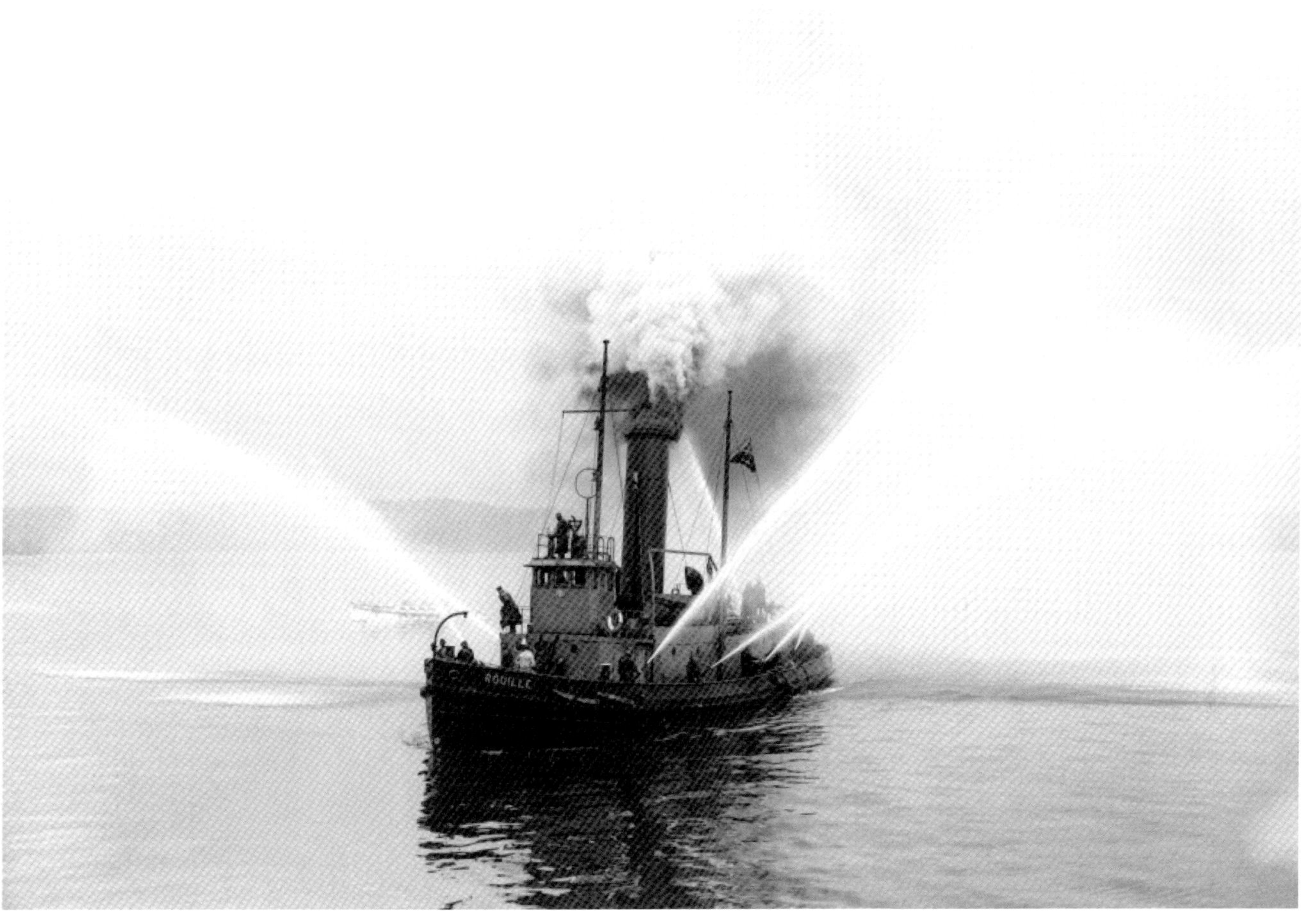
ROUILLE

ABOVE: *In spite of the very real danger from unpredictable and uncontrolled explosions of potentially deadly force, the fireboat* Rouille*, coming as close to shore as its draft allowed, pumped streams of water onto blazing buildings and piles of loose ammunition along the waterfront.*

RIGHT: *The magazine explosion aftermath: an unexploded projectile embedded in the road.*

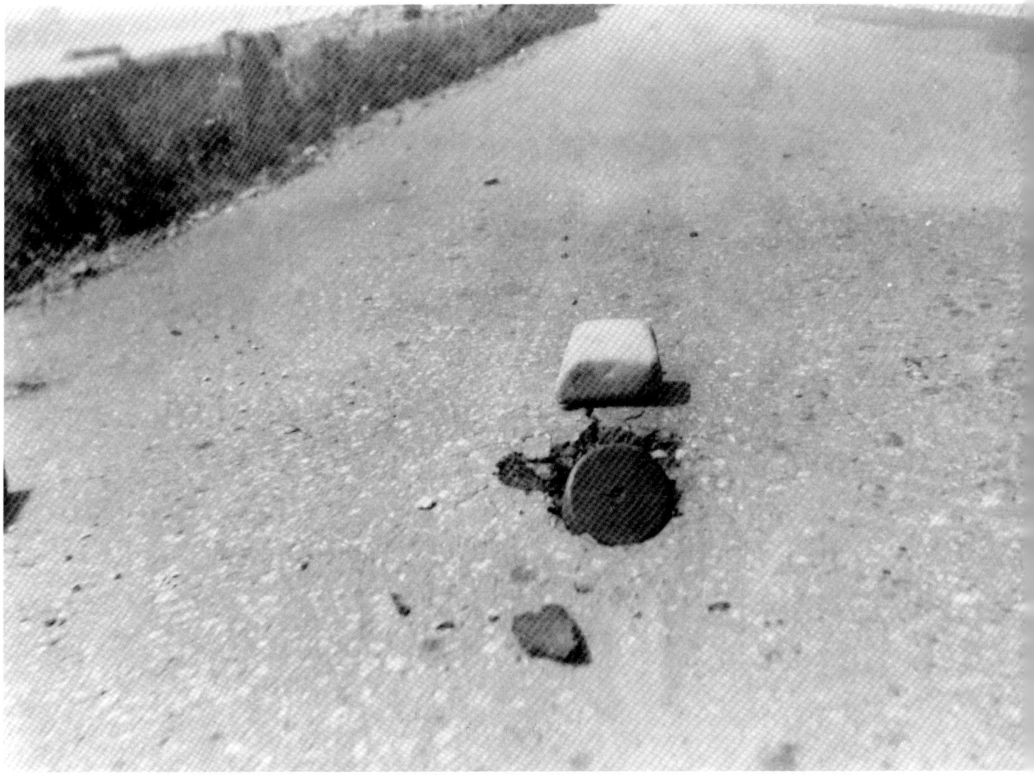

RIGHT: *The ceremonies of thanksgiving, the huge, spontaneous street gatherings, and even the more riotous, destructive behaviour all signaled the relief of war's end and the anticipation of the return of thousands of men and women who had been overseas, sometimes for years. Here RMS* Queen Elizabeth *arrives in Halifax with returning troops. Even though hundreds of liners, big and small, were recruited as transport for returning troops, for those itching to get home the wait in vast temporary camps in drab and war-weary Britain seemed endless.*

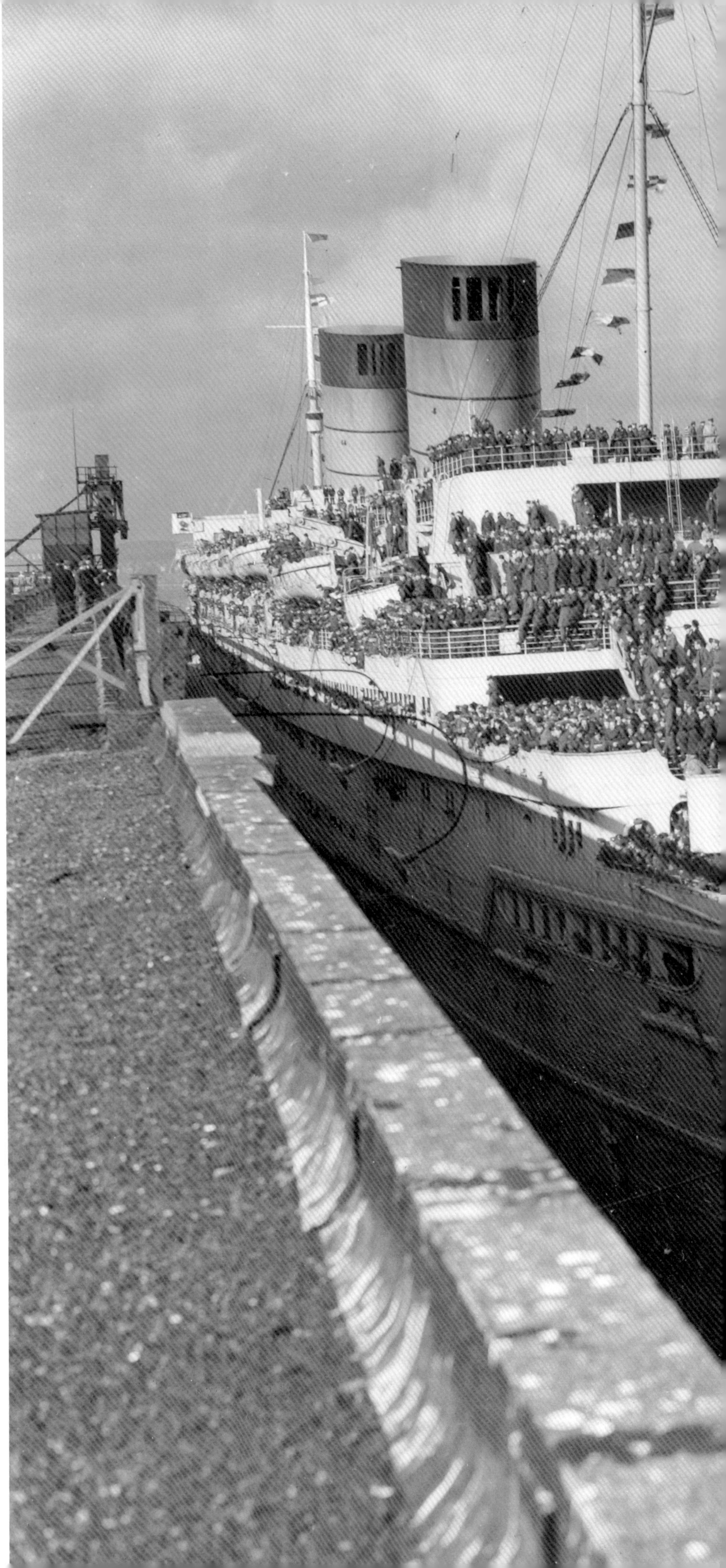

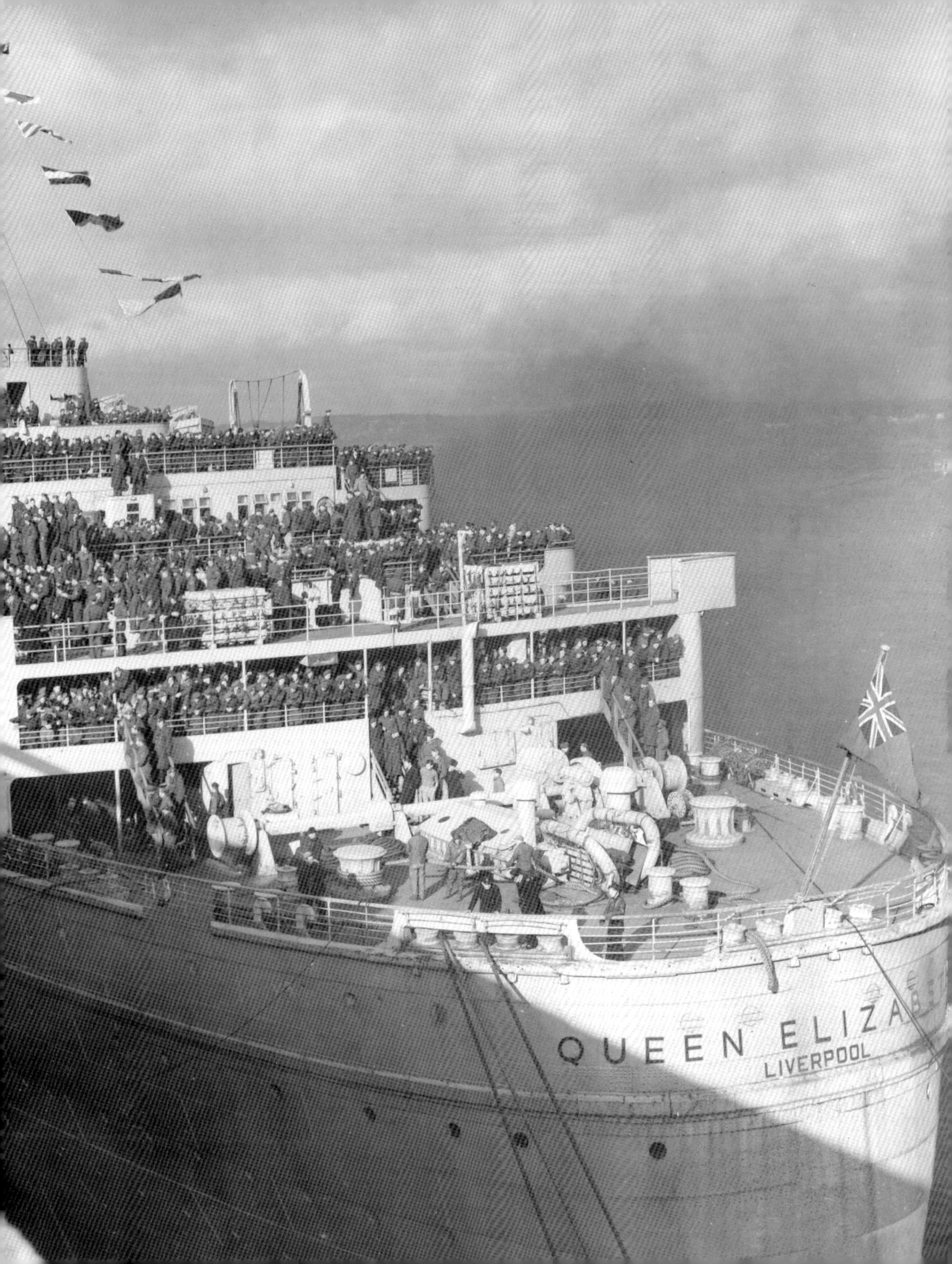
QUEEN ELIZA
LIVERPOOL

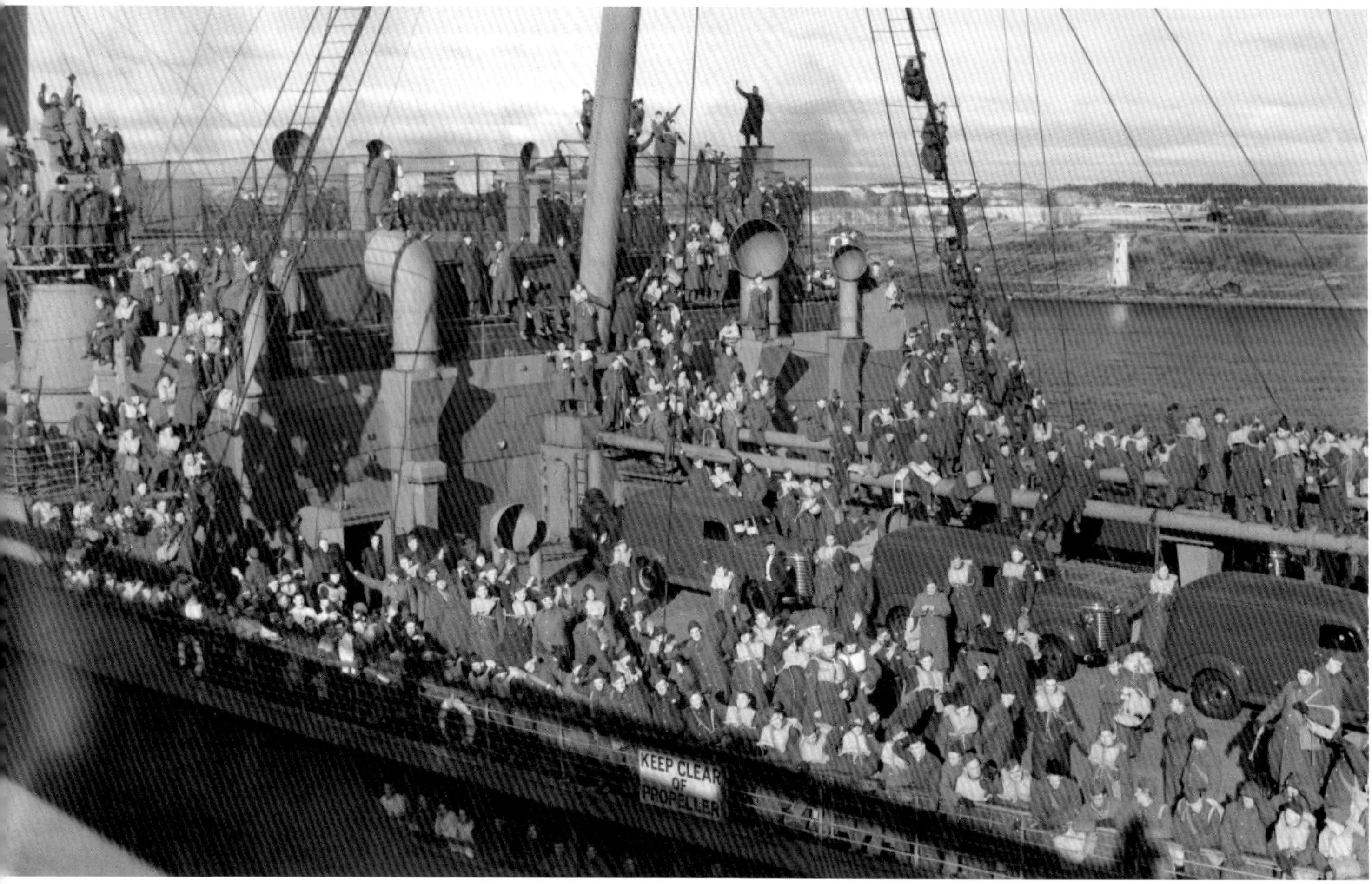
KEEP CLEAR
OF
PROPELLER

ABOVE: *It was now the time for which everyone had waited so patiently — the boys, and for the first time in a war, the girls in uniform were coming home. They shared the space on the troopships with hundreds of War Brides, crossing the Atlantic to join their soldier husbands met overseas. For almost a year the soldiers and sailors came by the thousands.*

RIGHT: *In June 1945, Canadian soldiers arrived from overseas aboard the troopship* S.S. Ile de France. *For this little boy, it may have been the first time meeting the father who had left home so long ago.*

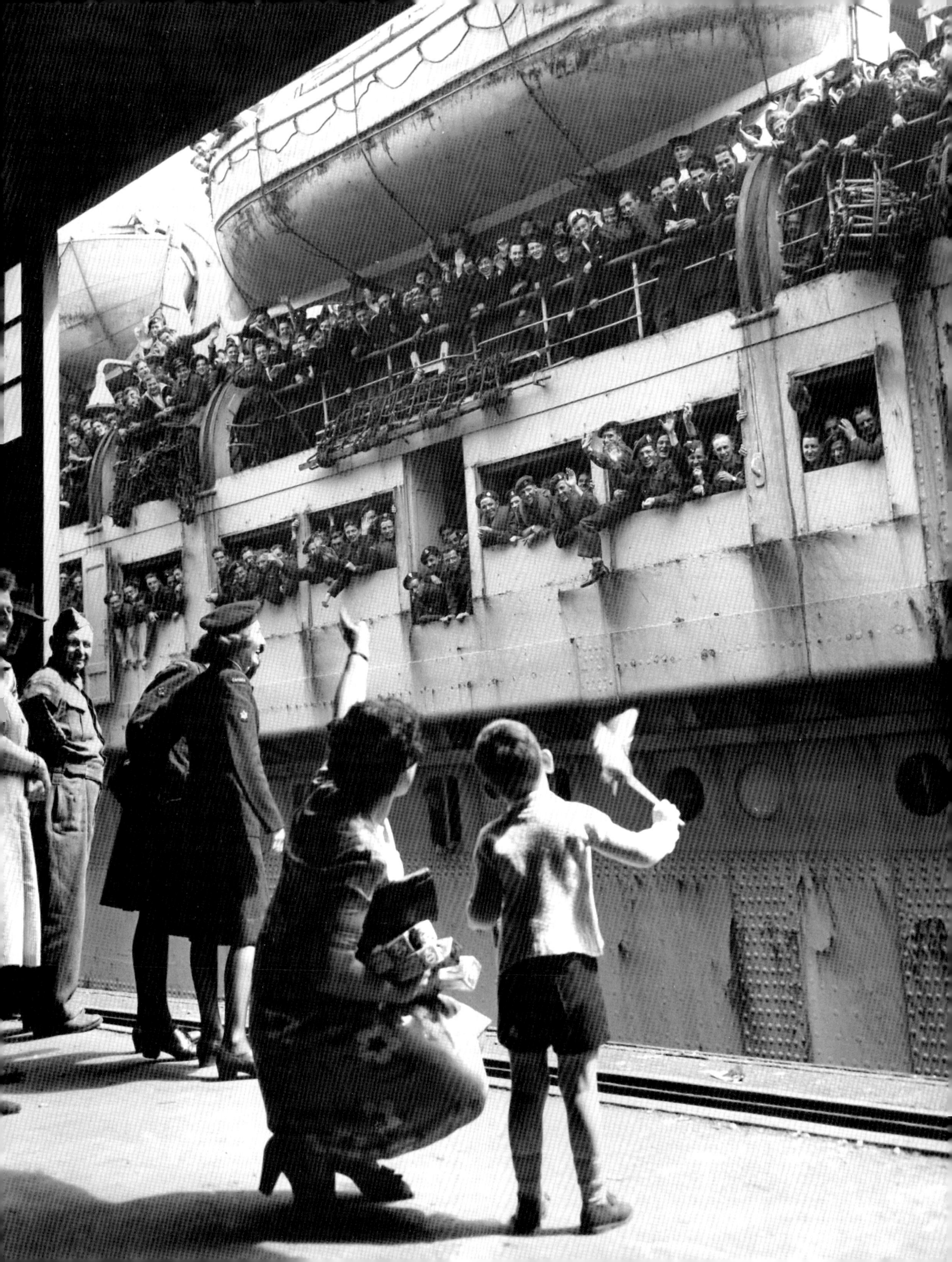

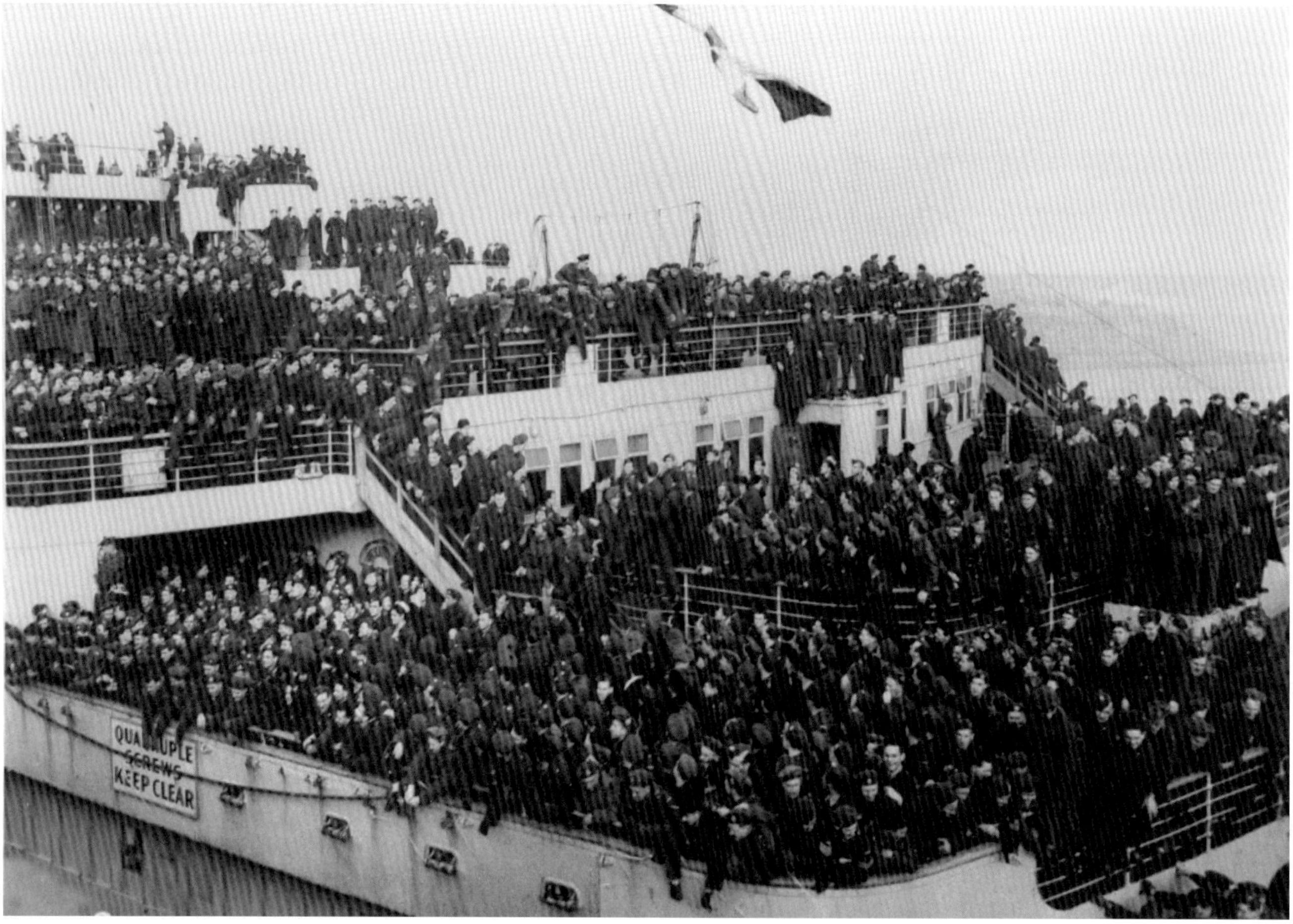
KEEP CLEAR

ABOVE: *RMS* Queen Elizabeth *with returning troops. The first complete unit to arrive in the port of Halifax was the Canadian Parachute Battalion on 21 June 1945. In spite of pouring rain, they marched through the streets to the welcoming cheers of thousands. The last Nova Scotia Regiment to reach home were the Pictou Highlanders, who arrived in April 1946, from garrison duty in the West Indies.*

RIGHT: *The* Ile de France *loaded with returning troops, with a tug pushing its bulk into the Seawall.*

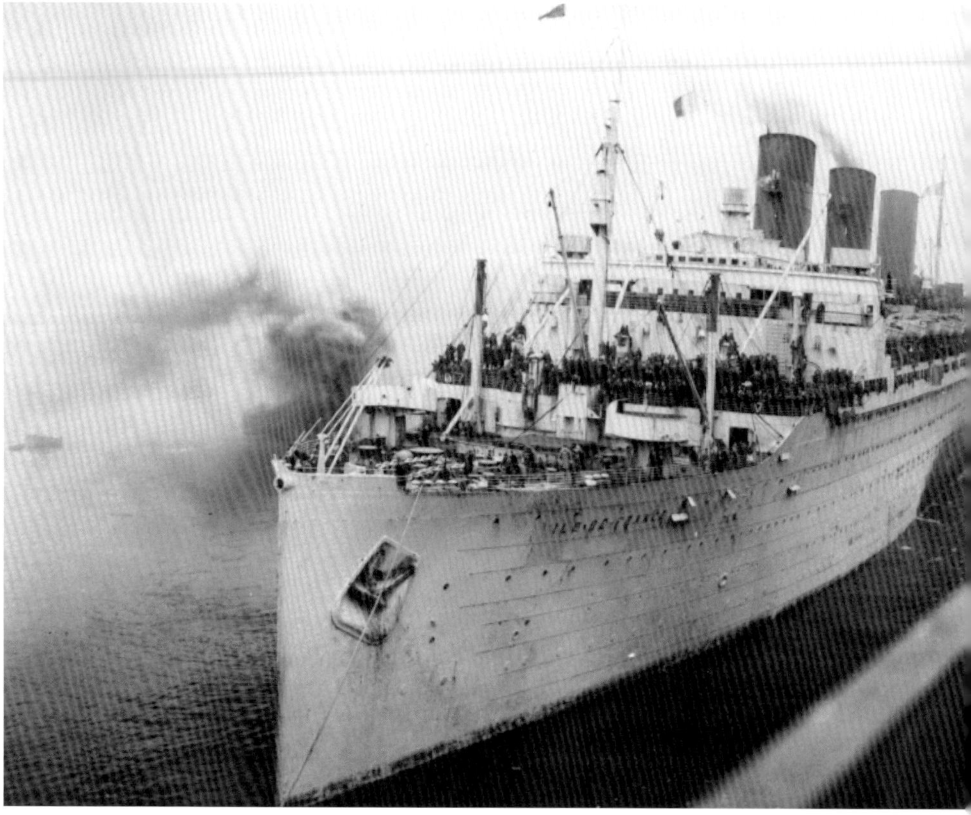

INDEX

PHOTO CREDITS

CST = Canadian Science and Technology Museum
HDC = Halifax Defence Complex
LAC = Library and Archives Canada
NA = National Archives Web site
NSARM = Nova Scotia Archives and Records Management
SAM = Shearwater Aviation Museum

T=Top, B=Bottom, C=Centre R=Right, L=Left

8	CST
8-9	NSARM
10-11	LAC PA 42043
11B	HDC 108-01-03-941-0037
12	CST
1-13	CST
14T	NSARM, Bollinger #106
14B	NSARM, Robert Norwood #413
1-17	LAC, Department of National Defence PA-190964
18T	LAC, Department of National Defence WRA-55
18B	NSARM, Bollinger #525A
19	HDC, Department of National Defence CT 311
20	NSARM, John F. Rogers #51
21	NSARM, Robert Norwood #278.1
22	NSARM, #18 Halifax Civil Defence Corps Fonds, Location 36-4-3
23	NSARM, Robert Norwood #408
24	NSARM, #74 Halifax Civil Defence Corps Fonds, Location 36-4-3
1-25	NSARM, #97 Halifax Civil Defence Corps Fonds, Location 36-4-3
26T	NSARM, #9 Halifax Civil Defence Corps Fonds, Location 36-4-3
26B	NSARM, #30 Halifax Civil Defence Corps Fonds, Location 36-4-3
28	LAC Department of National Defence PA-197864
29	NSARM, John F. Rogers Location 2004-0471, # 21
30T	NSARM, NSL&P Photo Album #49 - Ships WW II no. 75H
30B	NSARM, NSL&P Photo Album #49 - Ships WW II, no 75K
31	NSARM, NSL&P Photo Album #49 - Ships WW II no. 75E
32T	HDC, National Archives (NA) RG 24 vol 13129
32B	NSARM, Bollinger #458E
33	NSARM, Isabel McNeil Fonds, DAP/1995-176, loc 31.4.6 #74
34	LAC, Deptartment of National Defence PA-107099
34-35	NSARM, Isabel McNeil Fonds, DAP/1995-176, loc 31.4.6 #47
36	LAC, RCAF SD-172
37	HDC, NA PA 139862 or DND neg DH/K462
38	NSARM, Bollinger #328 H
39	NSARM, Bollinger #328B
40	LAC, DND Army WRC-577
41	NSARM, Bollinger #3283

42	HDC, "Canadian Army Photo", Directorate of History. Department of National Defence, Dhist 340.019 (D3) C60
43	NSARM, HB Jefferson 1992-304 loc 31.2.1, #54
44T	LAC, DND Army WRC-578
44B	HDC, "Canadian Army Photo", Directorate of History. Department of National Defence
45	LAC, Department of National Defence PA-105186
46	NA, Mikan #3393070
47T	Fort Sackville Hist Society #1485
47B	LAC, Department of National Defence, NLC NP-580
48	NA, Mikan #3571738
49	NSARM, HB Jefferson 1992-304 loc 31.2.1, #2
50	NA, Mikan #3571772
51	LAC, Department of National Defence PA-105362
52	SAM, Department of National Defence photograph
53T	SAM, Department of National Defence photograph
53B	SAM, Department of National Defence photograph
54	NSARM, Bollinger #328P
55	SAM, Department of National Defence photograph PL1185
56	NA, Mikan #3223037
58	NSARM, Bollinger #419B
59	NSARM, Bollinger #419 D
60	NSARM, Bollinger #419A
61	NSARM, Robert Norwood #62
62T	NSARM, Robert Norwood #370
62B	NSARM, Robert Norwood #369
64	LAC, Department of National Defence REA-426-47
66	NSARM, W. R. MacAskill #1987-453, Painting by Richard R. Rummell
67	NA, PA 105926
68	LAC, Department of National Defence PA-105926
69	NA, Mikan #3571311
70	LAC, NA GM 0451
70-71	NSARM, Robert Norwood #364
72T	NSARM, John F. Rogers #39
72B	LAC, National Film Board of Canada. Photothèque C-075212
73	LAC, National Film Board of Canada. Photothèque PA-105224
74T	NSARM, NSL&P Photo Album #49 - Ships WW II no. 41C
74B	NSARM, NSL&P Photo Album #49 - Ships WW II, no. 58E
76	NSARM, Bollinger #239 F
77	NSARM, John F. Rogers #49
78	Fort Sackville Historical Society #1393
1-79	NA, Mikan #3567374
80T	SAM, Department of National Defence photograph
80B	Joan Payzant Private Collection
81T	NSARM, Bollinger #234A
81B	NSARM, Bollinger #230A
82T	NSARM, Bollinger #317B

82B	NSARM, Bollinger #235B
83T	LAC, Department of National Defence PA-105191
83B	NSARM, Bollinger #270B
84	NSARM, Bollinger #654C
85	NSARM, Bollinger #269
86-87	LAC, DND RCAF BE-996
87	NSARM, Bollinger #465A
88T	NSARM, Bollinger #198D
88B	NSARM, Bollinger #198H
90	NSARM, John F. Rogers #37
91	NSARM, # 89 Halifax Civil Defence Corps Fonds, Location 36-4-3
92	NSARM, # 41 Halifax Civil Defence Corps Fonds, Location 36-4-3
93T	Ruth Teasdale Private Collection [from Joan Payzant]
93B	Joan Payzant Private Collection
94	NSARM, # 39 Halifax Civil Defence Corps Fonds, Location 36-4-3
95	NSARM, John F. Rogers, #25
96T	LAC, Department of National Defence PA-105768
96B	LAC, Department of National Defence GM-0916
98T	NSARM, Bollinger #462H
98B	NSARM, Edward J. Kelly 1985-417 Loc 34.17 #01
99	NSARM, Robert Norwood #383
100L	NA, Mikan #3523783
101	NA DND RCAF SD 115-G
102TL	NSARM, Bollinger #1
102TR	NSARM, Bollinger #6
102CL	NSARM, Bollinger #37
102CR	NSARM, Bollinger #31
102BL	NSARM, Bollinger #7
102BR	NSARM, Bollinger #44
103	NSARM, Edward J. Kelly 1985-417 Loc 34.17 #011
104	NSARM, Bollinger #319H
105	NSARM, Bollinger #320D
106	NSARM, Bollinger #265A
107	NSARM, Bollinger #665C
108T	NSARM, John F. Rogers #28
108B	NSARM, Bollinger #596-9
110T	NSARM, Kane Family Env 2 #22
110B	LAC, C-079561
111	NSARM, Kane Family Env 1 #7
112	NSARM, Kane Family Env 1 #8
113	LAC, C-079586
114L	NSARM, Kane Family Env 1 #9
114-115	LAC, C-079582
116	LAC, C-079567
117	NSARM, Kane Family Env 2 #20
118-119	NSARM, HB Jefferson 1992-304 loc 31.2.1, #49
120	NSARM, James McSwain, 1996-163, loc. 33-4-1, #6B
121T	NSARM, Bollinger #311D
121B	NSARM, Kane Family Env 2 #47
122-123	HDC, Hayward
124	NSARM, John F. Rogers #48
125	NA, Mikan #3616886
126T	NSARM, James McSwain, 1996-163, loc. 33-4-1, 6E #1
126B	NSARM, James McSwain, 1996-163, loc 33-4-1, 6E#2